What Has Been Will Be Again

RUSSELL NICKEL

ISBN 978-1-64299-132-1 (paperback)
ISBN 978-1-64299-133-8 (digital)

Christian Faith Publishing, Inc.
832 Park Avenue
Meadville, PA 16335
www.christianfaithpublishing.com

Printed in the United States of America

Contents

Introduction

It was probably a few months after Ginger and I were married in March of 1985, when I began to realize God was calling me to teach in the church setting. During this time I became more and more enthused with studying the Bible, especially any subject related to prophecy. During the 1980s and 1990s, I regularly watched a TV show called *Prophecy in the News*, hosted by J. R. Church. It would be several years later when I would invite J. R. to my hometown church in Helena, Oklahoma to speak on the subject of Bible prophecy. Other teachers of prophecy I enjoyed listening to during this time were Hal Lindsey, Gary Stearman, and Dr. Jack Van Impe.

My passion for studying the Bible continued to increase as I grew older. It was around 2005 when I began to realize the vast amount of information available on the internet. Instead of spending hours watching television, I would spend hours reading, listening, and watching various subjects related to history and Bible prophecy. I was amazed all a person had to do was type in any subject on a computer, and hours of information were immediately available for review. It was during time spent surfing the internet when I discovered other Bible prophecy teachers such as Chuck Missler, Tom Horn, and Patrick Heron. I give credit to Dr. Chuck Missler for helping me to nail down many of the questions I had concerning events occurring during the, "Days of Noah." Through the years I have come to realize maturing as a Christian is in many ways similar to building a house. When the foundational structure for your doctrinal beliefs are strong and secure, the rest of your spiritual house is much more square, plumb, and true. It reminds me of the story of the wise man who built his house upon a rock which was able to stand the storms of life, because it was built on the foundation of Christ.

I became troubled through the years while studying and teaching the Bible, because it appeared to me many verses and stories especially in the Old Testament seemed to be in conflict with the character of a loving, merciful God. I was also becoming frustrated, because it appeared the Bible is informing some events taking place especially in the Old Testament did not appear to agree with most church traditions and beliefs. One of the main events in the Bible I struggled with was the flood story recorded in the book of Genesis. Let me make clear I am not saying I struggled with any information the Bible was telling us, but I was beginning to struggle with how certain stories in the Bible were being inter-preted. It became more and more apparent to me as I continued to study and dig for answers, something much more serious and evil had taken place on earth than most people realize during the time before the flood. I began to believe the Bible was informing us something very sinister occurred on earth during this period of time which resulted in the corruption of all flesh on earth. I believe this corruption caused God to suddenly have no choice but to destroy all life on earth and start over.

Through the years I have grown to realize the Holy Spirit uses the Bible, personal experiences, and the words of others to confirm biblical truth. I have found in most cases, discernment of scripture comes only through diligent Bible study and prayer. I have come to understand many questions a person has about the Bible can only be answered through diligent Bible study. I have found the Bible will always be the best commentary to answer questions arising while studying the Bible. As I continued studying and researching the events recorded in the Bible, I began to realize reality is much more than what we can see, hear, and touch. I was steadily com-ing to the conclusion a spiritual battle between the forces of good and evil was much more a part of history than what we have been taught.

But as it is written, Eye hath not seen, nor ear heard, neither have entered into the heart of man, the things which God hath prepared for them that love him.

But God hath revealed them unto us by his Spirit: for the Spirit searcheth all things, yea, the deep things of God.

For what man knoweth the things of a man, save the spirit of man which is in him? Even so the things of God knoweth no man, but the Spirit of God.

Now we have received, not the spirit of the world, but the spirit which is of God; that we might know the things that are freely given to us of God.

Which things also we speak, not in the words which man's wisdom teacheth, but which the Holy Ghost teacheth; comparing spiritual things with spiritual.

But the natural man receiveth not the things of the Spirit of God: for they are foolishness unto him: neither can he know them, because they are spiritually discerned. (1 Corinthians 2:9–14)

Several years ago, I started spending time studying the literal hundreds of megalithic structures and pyramids located all over the world. I was amazed when I discovered the incredibly precise specifications these structures were built too. I knew then in my spirit there was more to these stories than we were being told. Gigantic stones used in these structures, some weighing as much as one thousand tons were cut and machined to tolerances within a few thousandths of an inch. Granite stones, many as large as four wheel drive tractors were cut, drilled, and machined within the tolerances of a human hair. These megalithic stones then were somehow carried or hauled to their final destination. We need to keep in mind we still to this day cannot replicate many of these machining and construction processes. When I watched videos informing me of the architectural design and history of the Egyptian pyramids, I realized there was no way on earth men with very primitive tools could possibly build such structures. For example, the base of the pyramid at Giza covers an area of approximately 13 acres, and after standing for thousands of years its base is currently less than one inch from being perfectly level.

I was also surprised when I discovered Egypt and Mexico are not the only places on earth where pyramids have been found. There are literally thousands of pyramids located all over the world in many different countries, and more are constantly being discovered. I literally spent hundreds of hours watching videos and reading articles researching the pyramids and other megalithic structures located around the world. During my studies, I continued to find many of these structures had unusual relationships to other structures, some being located thousands of miles apart from each other. Many of these structures have similar latitude and longitude alignments, and they interact with the position of the sun on certain days of the year. Many of these structures are also directly related to stars and constellations in the heavens which would be impossible to be planned and designed by man. For instance, I was very intrigued when I discovered a star shaft at the Great Pyramid of Giza appears to point directly to one of the brightest stars in the belt of the constellation Orion. It is also very interesting the constellation Orion is defined as, "The Mighty Hunter."

This historical information was fascinating to me, because the Bible also defines the person, "Nimrod," as a mighty hunter. It also appears the size and the positioning of the Giza pyramids are an exact representation on earth of the three stars located in Orion's Belt. I also became aware the ancient Egyptians worshipped a god by the name of, "Osiris." One of the many descriptions of the god Osiris is he is known as the god of the underworld and the dying and rising god. This appears to be why the Egyptians went to great lengths to prepare a body for the afterlife, because they believed these great rulers would one day rise again. I began to realize many of these ancient civilizations may have been in reality worshiping the same god who is known by many different names. The subject relating to the identity of Osiris was also interesting to me, because he is in many ways very similar to the man the Bible refers to as the, "antichrist," who the book of Revelation defines as Apollo. The Bible also describes the antichrist as being a god who once walked the earth, now is dead, and will one day rise again out of the abyss.

As a young man I was taught Darwin's theory of evolution in school. I have always believed this is a form of deception attempting to teach the theory people have evolved from lower forms of life. It did not make sense to me complex life forms such as us could evolve from lower forms of life. The Bible tells us we were created in the very image of God. Anyone who researches this subject will come to the conclusion past civilizations appeared to all of a sudden become extensively evolved using very complex mathematical skills and building techniques, some of which cannot be duplicated even today. The Bible presents to us a much different explanation than the theory of evolution, since God states in Genesis His creation in the beginning was, "Very Good." The biblical explanation of creation even agrees with the laws of physics and thermodynamics. God did not create life that was in the beginning flawed, disorganized, and improved over time. The Bible tells us God's creation was perfect, had no genetic defects, and because of the fall of man the entire creation developed genetic flaws. Many people who lived during the time of Genesis and throughout the Old Testament lived for hundreds of years.

> And God saw everything that he had made, and, behold, it was very good. And the evening and the morning were the sixth day. (Genesis 1:31)

I have told my wife I should have written this book fifteen years ago. Years ago I was discussing these subjects in Sunday school classes concerning what I believed the Bible was really informing us took place during the days of Noah. I was informing Bible study classes years ago of experiments being conducted in science labs involving the genetic manipulation and comingling of animals. I knew it wouldn't be much longer and scientists would be conducting genetic experiments on humans. It was a tough time for me during those years. I was feeling compelled to educate members in the church concerning information I believed the Bible wanted people to know. To be quite honest, discussions relating to these topics were shunned, and I could sense discussing these subjects made people feel very uncomfortable. I believed many in the church thought the information I was bringing to the classroom had no relationship with the Bible, and this information was not appropriate to discuss in the church setting.

I found hundreds of scripture references in the Bible constantly pushing me to find answers to what the Bible was trying to tell us about the past. One such example of this is where in many places the Bible makes reference to, "The Mountain of God." According to the Bible, the blueprint to the tabernacle of God Moses was given on Mt. Sinai was really an earthly picture of what existed in the heavens. I know many prophecy and Bible teachers have always believed, "The Holy City," pictured in Revelation descending down from heaven is in the shape of a cube based on the dimensions the Bible describes.

I have always wondered if this great, "Holy City," descending down from heaven was literally shaped like a mountain or pyramid. A pyramid can have a square base, and the length of each side could be equal to its height. It is said the great pyramid of Egypt may have once been covered by polished limestone, had a gold capstone, and this magnificent structure brightly gleamed in the sun. I believe there is much more truth to the past than we are being told. The following verse in the Bible is just one example causing me to believe some of the megalithic structures built all over the world, may actually be earthly symbols of what is real in the spiritual and heavenly realm.

> And he carried me away in the Spirit to a mountain great and high, and showed me the holy city of Jerusalem coming down out of heaven from God. (Revelation 21:10)

By the year 2000, I was noticing a prophetic relationship with books, TV shows, current events, and movies coming out in the secular media. The number of movies and shows I was witnessing dealing with the subject of aliens or extraterrestrial life was staggering. Pieces of the puzzle relating to the steady increase in spiritual warfare and deception of all people living on the earth was starting to come together for me. It was as if some unified force was trying to prepare the entire earth for some type of a deceptive event coming in the future, and I believed the force behind it was satanic in nature. I would regularly bring these biblical and prophetic conclusions to Bible classes for insight and discussion. I know many Christians are quick to quote the Bible verse stating, "We wrestle not against flesh and blood, but against principalities, against the rulers of darkness, and against spiritual wickedness in high places," but was there any real belief in the words the Bible was telling us. I have come to realize making a statement or quoting a Bible verse is a lot easier than a person placing their total faith in the written word of God. I would like to stress this book is in no way meant for the purpose of criticizing any church which is based on the foundation of Jesus Christ. I have been active in church most of my life. There are many brothers and sisters in Christ including pastors and teachers I love very dearly, and I have a tremendous amount of respect for. My major concern is I have been witnessing a major shift with what many churches today profess as truth. These past several years have been a huge struggle for me. During this same period of time, it has been a huge eye-opening experience as I started realizing the many ways the Bible is attempting to warn and educate the church concerning events occurring in the past.

In this book I will reveal what the scripture is trying to communicate to us about the past, the present, and what types of events are coming in the future. We will be taking an in-depth look at several Old Testament events, and how they will have a direct relationship to future events that will one day come upon those dwelling on the earth. It was when I came to understand the definition of one verse in Ecclesiastes, I realized it was the key to answering many of the questions we have concerning Bible history and prophecy. I have also dedicated the title of this book to this verse due to its historical and prophetic significance. One critical truth most churches need to realize is having an understanding of the past is extremely important. Knowledge of the past is the key to understanding the future. I now understand the entire world is being kept in the dark concerning the historical events of the past, and the reason is for the sole purpose of deception.

I would also like to thank my wife Ginger for encouraging me to write this book. I have never considered myself capable of taking on such a task as this, or being a public speaker for that matter. I am horrible with grammar, and it was a miracle I passed English in school. I believe the teacher gave me a passing grade because she just didn't want to deal with me another year. I would always tell my wife the information is in my head, but spending the time organizing twenty-five years of research and putting it down in words was a task I was unqualified to complete. Actually, I think the real truth was I really didn't want to put out the effort and lacked the confidence in myself to take on a project of this magnitude. This book will hopefully answer many of the questions countless numbers of people have concerning biblical history and prophecy.

I have struggled with many titles for the book. One title I was considering was, "Questions Christians Want to Know, but Are Afraid to Ask," because it definitely applies to this book. I am convinced the Bible has the answers to all our questions concerning history, the present time, and the future if we're just willing to dig. In this book, I will be giving the reader close to a twenty-five-year compilation of the research, study, and revelations I have come to over the years. I will be using the King James Bible for all scripture references. I understand talk is cheap, so I diligently try to back up everything said with the ultimate source of truth which is the Bible. If there is one thing the world needs today, it is truth.

My overall intention with this book is to provide biblically based answers to people in the churches who are struggling with the events they see taking place in the world today. Several books could have easily been written dealing specifically with the many subjects brought up in each chapter of the book. As always, I encourage everyone to take everything read in this book to the word of God making sure it can be accepted as truth. The Bible informs us in Acts 17:11 we must be a Berean, and we must do our own homework so we can define what is considered truth and what is known as false doctrine. There are four verses in the book of Ezekiel found in chapter 33 I have always taken very seriously, and these verses are a primary reason I am writing this book. When God reveals truth to us concerning His word, we have a duty to tell the truth to whoever will listen in the best way we know how.

> But if the watchman see the sword come, and blow not the trumpet, and the people be not warned; if the sword come, and take any person from among them, he is taken away in his iniquity; but his blood will I require at the watchman's hand.
>
> So thou, O son of man, I have set thee a watchman unto the house of Israel; therefore thou shalt hear the word at my mouth, and warn them from me.
>
> When I say unto the wicked, O wicked man, thou shalt surely die; if thou dost not speak to warn the wicked from his way, that wicked man shall die in his iniquity; but his blood will I require at thine hand.
>
> Nevertheless, if thou warn the wicked of his way to turn from it; if he do not turn from his way, he shall die in his iniquity; but thou has delivered thy soul. (Ezekiel 33:6–9)

The Journey Begins

My perspective on the Bible began to drastically change somewhere around 2002. I had been teaching in the church regularly since 1985. I trusted Christ as my personal Lord and Savior at the age of eight. My decision to trust Christ took place in the summer during a Larry Jones tent revival meeting in Seiling, Oklahoma. I grew up in a conservative Christian home believing the Bible was the inspired word of God and it could be taken as truth. I have attended church on a regular basis during my life.

In my early years of teaching and studying the Bible, I can remember coming across certain scriptural texts and would wonder to myself, what in the world is the Bible trying to tell us. Another issue I began to struggle with was the fact I had attended church all my life listening to sermons and actively participated in Bible studies, yet I never received answers relating to the biblical texts I was questioning. For years, certain Bible stories and verses continued to weigh on me. I would think to myself these verses and subjects I'm struggling with are in the Bible, so surely God would expect us to know and understand what the Bible is trying to tell us.

It was this consuming desire to search for biblical truth that would begin a several-year journey of personal study and research, which ended up being one of the main reasons for this book. In this book I will be giving conclusions to the numerous questions and struggles I've had over the years with certain texts and stories in the Bible. Another reason for the book was I was beginning to realize the entire church community failed to come up with answers to the same questions in the Bible I was struggling with. In fact, I have discovered many of these questions concerning the scriptures were not being researched, they are literally being suppressed and shunned in most churches today. Yes, I was beginning to realize tens, possibly hundreds of thousands of Christians could not answer many of the same questions I had concerning the Bible. Even worse, I was beginning to realize there might be a higher purpose as to why this information is not being taught in most churches today.

It was also during this time I continued to become more passionate with studying Bible prophecy always searching for answers as to where we were on God's prophetic timetable. I could see by watching the daily news reports, various TV shows, and witnessing the exponential growth in technology, I knew the world was changing fast, and there appeared to be an agenda behind what was going on. I noticed technology was advancing at such an alarming rate; by the time you purchased a new computer, took it home, it was already outdated. I also knew technology would play an important role in Bible prophecy especially as we draw closer to the end of this current age. The following verses in Revelation confirms the future role technology will one day have on the entire world.

> And he causeth all, both small and great, rich and poor, free and bond, to receive a mark in their right hand, or in their foreheads:
> And that no man might buy or sell, save he that had the mark, or the name of the beast, or the number of his name. (Revelation 13:16–17)

I understood from what the two above verses are telling us, these events will take place during a future rise of a coming world ruler the Bible refers to as the antichrist, and technology will play a major role in controlling the entire world's population. It is obvious extreme measures in controlling all forms of financial transactions will someday be put into place attempting to control all who dwell on the earth during this time. But I also knew total financial control would just be one facet of what is coming on the horizon. I wondered what could possibly be the source for all these so-called advancements in technology. Were people literally sitting around dreaming up new ideas creating highly advanced computer chip technologies, or was there a higher power actively involved working behind the scenes? I believe most people will be surprised when they realize the answers to these questions.

As time went on, I continued gaining wisdom and understanding of the scriptures. I began to realize studying the Bible must be somewhat like digging for gold. Sometimes you dig and dig and dig with no luck, but one day you find a nugget. I believe the following scriptures somewhat relates to this. I am firmly convinced there are spiritual truths hidden in the Bible only found by those who diligently search and seek God. In this book we will be looking into aspects to the scriptures some might consider very uncomfortable, but these studies will bring understanding to the Bible most people have never thought of before. I believe every verse in the Bible is there by design and is meant to be understood. There is no verse in the Bible that is off limits and should not be studied. Every verse in the Bible is given to us for instruction and learning.

> Ask, and it shall be given you; seek, and ye shall find; knock, and it shall be opened unto you: For every one that asketh receiveth; and he that seeketh findeth; and to him that knocketh it shall be opened. (Matthew 7:7–8)

> Call unto me, and I will answer thee, and shew thee great and mighty things, which thou knowest not. (Jeremiah 33:3)

> It is the glory of God to conceal a thing: but the honour of kings is to search out a matter. (Proverbs 25:2)

So as I continued to dig for truth in the scriptures more and more questions surfaced, but along with questions occasionally certain pieces of the puzzle would come together. So this is how this long several-year journey began for me. It is my desire this book clears up many of the questions others may have concerning God's word. I began to realize while on this journey when a person begins to understand the truth of what the Bible is really trying to tell us, the once thought problems and discrepancies in the Bible disappear revealing new truth.

One last comment before we move on. I have come to the realization many of the so-called traditions we have been taught about history, science, creation, religion, and even the Bible are filled with deception. Before we get into several very interesting and controversial topics, I want to express a warning to all who read this book. I am asking all people reading this book to not accept anything I state as truth. I ask each of you be diligent students and do your own homework. I also ask the reader to take everything discussed in this book to the word of God combining it with prayer making sure it lines up with scripture. Information confirmed by the word of God can be taken as truth. The Bible warns us in many places as we approach the end of this age deception will become the norm. The Bible warns us over and over again to not be deceived.

Study to shew thyself approved unto God, a workman that needeth not to be ashamed, rightly dividing the word of truth. (2 Timothy 2:15)

These were more noble than those in Thessalonica, in that they received the word with all readiness of mind, and searched the scriptures daily, whether those things were so. (Acts 17:11)

The Two Seeds

Approximately four years ago while instructing an adult Bible study session, I noticed an individual participating in the study seemed to become troubled concerning a statement I made during the class. One topic being discussed during this particular Bible study was dealing with the spiritual condition the Bible informs us all people are in apart from Christ. The Bible informs all people are sinners from the moment of birth. The particular individual mentioned above expressed open disagreement with my conclusion stating there was no way a newborn baby or young child in God's eyes could be born a sinner. To be quite honest, I was shocked this individual expressed this belief since this person was probably in their late sixties having attended the church as long as I could remember. One thing we need to understand is God has a special place in His heart for all children. According to the Bible, there will come a time in every person's life when they will be held accountable as to whether they will accept or reject Christ as Savior and Lord.

One thing I have learned as I have become older is to never get in an argument with anyone over a doctrinal or scriptural issue, no matter how certain you are of the answer. When a person asks me for an opinion concerning a spiritual or biblical matter I will give them my opinion, but I will always try to back up all possible statements and opinions with scripture. When it comes down to it, my or someone else's opinion on an issue really doesn't matter that much. The only thing important is the information the Bible gives us concerning the issue. It is going to be a very shocking time for millions of people when they one day stand in judgment before a holy God. During this event referred to as, "The Great White Throne Judgment," millions of people will attempt to inform God of their accomplishments during their time here on this earth. God will inform this group of people to depart from Him because He never knew them. The Bible goes on to tell us these people will then go into the eternal fires of punishment initially prepared for the devil and his angels.

The literal hundreds of questions and comments I have listened to people state in the church setting helped me to realize how little of an understanding most people have with the word of God. The Bible defines the mature Christian as a person who can eat and digest the meat of God's word. The babe in Christ or the immature Christian is portrayed as one who can only sustain themselves on the milk of God's word. Mature Bible study is intended for those who are able to digest the meat of the word. The sad thing is, most Christians end up living their entire lives incapable of participating in mature biblical studies. The following two scriptures clarifies this point. Paul here is dealing with the issue where church brothers and sisters are living their lives never being capable of participating in mature conversations concerning spiritual matters. The Bible contrasts spiritual immaturity to a ship tossed back and forth on the waves, and is not anchored on the truth of the Bible. Arguing, complaining, and gossiping are characteristics given to those who are spiritually immature.

> And I, brethren, could not speak unto you as unto spiritual, but as unto carnal, even as unto babes in Christ. I have fed you with milk, and not with meat: for hitherto ye were not able to bear it, neither yet now are ye able. (1 Corinthians 3:2)

> For when for the time ye ought to be teachers, ye have need that one teach you again which be the first principles of the oracles of God; and are become such as have need of milk, and not of strong meat. (Hebrews 5:12)

The above scripture references point out the reality many believers will never reach a maturity level where they are able to digest the meat of God's word. Some of the subjects discussed in this book will challenge most believers, since it will bring a new perspective to the ways the stories of the Bible have traditionally been taught. There will be some people who will become upset when they read this book, because they will not be able to deal with the spiritual and prophetic truths being discussed.

Now, continuing with the question raised during Bible study dealing with what time in a person's life they become sinners needing a Savior. The great thing about this question is the Bible clearly gives us the answer. The answer to this question is found in many places, but let's look at the answer the Bible gives us in the book of Romans.

> Wherefore, as by one man sin entered into the world, and death by sin; and so death passed upon all men, for that all have sinned. (Romans 5:12)

> For as by one man's disobedience many were made sinners, so by the obedience of one shall many be made righteous. (Romans 5:19)

From what we read above in the book of Romans, the Bible informs us we are all sinners at birth. Now that we have biblically established the truth of when a person becomes a sinner, notice the statement Paul tells us in Romans 5:19. Paul explains through the disobedience of one man named Adam many became sinners, but through the obedience of Jesus Christ many are made righteous. So now we must deal with the question relating to what ways Jesus Christ was so much different than Adam?

> For he hath made him (Jesus Christ) to be sin for us, who knew no sin; that we might be made the righteousness of God in him. (2 Corinthians 5:21)

> And the Word was made flesh, and dwelt
> among us, (and we beheld his glory, the glory as
> of the only begotten of the Father), full of grace
> and truth. (John 1:14)

> The next day John seeth Jesus coming unto
> him, and saith, Behold the Lamb of God, which
> taketh away the sin of the world. (John 1:29)

Many books have been written dealing with the subject of who Jesus was and the authority given to Him by the Father. Notice the Bible informs us Jesus Christ literally is the, "Word of God," who was made flesh and unlike Adam, He knew no sin. Since we have established the spiritual differences between Adam and Jesus, we can now move on to the purpose of this chapter. I will in this book many times use more than one scriptural reference to nail down doctrinal issues and validate truth. It is interesting a person will find all essential spiritual truths will be recorded more than once in the Bible. One example of this is where we find several instances where multiple authors refer to the birth, death, and the resurrection of Christ. Not only are many of these similar references stated by multiple authors, but they will usually be validated in both the Old and New Testaments.

> This is the third time I am coming to you.
> In the mouth of two or three witnesses shall every
> word be established. (2 Corinthians 13:1)

> One witness shall not rise up against a man
> for any iniquity, or for any sin, in any sin that
> he sinneth: at the mouth of two witnesses, or at
> the mouth of three witnesses, shall the matter be
> established. (Deuteronomy 19:15)

One of the many spiritual revelations I came to years ago is found nowhere else but in the book of Genesis. This event takes place after the famous incident in the garden with God, Adam, Eve, and the Serpent. This event relates to how Satan physically appeared and interacted with Eve when he tempted her in the garden that most Christians do not realize and have not been taught. The Hebrew word used in Genesis for Serpent is the term, "Nachash." The Hebrew meaning for this word literally is defined as a spiritual being who, "Brilliantly Shines," or is, "The Shining One." According to the Hebrew definition, it appears Satan here in Genesis presents himself to Eve as a beautiful shining being, not literally in the form of a slithering serpent. It is after Satan tempts Eve, the Bible records in Genesis 3:14 the Serpent is cursed above all cattle, above every beast of the field, and was informed by God from now on upon his belly he would eat dust the rest of his life. It is no accident the Bible in many places describes Satan as an, "Angel of Light." It is no accident the occult and false religions refer to Satan as, "The Light Bearer," or, "The Illumined One." We see here in the following verse after Adam and Eve disobeyed God and sinned, God makes a very unusual statement to Satan recorded in Genesis chapter 3.

> And I will put enmity between thee and the woman, and between thy seed and her seed; it shall bruise thy head, and thou shalt bruise his heel. (Genesis 3:15)

When I finally understood the true meanings behind this verse, many questions concerning events in the Old Testament, the New Testament, and prophecy finally started to make sense. The events which took place in the garden between God, Adam, Eve, and Satan would change the course of history for thousands of years to come. The first word in this verse that sticks out like a sore thumb is the word, "Enmity." When there is enmity between two people there is usually opposition, but many times it involves outright hatred or hostility between two parties. God is informing us here in Genesis from this moment in time, until sin, death, and Satan will one day be defeated, enmity will continue between the woman and Satan. Until Satan is one day judged, bound, and thrown into the Lake of Fire, hatred will continue to exist in this world especially toward Israel and Christianity.

God answers the question in Genesis why Satan will have hatred towards Eve, as well as all women. The statement God makes directly to Satan also gives us valuable insight as to the differences between God and Adam. Satan will have a constant hatred towards women, because here in Genesis he discovers it would be through the seed of a woman, not the seed of a man, Jesus would be born. It is only through the seed of a man, not the seed of a woman, sin passes from one generation to the next. We will discover the term, "Woman," has a dual meaning throughout the Bible referring not only to women in general, but also to the woman, "Israel," that would one day give birth to the Messiah. This is interesting, because Daniel 11:37 informs us a characteristic of the antichrist is he will not be a respecter of women.

This revelation was very shocking for me, because it really is amazing what God is revealing to us here in this verse. Here in Genesis chapter 3, we are being instructed by God in a sense as to how the story will ultimately end. Here also in this same verse we are given the prophetic picture of Christ's death on a cross where Satan would bruise His heel. We are also given a prophetic picture where Satan receives a deadly head wound when he will be one day bound, and cast into the, "Lake of Fire."

> And the devil that deceived them was cast into the lake of fire and brimstone, where the beast and the false prophet are, and shall be tormented day and night for ever and ever. (Revelations 20:10)

This one verse in Genesis nailed down for me the doctrinal truth God has always been in complete control of all events, whether past, present, or future before the heavens and earth were created. A person needs to recognize there is nothing that surprises God. God foreknew a man called Jesus would be born of a woman, and He would die a horrible death on a cross for the sins of the world before it was created. God saw the final fate of Satan and his demonic armies before Adam and Eve were created and placed in the garden. It was no surprise to God that Adam and Eve would flunk the test of obedience and would sin in the garden. It was no surprise to God He would have to send His Son to save the world from their sins.

Although this verse has revealed some amazing things so far, there's much more we need to understand about this verse. We have spent some time discussing the issue of, "The Seed of the Woman," but we still need to discuss and define the identity of, "The Seed of the Serpent." Notice this verse in Genesis uses the words, "Thy Seed," which seems to suggest something most never realize and are not taught in most churches and seminaries today. Other versions of the Bible will sometimes use the word, "Offspring," in place of the word, "Seed," used here in the King James. The actual Greek interpretation of the word, "Seed," literally refers to reproductive seed or sperm, and also refers to a person's, "DNA," or the term, "Genetics."

We know from scriptures the concept of reproductive seed is correct due to the fact Jesus Christ was literally born of a woman being conceived by the Holy Spirit. Jesus truly was born of the seed of a woman because He had no earthly father. We serve a God that as the Bible states, was and is personally involved in the intimate fabrication of our bodies. It is interesting science has now proved each individual person truly is unique and can be individually identified by their DNA. Our bodies literally were as the Bible states meticulously woven together, and each individual person has been given their own unique digital code. A person needs to understand, digital codes do no occur randomly. Digital codes are designed and input by a digital coder. Anything exhibiting intricate design has a designer.

> And in the sixth month the angel Gabriel was sent from God unto a city of Galilee, named Nazareth,
> To a virgin espoused to a man whose name was Joseph, of the house of David; and the virgin's name was Mary.

And the angel came in unto her, and said, Hail, thou that art highly favoured, the Lord is with thee: blessed art thou among women.

And when she saw him, she was troubled at his saying, and cast in her mind what manner of salutation this should be.

And the angel said unto her, Fear not, Mary: for thou hast found favour with God.

And, behold, thou shalt conceive in thy womb, and bring forth a son, and shalt call his name Jesus.

He shall be great, and shall be called the Son of the Highest: and the Lord God shall give unto him the throne of his father David:

And he shall reign over the house of Jacob forever; and of his kingdom there shall be no end.

Then said Mary unto the angel, How shall this be, seeing I know not a man?

And the angel answered and said unto her, The Holy Ghost shall come upon thee, and the power of the Highest shall overshadow thee: therefore also that holy thing which shall be born of thee shall be called the Son of God. (Luke 1:26–35)

I would like to discuss a few more quick points mentioned in the book of John before we move on due to its doctrinal importance. We notice more than once the Bible informs us Mary was a virgin. Mary even informed the angel Gabriel there was no possible way she could have a child due to never having sexual relations with a man. The angel Gabriel informs Mary the conception would literally be a supernatural event coming from God. Gabriel instructs Mary to name her son Jesus because He literally would be the, "Son of God." Another prophetic statement Gabriel tells us was Mary's son, "Jesus," would literally be, "The Son of the Most High God," who would one day rule from Jerusalem on David's throne. Many churches today deny Jesus Christ will literally one day rule the entire earth from Jerusalem. Gabriel prophesied to Mary this event would take place during Christ's, "Thousand-Year Millennial Reign," spoken of in the book of Revelation, as well as in other scriptures. The verses below recorded in the book of Psalms also gives prophetic relevance to the credibility of this future event.

> He that sitteth in the heavens shall laugh: the Lord shall have them in derision.
> Then shall he speak unto them in his wrath, and vex them in his sore displeasure.
> Yet have I set my king upon my holy hill of Zion.
> I will declare the decree: the Lord hath said unto me, Thou art my Son; this day have I begotten thee.
> Ask of me, and I shall give thee the heathen for thine inheritance, and the uttermost parts of the earth for thy possession.
> Thou shalt break them with a rod of iron; thou shalt dash them to pieces like a potter's vessel. (Psalm 2:4–9)

It is very important we establish exactly what the text is trying to tell us here in Genesis. We are talking about two literal prophesied beings who have walked the earth in the past and will again walk the earth in the future. The seed of the woman being discussed in Genesis is referring to Jesus, "The Son of the Most High God." The seed of the serpent we will call for now, "the antichrist." The Bible gives us many characteristics and many names for this person known as the antichrist. A few names the Bible identifies this person by would include; Apollo, The Destroyer, The Son of Perdition, The Man of Sin, The King of Fierce Countenance, the Beast, The Little Horn, the Assyrian, and the god of many names. This is where the journey started getting interesting for me. The Bible gives definitions of Jesus and the antichrist in the following verses. Please notice the similarities and the differences the Bible gives us of these two individuals in the verses below.

> **Jesus:** "I am Alpha and Omega, the beginning and the ending, saith the Lord, which is, and which was, and which is to come, the Almighty." (Revelation 1:8)

> **Antichrist:** "The beast that thou sawest was, and is not; and shall ascend out of the bottomless pit, and go into perdition: and they that dwell on the earth shall wonder, whose names were not written in the book of life from the foundation of the world, when they behold the beast that was, and is not, and yet is." (Revelation 17:8)

The definition of the antichrist is usually defined as someone who is against Christ which definitely does hold truth and appropriately defines this man. Another definition or characteristic of this man a person needs to consider is he is someone who will come in the place in Christ. When I began to understand this scriptural truth, more pieces of the puzzle started coming together for me. The reality is, there is a man who will be allowed to come on the world scene during God's appointed time who the Bible refers to as the antichrist. This man will deceive all dwelling on the earth into believing he is, "The Christ." I believe this man literally will be the son and of the seed of Satan. In other words, the antichrist will more than likely be Satan's offspring. For now, we need to realize we are talking about a literal future event dealing with a literal spiritual being, and not just a mortal man. If we today would be teaching a literal interpretation of God's word, most people in the churches would not one day be deceived by the coming of this man. We will be taking a deeper look into this subject later on in the book. If the church today would believe the truth of what the Bible is telling us about the past, the biblical prophecies of the future wouldn't be so impossible to believe.

During a future time known as the, "Second Coming," Jesus Christ will descend from heaven. The Bible tells us, "All eyes will see Him," as He interrupts the evil plans of those dwelling on this earth. Before this event takes place at the end of a time of Great Tribulation, a counterfeit Christ will walk the earth again descending not from heaven, but coming out of a bottomless pit. During this time on earth an evil trinity will be allowed to rule the world for an appointed time. We will during this time see Satan playing the role of God which has always been his ultimate goal. The antichrist will play the role of Christ, and a person the Bible refers to as the false prophet will play the role of the Holy Spirit. Satan, the ultimate deceiver and counterfeiter, will establish an, "Unholy Trinity," ruling the entire earth during a time of, "Great Tribulation." I am convinced the mark of the beast forced upon all dwelling upon the earth will be a counterfeit mark guaranteeing all who take it eternal damnation. The mark of the beast will be in direct opposition to the mark of the Holy Spirit which as the Bible states is a deposit guaranteeing all who receive it eternal life.

During this future event, those dwelling on the earth will be deceived, and the antichrist will be given authority to overcome and kill the Saints. The meaning of the word, "Saints," here in this context is not referencing the bride of Christ, or those being, "in Christ." A person must realize the Old Testament and the Tribulation saints are not members of the group the Bible refers to as those, "in Christ." I am not stating in any way Jesus and the antichrist are equal spiritual beings. Nothing could be further from the truth. The Bible teaches us the antichrist will come to earth with such power and deception, most dwelling on the earth during this time will be deceived and will be overcome and killed by the antichrist during this time. Jesus Christ is the, "Son of God," and scripture states He is one with the Father. Satan is a spiritual being created by God, and according to the words in Ezekiel, he is a mighty cherub.

The verse in Genesis chapter 3 concerning the two seeds gives clarity to the reason behind many biblical events. When God informed Satan a woman would give birth to a Savior who would bridge the gap between sinful man and a loving God, we see from this moment on Satan taking steps throughout the Bible to overthrow God's plans. We can now see the Genesis chapter 3 prophecy relating to the, "Two Seeds," being directly linked to the days of Noah, the Egyptian captivity, and Israel's entrance into the promised land. Now the repeated problems Israel faces both in the past and in the future makes perfect sense. We need to remember God informs us in Genesis there would be enmity between Satan, the woman, and between their seed. Satan hated Mary, who brought forth the baby Jesus. Satan hated Jesus, who was born of the seed of a woman. Satan hated Israel, the nation who would give birth to the Messiah. We should also understand Revelation chapter 12 gives us a prophetic picture where the nation Israel is referred to a woman being with child. She is crying out in labor, and bringing forth a child who would one day rule the world with a rod of iron. Notice Revelation chapter 12 mentions Satan waiting to kill the baby Jesus upon His birth. Here in Revelation 12, the Bible gives evidence of the woman being a spiritual picture of Israel, and the child symbolizing Jesus the Lamb of God. We also see evidence for the centuries of hatred Satan will have toward women in general, Israel, Jesus, the church, and any other thing representative of God.

God Wipes the Slate Clean

Another interesting story in the Bible is the story of Noah and the Flood account. I would remember as a young child participating in Sunday school class being fascinated with many Bible stories including the flood of Noah. I can remember as a young boy completing craft projects relating to the flood including pictures of a boat loaded with various types of animals. I can remember being taught as a young child, the purpose for the, "Flood," was due to sin and evil being present in men's hearts. I grew up with the belief God sent the flood upon the earth, because people were sinning and committing evil acts with one another to the extent God had to destroy all flesh living on the earth. This reason seemed to work for me for several years even into my early years as a teacher.

As I became older my desire for studying the Bible increased, especially in the area of Bible prophecy. As I continued to study the Bible, I began to wonder if there was more to the story of the Flood than I was taught. Several questions concerning the Flood account began to surface in my mind the more I studied the Bible. It became more and more interesting to me the Bible gives us a description of two distinct worldwide events where God pours out His wrath upon those living on the earth. We understand one of these events is referring to the flood of Noah which has already taken place. We are given extensive details relating to the second event in the book of Revelation. As I continued to mature as a believer, the flood story began to bother me a great deal. The reason for my frustration had to do with why God suddenly came to the conclusion all flesh on the earth must be destroyed. This event surely didn't occur just because

God became upset with the spiritual condition of people, because this event dealt with the sudden destruction of all God's creation on earth.

> But as the days of Noah were, so shall also the coming of the Son of man be.
>
> For as in the days that were before the flood they were eating and drinking, marrying and giving in marriage, until the day that Noe entered into the ark.
>
> And knew not until the flood came, and took them all away; so shall also the coming of the Son of man be. (Matthew 24:37–39)

> For if God spared not the angels that sinned, but cast them down to hell, and delivered them into chains of darkness, to be reserved unto judgment;
>
> And spared not the old world, but saved Noah the eighth person, a preacher of righteousness, bringing in the flood upon the world of the ungodly;
>
> And turning the cities of Sodom and Gomorrah into ashes condemned them with an overthrow, making them an ensample unto those that after should live ungodly;
>
> And delivered just Lot, vexed with the filthy conversation of the wicked;
>
> For that righteous man dwelling among them, in seeing and hearing, vexed his righteous soul from day to day with their unlawful deeds;
>
> The Lord knoweth how to deliver the godly out of temptations, and to reserve the unjust unto the day of judgment to be punished. (2 Peter 2:4–9)

One of the things that became very interesting to me was the way the above verses referred to the Flood story. You will notice Jesus directly refers to the, "Days of Noah," as a time that will be similar to His return one day to earth a second time. Jesus goes on to explain the similar characteristics people will have during both of these worldwide wrath events. The words of the Bible informs us the Flood appeared to be somewhat of a surprise to the people living on the earth during this time, except for Noah. Most would understand the acts of eating, drinking, and giving in marriage are not in themselves evil, so what was Jesus trying to tell us about this time. This warning from Jesus seems to be inferring the people living during this time were so caught up in life and the affairs of the world, they failed or refused to recognize the state of the world's sinful condition. The Flood caught those people living on the earth who were spiritually blind by surprise, resulting in their death. Jesus warns a worldwide spiritual blindness resulting in people being unable to recognize the signs of evil going on around them, will again take place in the future.

When I continued to look at other biblical references concerning the flood event being described in the book of Peter, more pieces of the puzzle started coming together for me. I know the word, "Denial," is a strong word, but the words of Peter are clearly informing us the Flood of Noah apparently took place because of some event taking place in the spiritual realm. The book of Peter relays to us some very bizarre information describing angels who evidently got into some very serious trouble, and were severely disciplined by God. A person also needs to notice these events seem to have taken place during the time before the Flood. Evidently, these angels were put in chains, and were cast into the lowest chambers of hell for some type of crime they committed on earth before the Flood occurred. Peter appears to be linking this past strange event involving angels with the worldwide destruction from God of all flesh on earth, the eternal incarceration of a select number of angels, and the saving of Noah and his entire family from God's wrath. The question I struggled with for years, related to why the Bible informs us in several texts angels are still to this day incarcerated and chained, because of some event they participated in before the flood. What types of sins could these fallen angels participated in making God so angry they were bound in chains, currently awaiting future judgment in the lowest levels of hell?

Peter also informs us through the wisdom of the Holy Spirit that Noah was a preacher of righteousness. I am not aware of any place in the scriptures where it states how long Noah and likely his sons spent building the ark. I know many people use the scripture reference below in Genesis referring to 120 years. I believe this scriptural reference relates to the amount of time God would continue to tolerate these types of sins being committed on the earth. God is telling those living on the earth during that time they had 120 more years to clean their lives up, or the hammer of God's judgment would fall.

> And the Lord said, "My Spirit shall not strive with man forever, because he also is flesh; nevertheless his days shall be one hundred and twenty years." (Genesis 6:3)

The above scripture text references the time frame before the flood God would give mankind the opportunity to repent and turn from their evil ways. For some reason, it appeared as though God had changed His mind and had enough with the amount of evil existing on the earth during this time. Although no one knows for certain, I believe it very likely took Noah and his family ten to twenty years to build the ark. I'm sure the people dwelling on the earth during this time heard about the Ark Noah was building. I'm sure thousands of people walked by admiring this monstrous boat, and they heard the preaching coming from Noah pleading with them to repent, and turn towards God. The Bible seems to be informing us Noah could convince none living on the earth during this time judgment was coming. Noah and his family were the only people that were saved from God's wrath on the entire earth. The fact Noah was preaching to those dwelling on the earth and could not persuade one person to repent of their sins, should give all people insight concerning the spiritual condition of men's hearts on the earth during this time. At least Noah was able to convince his own family to enter the ark. We will be taking a look later on in the book at a man by the name of Lot who was unable to convince his immediate family God's wrath was coming. These Bible stories should all be taken as spiritual pictures and patterns of what will again be the spiritual condition of men's hearts dwelling on the earth during the end of this age.

Just think of it, there were more than likely millions of people living on the earth during this time, and according to the Bible Noah was the only man recorded as being righteous. This was an astonishing moment for me when I realized this truth. This realization now brings new meaning to the words of Jesus stating the future time during His second coming would be like the days of Noah. But this is not the end of the story, it's just the beginning. One of the main points I am trying to stress to people is the Bible gives us many clues if our eyes are spiritually open. A question people constantly ask me is, "Will God, one day pour out His wrath on the righteous." My response to people when I am asked this question is to ask them how many righteous people perished during the Flood. Of course, the answer to this question is not one person. The key to understanding the future is to understand the past. This reminds me of another clue Jesus gives us concerning the condition of men's hearts at the coming end of this age.

> I tell you that he will avenge them speedily.
> Nevertheless when the Son of man cometh, shall
> he find faith on the earth? (Luke 18:8)

What is Jesus trying to tell us here in this verse? Jesus is saying the situation on earth right before His second coming will be similar to the way it was when Noah was living on the earth. Just as it was in the days of Noah, during a future time of tribulation coming on the earth, those dwelling on the earth will again have no faith or belief in God. There is coming a time in the future and only God knows this time, when men will no longer be receptive, and they will completely refuse the gospel message of salvation. It will truly be just like it was in the days of Noah.

I would like to bring up a couple more points on the above verses in the book of Peter. Notice the Bible also links the events of the Flood to the destruction of Sodom and the cities of the plain. The Bible also tells us a story of a man named Lot who lived in the city of Sodom. The Bible informs us Lot was greatly troubled with the constant acts of unrighteousness he witnessed every day in this city. I also began to realize this story gives us many answers of what again will take place in the future. Yes, what has happened in the past is extremely important and valuable for all people willing to open their spiritual eyes and ears. For some reason this information on biblical history is not being discussed in most churches today. We will be taking a closer look at the story of Lot and the cities of the plain later on in the book.

The second chapter of 2 Peter gives us more very valuable information concerning God's love for the righteous. Verse 9 in the book of Peter tells us God is very capable of taking care, protecting, and even rescuing those who are righteous, while at the same time pouring His wrath out on the ungodly. Noah and his family being literally shut in the ark by the hand of God is a powerful example of this spiritual truth. We will also discover the story of Lot also shows the love and protective power God displays for His children. What I have discovered as I have studied the Bible, is there appears to be story patterns I believe God has put in place for those who pay attention and are able to discern them. I have discovered there are many story patterns with this same overall theme repeated over and over throughout the Bible, and I am certain these verses are not there by coincidence. I have also discovered word patterns are used throughout the Bible being extremely important for God's children to pay attention too. Examples of such word patterns would include people the Bible refers to as; righteous, just, godly, overcomers, clothed in white, spiritually alive, and able to spiritually see and hear. Some examples of people the Bible refers to as unrighteous would be those referred to as; unjust, blind, naked, spiritually dead, and those who dwell upon the earth.

As we continue to look at other subjects in the Bible, these story and word patterns will become more and more evident to the reader.

The Bible comes right out and tells us many of the events referred to in the Old Testament are not just stories of historical events that have taken place, but are actual warnings of future events yet to take place. As my Bible studies continued, I began to realize there seems to be no end to the biblical patterns in the Bible. Not only are there story and word patterns, there are name, place, date, number, and even patterns in the heavens pointing to the awesomeness of God, and the validity of the Bible. The awareness of these truths has confirmed in my heart the Holy Bible is without question written under the inspiration of God. The Bible says what it means, and means what it says.

All scripture is inspired by God and profitable for teaching, for reproof, for correction, and for training in righteousness (2 Timothy 3:16).

The heavens declare the glory of God; and the firmament sheweth his handywork.
Day unto day uttereth speech, and night unto night sheweth knowledge. (Psalms 19:1–2)

Let's take a look at the Hebrew meaning of one Bible character to prove a point. I need to give credit to Dr. Chuck Missler for sharing this information. This example relates to the biblical character Methuselah. We know according to the Bible, Methuselah was the son of Enoch, and he was the grandfather of Noah. The Bible records Methuselah lived to be 969 years of age, and according to information given by Dr. Missler there is evidence Methuselah may have died the very year the flood came. Dr. Missler shares on a YouTube video dealing with the, "Days of Noah," the meaning of the name Methuselah could mean, "His Death Shall Bring." I will also state *Hitchcock's Bible Names Dictionary* defines Methuselah as meaning, "He Has Sent His Death," which appears to have similar meaning. Dr. Missler believes the Bible could be informing us the name, "Methuselah," may be a prophetic warning informing people living during those days, failure to repent would bring divine judgment from God. So if the very names of the Bible reveal prophetic truths, the name Methuselah may not only be a picture of judgment, but also a picture of God's mercy, and His patience with sinful man. I would say if God would be willing to wait 969 years before sending wrath upon His creation, this is definitely a picture of a merciful God.

Let's continue with a few more verses from Genesis relating to the biblical flood and its purpose. You will notice for now I am skipping the first four verses of Genesis chapter 6. We will in the following chapter take a closer look at these four verses along with other scripture references, where the Bible will literally define for us the identity of, "The Sons of God."

> And God saw that the wickedness of man was great in the earth, and that every imagination of the thoughts of his heart was only evil continually.
>
> And it repented the Lord that he had made man on the earth, and it grieved him at his heart.
>
> And the Lord said, I will destroy man whom I have created from the face of the earth; both man, and beast, and the creeping thing, and the fowls of the air; for it repenteth me that I have made them.
>
> But Noah found grace in the eyes of the Lord.
>
> These are the generations of Noah: Noah was a just man and perfect in his generations, and Noah walked with God.
>
> And Noah begat three sons, Shem, Ham, and Japheth.
>
> The earth also was corrupt before God, and the earth was filled with violence.
>
> And God looked upon the earth, and behold, it was corrupt; for all flesh had corrupted his way upon the earth.
>
> And God said unto Noah, The end of all flesh is come before me; for the earth is filled

with violence through them; and, behold, I will destroy them with the earth. (Genesis 6:5–13)

But with thee will I establish my covenant; and thou shalt come into the ark, thou, and thy sons, and thy wife, and thy sons' wives with thee. (Genesis 6:18)

And the Lord said unto Noah, Come thou and all thy house into the ark; for thee have I seen righteous before me in this generation. (Genesis 7:1)

For yet seven days, and I will cause it to rain upon the earth forty days and forty nights; and every living substance that I have made will I destroy from off the face of the earth. (Genesis 7:4)

And it came to pass after seven days, that the waters of the flood were upon the earth.

In the six hundredth year of Noah's life, in the second month, the seventeenth day of the month, the same day were all the fountains of the great deep broken up, and the windows of heavens were opened. (Genesis 7:10–11)

And they went in upon Noah into the ark, two and two of all flesh, wherein is the breath of life.

And they that went in, went in male and female of all flesh, as God had commanded him: and the Lord shut him in. (Genesis 7:15–16)

And every living substance was destroyed which was upon the face of the ground, both man, and cattle, and the creeping things, and the fowl of the heaven; and they were destroyed from the earth: and Noah only remained alive, and they that were with him in the ark. (Genesis 7:23)

In my opinion, the Flood of Noah is probably one of the most popular stories ever recorded in the Bible. You will notice I really don't deal with the issue of whether or not there was a literal biblical flood. Since there are at least five hundred recorded stories and legends of a cataclysmic flood event besides the biblical account, I see no point in taking the discussion any further. If someone wants to argue no such event as the flood of Noah ever took place which according to the Bible was a worldwide flood, all I can say is the evidence is overwhelming once a person does the research.

The Flood event was one of the stories I began to question in my early years of teaching. Keep in mind, I wasn't ever questioning the fact the flood of Noah actually took place as was described in the Bible. My question has always been related to why the flood occurred in the first place. One of the points Genesis appears to bring out is God seems to be talking in a manner leading a person to believe He was sorry or disappointed He ever created man in the first place. This bothered me a great deal since I understood the scriptural truth God is, "All Knowing." It is obvious God was since, "The Garden of Eden," and, "The Cain and Abel," events not surprised man all of a sudden had the capacity to sin, and they had a problem with disobedience. It was also obvious from Genesis chapter 3 and other scriptural references, God from the beginning of time knew a Redeemer would be needed to save mankind from their sins. The idea of God becoming surprised when Adam and Eve sinned in the garden, and mankind continuing to sin caused God to destroy all flesh, to me was an impossible conclusion. I knew in my heart there was more the Bible was trying to tell us.

Verse 7 in Genesis chapter 6 even brought up more questions for me. Not only does it appear God seems to be sorry for creating mankind, but God now expresses He regrets creating all living things. I would think to myself, I can somewhat understand God becoming upset with people because of the sins they were committing, but why would God suddenly decide to destroy every living creature on earth. We need to remember this is the same God that states the following.

> And God saw everything that he had made, and, behold, it was very good. And the evening and the morning were the sixth day. (Genesis 1:31)

Notice God states everything He made was, "Very Good." Here we have a picture of God's creation before the fall. Here God gives us a spiritual and scientific truth man continues to deny every day. When God created everything, it was perfect and it was flawless. So the question is, what could have been the reason for causing God to destroy all flesh? As a Christian and a Bible teacher I continued to search for the answer. I knew there must be a reason. Over and over in these verses, God seems to be exhibiting deep grief and anguish over considering the possibility of destroying His creation. I can understand God's frequent disappointment with our behavior, but why was there a need to destroy all flesh?

But in the midst of what seemed like a frustrating and disappointing moment for God, there seems to suddenly be hope for all life. In verse 8 the Bible informs us Noah found grace in the eyes of the Lord. Of course, we know the definition of grace is unmerited favor. Notice here in verse 8 God mentions the name of one person. No other names of the millions of people living on the earth during this time are mentioned. The earth during this time is more than likely inhabited with millions of people, and God mentions the name of one person who He finds grace with. Are you kidding me? Could the Bible be telling us there is only one righteous man living on the earth during this time? Yes, I believe this is exactly what the Bible is telling us. Notice the interesting parallels the Bible gives us concerning this lack of righteousness being present on earth also occurs during an event referred to as the, "Day of the Lord," in Isaiah.

> And I will punish the world for their evil, and the wicked for their iniquity; and I will cause the arrogancy of the proud to cease, and will lay low the haughtiness of the terrible.
>
> I will make a man more precious than fine gold; even a man than the golden wedge of Ophir. (Isaiah 13:11–12)

Continuing on with verse 9, the Bible informs us Noah was a just or a righteous man, he was perfect in his generations, and he walked with God. The fact Noah found grace in God's eyes, God calls him righteous, and he walked with God did not trouble me. It was the comment the Bible makes concerning Noah being perfect in his generations I did not understand. Why was God so concerned about Noah being perfect in his generations? We find the literal Hebrew interpretation of the word, "Perfect," means to be, "Without Spot or Blemish." Is the Bible trying to tell us Noah was perfect like Christ? I don't believe so, because according to the Bible all have sinned and come short of the glory of God. The Bible here is trying to tell us Noah had, "No Spot," or, "Blemish," in his generations, and he is considered by God as righteous. The definition here of the word, "Generations," has to do with what would be referred to as a person's, "Genetics," or, "DNA." Something very strange went on during the days of Noah, possibly having something to do with the genetic corruption of all life on earth.

Evidently God has become so upset due to the corruption of all flesh on the earth, He instructs Noah to build an ark. God informs Noah a flood is coming which will destroy all life on the earth. God also gives Noah specific instructions as to how the ark should be built. We will not be spending much time dealing with the measurements and dimensions of the ark. An entire Bible study could be conducted relating to the specific size, and the symbolic nature of the ark. I will state one interesting fact relating to Noah's ark, is many large ships even today are built to the exact ratio and dimensions God gives Noah, due to the stability and buoyancy a ship with these dimensions will have while floating in the water.

God informs Noah it was with him only He would establish His covenant. Another interesting point most miss is the fact God also informs Noah in Genesis chapter 7 the number of days before the flood was to come upon the earth. It was no surprise to Noah God's wrath was coming upon the earth, and he even knew the day it would commence. Since I believe the Bible uses patterns to inform and warn the believer, it should not surprise us to find other scripture references directly informing and warning the church saints, in similar ways God spoke to Noah.

> But of the times and the seasons, brethren, ye have no need that I write unto you.
>
> For yourselves know perfectly that the day of the Lord so cometh as a thief in the night.
>
> For when they shall say, Peace and safety; then sudden destruction cometh upon them, as travail upon a woman with child; and they shall not escape.
>
> Be ye, brethren, are not in darkness, that that day should overtake you as a thief.
>
> Ye are all the children of light, and the children of the day: we are not of the night, nor of darkness.
>
> Therefore let us not sleep, as do others; but let watch and be sober.
>
> For they that sleep in the night; and they that be drunken are drunken in the night.
>
> But let us, who are of the day, be sober, putting on the breastplate of faith and love; and for an helmet, the hope of salvation.
>
> For God hath not appointed us to wrath, but to obtain salvation by our Lord Jesus Christ. (1 Thessalonians 5:1–9)

A couple quick points on the above nine verses. So far, I've stressed over and over the importance of biblical patterns. When the

Bible gives us specific information stating it over and over again, God is more than likely wanting to make sure we get the message. It is important to first define Paul is speaking here to the brethren, to those who are part of the body of Christ. Paul is also stating there should be no doubt for the Christian whose spiritual eyes are open, where we are in God's prophetic timetable. Another prophetic pattern most people miss would be to understand what groups of people are being addressed in the text. For example, there is a big difference between using the words, "Them," or, "Us," when referencing a group of people. A person needs to understand these same word patterns carry on through the entire Bible. In the book of Revelation for example, we keep running into the phrase, "Those who dwell on the Earth." When we begin to pick up on these biblical truths, there is tremendous spiritual insight that is gained.

When a person reads verse 9 in 1 Thessalonians, the Bible again informs us of another biblical truth recorded over and over in the Bible, and I am constantly shocked most Christians do not grasp this concept. The Bible promises the true church, the brethren, or the bride of Christ have not been appointed to God's wrath, but to salvation. When the Bible tells us we have been saved from the wrath of God, the Bible means what it says, and says what it means. In the same way Noah was spared from God's wrath being sent upon the earth, so too will the Bride of Christ be one day saved from the wrath to come. This is the very reason the Bible states we in the church body are to comfort one another with these words.

> Much more then, being now justified by
> his blood, we shall be saved from wrath through
> him. (Romans 5:9)

The Bible states Noah was obedient with all the instructions God gave him. The Bible also states Noah was six hundred years of age when he walked into the ark. Notice the Bible informs us the very month and day the wrath of God came upon those dwelling on the earth. Here, the Bible again gives us a scientific fact related to the lifespans of individuals living during this time. It was not unusual for people living during this period of time to have lifespans lasting hundreds of years. These biblical facts are in direct contrast to the theory of evolution which is widely taught today in most schools. It is interesting the second law of thermodynamics states things tend to go from order to disorder. Things do not appear to become better with time, they tend to become disorderly and develop flaws. I am currently fifty-six years of age, and yes I have definitely evolved. I take more and more ibuprofen, the more evolved I become. Your lawnmower or the engine in your car doesn't improve with time, they require overhauls.

Another point almost always overlooked is the fact the Bible mentions the Flood event was not only the result of flooding rains, but was also the result of the fountains of the deep breaking up, and spewing forth water. The Bible here is giving us another clue of what was occurring on the earth during this time. The Flood of Noah was evidently not just a time of tremendous flooding. The Flood was also a time when great cataclysmic events took place on the earth. I believe it was at this time there were extremely violent geologic earth changes being similar in nature to future events yet to take place, and are discussed in great detail in the book of Revelation. Revelation refers to geologic and heavenly events coming on the earth being so severe, every mountain and island will be removed from their place. So here again, the Bible is attempting to inform and help us to understand what took place during the Genesis Flood event, should give us the spiritual insight to better understand what will again happen in the future. I see today a complete absence of this teaching and biblical understanding in most churches today.

Just a couple more points the Bible makes concerning the Flood. Some will argue the Bible may indeed be describing a historical flood, but it was more than likely a regional event and not a worldwide event. The problem is, this is not the facts the Bible or the historical record is presenting to us. This argument is also in direct opposition to hundreds of stories and historical accounts. The Bible makes it perfectly clear, the ark was lifted up above the earth, the ark floated upon the face of the waters, and all high hills on the surface of the earth were covered with water. The Bible also continues by stating the flood waters rose fifteen cubits above the mountains and covered them. It is also amazing the spiritual picture these verses portray to us when the Bible states the ark was lifted above the earth. The ark that held Noah, his family, and the animals were supernaturally protected from the wrath of God.

One last point I would like to make before we move on, is the Bible records in Genesis the ark had one door. The Bible records once Noah, his family, and male and female animals of every kind entered the ark, God shut the door. Noah did not shut the door. God shut the door. The fate of those people inside and those people outside the ark was eternally sealed by God. This is a prophetic picture of what will take place again.

> I am the door: by me if any man enter in, he shall be saved, and shall go in and out, and find pasture.
>
> The thief cometh not, but for to steal, and to kill, and to destroy: I am come that they might have life, and that they might have it more abundantly.
>
> I am the good shepherd: the good shepherd giveth his life for the sheep. (John 10:9–11)

Jesus truly is the door. All who were in the ark were saved. All life outside the ark was destroyed. The Old Testament stories are very important for us today. They contain spiritual truths that apply to our daily lives, as well as inform us of events that will take place in the future. The biblical Flood story is a warning to all that read it. The Flood story should now bring new understanding to those who are spiritually awake when Jesus stated to all who would listen, today is the day of salvation. In the same way God sealed the door to the ark with an eternal finality, according to the Bible, a future similar event will again have the same eternal circumstances.

One of the main reasons I am writing this book is because God has given me a deep conviction concerning the spiritual decisions people are making today. I see people living today being consumed by materialism, keeping up with the neighbors, and constantly striving to find ways to find happiness to fill a void in their lives only God can fill. Quite honestly, most people are living their lives and making the same types of spiritual decisions people were making during the days of Noah. The ark was meant to be a spiritual picture of Christ. The door to the ark of Christ is open. Run into the ark of Christ while you still can. The flood of Noah is not just another allegorical story. This is a lie from the father of lies, Satan.

Babylonian winged god, "Marduk." A god of many names.

There were giants in the earth in those days; and also after that, when the sons of God came in unto the daughters of men, and they bare children to them, the same became mighty men which were of old, men of renown. Genesis 6:4 KJV

The Sons of God

I must confess right up front the subject dealing with identifying, "The Sons of God," discussed in Genesis, has been one of the most eye-opening and interesting biblical subjects I have ever studied. It is my belief this chapter will contain some of the most shocking information it will cause even the most mature Christian to struggle with, and many people will be unable to spiritually handle and digest this information. I have found over 90 percent of the church population has no earthly idea what the Bible is really trying to tell them concerning this subject. If you can recall several pages back, I discussed scripture references relating to the subject of a person's spiritual maturity.

In 1 Corinthians chapter 3, Paul reminds the brethren there were various biblical subjects he would like to teach or discuss with them, but he was unable to do so. Paul goes on to state these immature brethren would be unable to handle some biblical truths, because of their spiritual immaturity. Paul calls these immature Christians carnal, meaning their spiritual condition was temporal and worldly. Paul compares these brethren to infants being only capable of drinking spiritual milk.

So as we dig into this study concerning the identity of who these Sons of God really were, I would like to give the reader a word of warning before we proceed. I would ask each of you read and study this subject very carefully, take every fact presented by the Bible, pray, and draw your own conclusions. I have stated many times in my classes, too many people today receive information whether it comes from a pastor, teacher, professor, or even a scientist, and they fail to do their homework on the issue.

I have come to the conclusion this lack of spiritual maturity will be the primary reason for a worldwide deception that has already began, and will climax during a future, "Great Deception," God literally allows to take place. We will later on take a closer look at the events relating to this coming deception. We must remember the only real truth we have is the word of God. The verses below in Isaiah and Hosea reminds us of this fact.

> My people are destroyed for lack of knowledge: because thou has rejected knowledge, I will also reject thee, that thou shalt be no priest to me: seeing thou hast forgotten the law of thy God, I will also forget thy children. (Hosea 4:6)

> Therefore my people are gone in captivity, because they have no knowledge: and their honourable men are famished, and their multitude dried up with thirst. (Isaiah 5:13)

In the beginning of the book, I shared some of my struggles as an early Christian and teacher. As I have studied the Bible throughout the years, several questions concerning biblical stories, events, and prophecies continued to arise and bother me. I knew from a prophetic perspective, deception would play a key role as we approached the end of this age. The books of Revelation and Daniel have always been two books that have fascinated me, partly because I understood both of these books were key in understanding what will take place in the future. It was several years ago while conducting a study in Revelation, I stumbled across a YouTube video dealing with the sixth chapter of Genesis. The person presenting this video was Dr. Chuck Missler. The biblical flood account was a Bible story bothering me a great deal due to the mystery regarding the sudden change in God's character, and the purpose for the flood in the first place. It seemed to me if God was going to wipe the slate clean, the time of Adam and Eve's disobedience, or the incident with Cain when he murdered his brother Abel would be a more reasonable time to start over with creation. The question relating to the flood being the result of people becoming increasingly evil was one issue I could understand, but what could be the reason as to why God suddenly saw the need to destroy His entire creation. What could the destruction of all animal life on earth have to do with man's disobedience to God?

When looking at the Genesis chapter 3 prophecies dealing with the two seeds, I believed God was letting us know He had already made a way to deal with sin by one day sending a perfect Lamb who was Jesus, God's only Son. So out of curiosity I listened to the YouTube video presented by Dr. Missler stating his case for the cause of the Genesis Flood account. As I listened to the video, I knew in my spirit the words this man was speaking were truthful because they were first of all backed with scripture. For the first time after years of research, many of the questions I had been searching for answers to for years, and the ideas I had concerning the flood were being confirmed in my spirit. Finally, I was beginning to understand fully the truth of what the Bible was really trying to tell us. I give Dr. Missler credit for bringing sanity to my spirit relating to the issue of what really took place during the days of Noah. For the first time in my life, I had a brother in Christ telling me the information I needed to hear. For the first time in my life, I was receiving confirmation of what the Bible was literally trying to tell me, and the real reason God sent a worldwide flood. I was now certain Noah's flood was sent by God due to disobedience and apostasy in the spiritual realm.

As time went on, the more I studied, the more sense the Bible was making to me. The more my knowledge of the Bible increased, the more I would want to share my newfound information with my brothers and sisters in Christ. Here I was, a man in his late forties, a man who had been in church all his life, a church member, a born-again believer, and a man who had never heard or been taught this information before. So in a sense, this is how the desire to write a book began. So I begin to do what all excited Christians do when they discover biblical truth, I began to share this information with others.

As I began to teach and share the truths I was learning, I became shocked with the responses I was getting from my own brothers and sisters in Christ. I began to feel a sense of alienation from my own Christian friends when discussing this issue. Many of my own friends were treating me like someone who was upsetting the boat of church traditionalism and was going against church doctrine. I went through a very depressing time in my Christian life struggling with my desire and calling to teach the truth of God's word. The truths of the Bible were becomings more and more transparent to me, but very few in the church wanted to listen, or was afraid to listen to this message.

My spiritual struggle continued for approximately three years. I became somewhat disinterested and disconnected with church. To be honest, my views and scriptural interpretations of many Bible verses were seen by most Christians as being almost radical and heretical. I would describe my teaching style as one causing a person to come to their own conclusions relating to the interpretations of scriptures, using the Bible as the sole source for truth. I have always held to the belief, it is good for a person to be able to answer questions dealing with why and how they believe what they believe concerning their Christian faith. It is amazing how many people take a stance on a biblical topic based solely on traditions, and long held family interpretations and superstitions.

My goal as a teacher was always to try to make the Bible come alive in class by bringing up current events, and relating them to specific biblical texts. What I was noticing in churches today was a disbelief and a disconnection with what the Bible was literally informing the church concerning spiritual issues, and our individual daily Christian walk. I have discovered the idea of studying Bible prophecy subjects in the church setting is really not welcomed in most churches today, and it seems to be directly linked with the interpretations a person has with the Bible. I was witnessing in the church, the steady decline in the belief of a literal interpretation of scripture, and an increase in the belief the Bible is a book of moral teaching and allegorical stories. The Bible warns the church in several places a falling away from sound doctrine is a sign we are living in the end times, which will climax to the point sound doctrine will literally one day be refused in most churches. The coming one day world religious system will be made up of many religions worshipping together under one roof. The problem with this is in order to achieve this goal, conservative and literal views concerning the Bible must be done away with. The belief Jesus Christ is the only way, the only truth, and the only life will in the future be completely rejected by the church.

It was my lovely wife Ginger who would occasionally tell me after seeing and feeling my day-to-day frustration, that I should write a book. My wife would tell me, "Russ, you walk around with all this information in your head, and you need to find a way to share it with the world." I thought to myself, "That's the craziest thing I've ever heard." I believed God had called me to teach, God didn't call me to write a book. I was trying to make myself believe there was no way possible I could write a book, because I believed I didn't have the qualifications. I didn't graduate from a seminary or with a doctorate in theology. I was just a simple country boy who nobody would want to listen too. The seed God planted in my heart through the encouragement of my wife slowly began to take root. It would take three years of God continuing to work on my heart, finally causing me to accept God's calling. Sometimes it takes time for God to get a person to the point He can use them. I am definitely one of those examples.

Now that I've given some background information relating to my past experiences, I would like to take a little deeper look into the Genesis flood account. I would also again like to give credit to Dr. Chuck Missler for playing a part in my understanding of some very key truths in the book of Genesis, I now realize greatly impact the message of the entire Bible. One thing I have learned through the years, is truth always comes directly from the Bible. It is when man gets involved with the interpretation of scripture, errors arise. So with that being said, let's take a look at the first four verses in Genesis chapter 6.

> And it came to pass, when men began to multiply on the face of the earth, and daughters were born unto them,
>
> That the sons of God saw the daughters of men that they were fair; and they took them wives of all which they chose.
>
> And the Lord said, My spirit shall not always strive with man, for that he also is flesh: yet his days shall be an hundred and twenty years.
>
> There were giants in the earth in those days; and also after that, when the sons of God came in unto the daughters of men, and they bare children to them, the same became mighty men which were of old, men of renown. (Genesis 6:1–4)

I will begin by saying there is a tremendous amount of controversy relating to these four verses in Genesis 6. I will admit, for close to forty years I read these verses and didn't have a clue as to their real meaning. For years, even as a teacher these four verses bothered me as much as any other verses in the Bible. What became more interesting over time, was when I started asking questions relating to this subject to other mature Christians, teachers, and even pastors, I realized most people had no clue to the real meaning of these verses either.

To try to explain this subject as simple as possible, most if not all seminaries, churches, and pastors hold to a view known as the, "Sethite," view. Simply put, the Sethite view teaches the interpretation of Genesis chapter 6 deals with a righteous line of people, referred to in the Bible as, "The Sons of God," comingling themselves with an unrighteous line of people. These people are referred to in the Bible as the, "Daughters of Adam." Another way of describing the reason for such abhorrent wickedness on the earth, was due to righteous, "Sethite," males intermarrying with the evil daughters of Cain. This intermarriage between righteous and unrighteous people according to this view, is what caused God to become so distraught He decided to destroy all life on earth and start over. A person needs to keep in mind, according to this view there is nothing mentioned of the possibility of righteous, "Sethite," females marrying the evil sons of Cain.

So according to the, "Sethite," view, it is this apparent unholy union between, "Sethites," and the daughters of Cain, causing Giants to be born on the earth during this time. Keep in mind, this belief is what most churches and seminaries hold to today. There is one major problem with this view. When a person reads Genesis chapter 6 or anywhere else in the Bible, a person will not find one single verse supporting evidence for this view. Quite honestly, the biggest problem with the, "Sethite," view, is it clearly is not what the Bible is telling us.

According to research conducted by Dr. Chuck Missler, the Sethite view has been around since the fifth century. It was during this time, a man named Julius Africanus came up with this view as an alternate explanation to the literal interpretation of scripture. In other words, the thought or idea was surely the scriptures can't be referring to angels committing sins with women; therefore, the Bible must be referring to the intermarrying between righteous and unrighteous groups of individuals. Further study tells us Augustine also embraced the, "Sethite," doctrine, and it became the general orthodox view continuing to this day. This view has also spilled into the early Protestant churches, and also continues to be taught in most churches and seminaries during the present time.

Let's now take an in-depth look at what the Bible is trying to tell us in Genesis. A couple points I would like to make as we look into Genesis chapter 6, is you will notice this extremely controversial subject seems to take place in the scriptural context of the flood, suggests this event takes places before the flood, and appears to be a direct cause for the flood.

When we take a closer look at the first verse in Genesis 6, we will see the Bible is referring to a time when men were multiplying on the earth, and for some reason makes the point this event occurred during a time when daughters were being born. When we look at the Hebrew translation for the word, "Men," used in this verse, we find the actual translation refers to men who were born of Adam. This is a reference relating to, "All Men," since all men are born of Adam's seed. We also find the Hebrew translation for the word, "Daughters," seems to be referencing, "All Women," since all women are also born of Adam's seed. So we can see the first verse is trying to inform us this event evidently happened in the past during a time when men, "Adomites," were populating the earth, and daughters, "Daughters of Adam," were being born. This is simply what the scripture is trying to tell us. No more and no less.

It is when we take a look at the second verse in Genesis chapter 6, the story starts getting a little more interesting. The Bible informs us during this time when men were populating the earth, and daughters were being born, "The Sons of God," whoever they were, looked or lusted after these "Daughters," taking wives of all they desired. It is in verse 2 of this chapter, the Bible lists two groups of people that will be crucial in understanding the purpose for the flood event. What I discovered is the Bible will define for us who these two groups of people are.

When looking at the words, "Sons of God," we find this translation comes from the Hebrew word, "Bene ha Elohim," which literally means, "Sons of God." When we go through the entire Old Testament scriptures, we find four other examples where this exact Hebrew term is used. Below is a list of these four scriptural references all found in the Old Testament.

> Now there was a day when the sons of God
> came to present themselves before the Lord, and
> Satan came also among them. (Job 1:6)

> Again there was a day when the sons of God
> came to present themselves before the Lord, and
> Satan came also among them to present himself
> before the Lord. (Job 2:1)

> Who hath laid the measures thereof, if thou
> knowest? or who hath stretched the line upon it?
> Whereupon are the foundations thereof fas-
> tened? or who laid the corner stone thereof;
> When the morning stars sang together, and
> all the sons of God shouted for joy? (Job 38:5–7)

> For who in the heaven can be compared
> unto the Lord? who among the sons of the mighty
> can be likened unto the Lord? (Psalm 89:6)

When a person searches through the entire Old Testament and studies the scriptural references listed above for, "Sons of God," the Old Testament in every text confirms this phrase is referring to angels. I will also add, when a person investigates the Septuagint definition of this term which is the Greek translation of the Old Testament, the phrase, "Sons of God," is translated as angels. One can find no place in the entire Old Testament where the term, "Sons of God," is referring to men born of Adam or Seth for that matter. Notice, I state men born of Adam. Adam and Eve were the only two created human beings mentioned in the Bible having no earthly father besides Jesus Christ. Adam and Eve were both created personally by God. Jesus, who the Bible declares was overshadowed by the Holy Spirit, literally was the, "Son of God," because God literally was His Father. This also explains the reason I earlier went into such detail concerning the state of an individual's spiritual condition in the eyes of God. Since all men born with the exception of Adam and Eve are born of Adam's seed, the Bible declares we are all born in sin needing a Savior from the moment of birth. Actually if we want to get it technically correct, it is during the very act of conception the seed of sin passes from the father to the child.

Another question that always comes up relating to the identity of these, "Sons of God," is the New Testament tells us those, "In Christ," are also referred to as being "Sons of God." The verses below deal with this question.

> But as many as received him, to them gave
> the power to become the sons of God, even to
> them that believe on his name. (John 1:12)

> Behold, what manner of love the Father
> hath bestowed upon us, that we should be called

the sons of God: therefore the world knoweth us
not, because it knew him not.

Beloved, now are we the sons of God, and
it doth not yet appear what we shall be: but we
know that, when he shall appear, we shall be like
him; for we shall see him as he is. (1 John 3:1–2)

Therefore if any man be in Christ, he is a
new creature: old things are passed away; behold,
all things are become new. (2 Corinthians 5:17)

In the verses above, we see what many people would refer to as
a contradiction in the scriptures. How can the, "Sons of God," spoken of in the Old Testament be referring to angels, when we read in
the New Testament, those, "in Christ," are also referred to as being
a, "Son of God." As always, we will find the answer in the Bible,
and we notice the verse above in 2 Corinthians gives us a clue to this
answer. Notice in Corinthians it mentions those, "In Christ," are
worthy to be called, "Sons of God," because they have recognized
their spiritual condition apart from Christ. These people realize
apart from God's grace they are sinners in need of a Savior. When
God through the Holy Spirit convicts an individual of sin in their
life and they receive Christ, he or she literally becomes a new creature. According to the Bible, when an individual professes Christ as
Lord and Savior, God literally recreates and restores their spiritual
relationship with Him. This is where we get the term, "Born Again."
This reminds me of the conversation a Pharisee named Nicodemus
had with Christ.

Jesus answered and said unto him, Verily,
verily, I say unto thee, Except a man be born
again, he cannot see the kingdom of God.

Nicodemus saith unto him, How can a man
be born when he is old? can he enter the second
time into his mother's womb, and be born?

Jesus answered, Verily, verily, I say unto thee, Except a man be born of water and of the Spirit, he cannot enter into the kingdom of God.

That which is born of the flesh is flesh; and that which is born of the Spirit is spirit. (John 3:3–6)

So here again we see the Bible answering the question for us. Who born of Adam has the right to be called a, "Son of God?" It is those having professed Christ as Lord and Savior, and only those who have been born of Spirit, not of flesh. So those who trust Christ can be called, "Sons of God," due to becoming literal children and joint heirs with Christ.

So who are these, "Sons of God," spoken of here in Genesis. They are the angels of God being present with Him before the foundations of the world were created.

Now let's take a look at the phrase, "Daughters of Men," mentioned in Genesis 6:2. The Hebrew meaning for the term, "Daughters of Men," is here defined as the, "Daughters of Adam." According to the Hebrew definition, this phrase is defining all women born on the earth.

When I realized the literal biblical conclusion of the first two verses in Genesis, I came to some very startling conclusions. The Bible seems to be informing us the reason for the flood was because fallen angels lusted after women, took them as wives, and committed sexual sins with them resulting in the genetic corruption of mankind. We will find the Bible also informs us this corruption not only included people, but also included animals. All flesh on the earth was corrupted by these angels.

Let's now take a closer look at verse 3 in Genesis chapter 6 to see what else the Bible can tell us. Taking in consideration what the Bible tells us in the first couple verses, we see God establishing a timeline of 120 years these types of behaviors would be allowed to continue. God appears to be warning those dwelling on the earth before the flood they have 120 years to get it right, or judgment is coming. I believe this 120 year period gives evidence God patiently waited for repentance in the hearts of people during the days of Noah, just as He is patiently waiting today for people to repent, and turn towards Him.

When we read the fourth verse in Genesis chapter 6, we encounter a very strange and interesting term. This verse was one I had struggled with for several years. I have to admit, for years I would just read through these verses, wonder about them for a while, then just move on to what I thought were more important subjects to study. It would be several years later I would realize understanding Genesis chapter 6 would play a key role in understanding a good part of the Old Testament, the New Testament, and most Bible prophecies.

Verse 4 in the King James tells us before the flood and also again after the flood, there were Giants on the earth. You will also notice some versions of the Bible will use the word, "Nephilim," in place of the word, "Giants." The word, "Nephilim" is the actual Hebrew word and it does refer to Giants, but a more accurate definition would define the word as, "The Fallen Ones." The word, "Nephilim," only appears twice in the Bible. We find this term once in Genesis and the other instance is in the book of Numbers chapter 13, during the time the children of Israel were spying out the promised land. The real reason the children of Israel died in the wilderness is because they lacked the faith God would give these giants over to them to be slain. When the Bible states in the book of Numbers the children of Israel were as grasshoppers in the sight of these giants, this is exactly what the Bible is trying to tell us.

The Bible informs us, "The Sons of God," who the Bible defines as angels, evidently sinned with women and the birth of Giants is the result of this relationship. It also appears the offspring of this unholy union are recorded as being, "The Heroes of Old," who were the cause of many legends and fables being told until the end of time. I believe the stories and legends of Greek mythology has its origins in the Genesis 6 event which occurred on earth before the flood. According to Greek mythology, Hercules had a father who was a god or fallen angel, and his mother was a mortal woman, so he would fit the biblical definition of a, "Nephilim," a hero of old. Taking a literal interpretation of the scriptures seems to give valid reasons to why God all of a sudden decided to destroy all flesh on the earth and needed to wipe the slate clean. This literal conclusion of the Genesis 6 verses also answers questions related to many events recorded in the Old Testament. These verses also then connect the dots of the Genesis chapter 3 scriptures dealing with the, "Seed of the Serpent," and how the coming antichrist will literally be Satan's offspring. Here in Genesis chapter 6, we see a literal example of giants being born from the seed of fallen angels or serpent seed.

Now I was beginning to understand why this information has been avoided and covered up. First of all, the thought of an event like this taking place is very hard for anybody to accept, let alone for the church to accept. Believe me, it is many times a lot easier to ignore what the Bible is trying to tell us, or deny this event ever occurred in the first place. The problem with this is, as I continued to study and dig into the scriptures I began to realize there is a connection with what has happened in the past and what will happen in the future. Accepting the Bible as God's literal word reveals truth and wisdom we would otherwise miss out on.

If we look at other texts in the scripture, we now clearly see God became extremely upset with the sinful acts committed by a group of angels. Angels are beings created by God, but evidently angels just like us are given some degree of free will. Remember, the scriptures inform us one third of the angels fell with Satan. Below is a list of Bible verses validating the literal interpretation of the biblical flood, by informing us angels were severely punished for sins they committed during the days of Noah.

> And the angels which kept not their first estate, but left their own habitation, he hath reserved in everlasting chains under darkness unto the judgment of the great day. (Jude 1:6)

> For Christ also hath once suffered for sins, the just for the unjust, that he might bring us to God, being put to death in the flesh, but quickened by the Spirit: By which also he went and preached unto the spirits in prison; Which some-

time were disobedient, when once the longsuffering of God waited in the days of Noah, while the
ark was a preparing, wherein few, that is, eight
souls were saved by water. (1 Peter 3:18–20)

For if God spared not the angels that sinned,
but cast them down to hell, and delivered them
into chains of darkness, to be reserved unto judgment. (2 Peter 2:4)

The Bible gives us similar accounts in the books of Jude and
Peter informing us during the days before the flood angels had crossed
the line, they broke spiritual rules, and God was very upset about it.
The words in Jude states these angels leaving their own habitation
evidently relates to these angels somehow leaving or forsaking their
created purpose, taking on human forms, and coming into our reality in order to participate in such mischief. I also found it interesting
in 1 Peter chapter 3, the verse stating Jesus "Preached," unto the
spirits in prison is misleading. The Greek word for, "preached," is,
"Kerysso," which means, "To herald or proclaim a message with conviction." Christ was not preaching to, "Spirits," in the abyss trying
to convince them they were sinners needing to trust in Him. Christ
is pictured in this text heralding and proclaiming to these evil spirits imprisoned in the lowest levels of Hell, He defeated death, hell,
and the grave, and He was victorious over Satan's plans to destroy
Him along with His creation. Notice 1 Peter outright informs us this
event occurred when angels left their first estate and were disobedient
during the days of Noah.

The Bible also states this group of angels participating in these
horrible sins were thrown into the abyss, and are still this very day
in chains awaiting future judgment. It is for this reason, God had no
choice but to destroy all flesh living on the earth during this time. It is
for this reason, God instructed Noah who was righteous in the sight
of God to build an Ark. A shocking truth that hit me like a hammer,
was when I realized the lengths God went to save just one man and
his family. Another shocking reality is when I realized during the

days of Noah of the millions of people on earth, only one man could be found that was righteous, and God saw to it he survived. Several times in this book I mention the idea of patterns running throughout the entire Bible. Here we see an example of a spiritual truth repeating itself over and over again. The truth is, God loves and goes to great lengths to protect the righteous.

In closing out this chapter, I would like to discuss the subject of Giants a little more. The Bible is informing us angels literally did marry the daughters of men, and they had sexual relations with these women resulting in the birth of giants. The Bible informs us stories, fables, and legends will be told until the end of time, and refers to these offspring as the, "Men of Old, The Men of Renown." I personally believe the birth of these giants explains and gives reasons for the legends of Greek mythology, as well as the reason for building megalithic temples, pyramids, and structures all over the world. I believe these structures were built before the flood of Noah when angels literally walked on earth and had literal offspring. This incursion of fallen angels coming down to earth also explains the worshipping of many gods, and the existence of the many different religions we have in the world. This also gives understanding to the many historical stories relating to, "Star People, gods, or extraterrestrials," coming down to earth, and interfering in the lives of men.

It is interesting in Greek mythology, Zeus is known as the king of the gods who ruled from Mt. Olympus. Zeus supposedly became the ruler of the heavens after revolting against his father Cronus. It is also interesting the name Zeus means, "Bright," or, "Sky." We find scripture in the book of Isaiah where the Bible defines Satan's ultimate goal is, "To be like the Most High." The Bible also refers to Satan as, "The god of This World," and the, "Angel of Light." As stated earlier, I believe this spiritual incursion upon earth also explains the reasoning behind the worshipping of many ancient gods of Greek mythology, astrology, and many other pagan religions. I believe these stories, legends, and religions came as the result of this incident in Genesis chapter 6, since the Bible refers to these men as the, "Men of Old, the Men of Renown."

One quick point I need to again stress, is this disobedience in the angelic realm now explains the reason for God to send a flood wiping out all flesh. Historic texts as well as many other religious texts informs us these angels also corrupted the animals by committing sexual acts with them. It is interesting we also find several stories and legends relating to half-man, half-animal creatures that once walked the earth. Before you start thinking I'm out of my mind, I would suggest researching a subject referred to as, "Transhumanism." You will find out for many years, scientists have been experimenting with ways to mix the genes of different species of animals, and we are even currently mixing the genes of animals with humans. For anyone wanting to further research the subject of transhumanism, I would strongly recommend the research a person named Tom Horn has completed on this subject.

Here is a list of Bible verses proving giants once existed on the earth. I have come across many of these verses over the years, and would wonder what exactly they were referring to. One of the most interesting verses has to do with the real reason the children of Israel were delayed in inhabiting the promised land. The incident in Genesis 6 also answers the question as to why a loving God commanded the children of Israel to kill every man, woman, and child when they encountered groups of people such as the, "Anakims," who were of the sons of Anak. It is because these people were of evil seed, the seed of the serpent. Other groups of giants listed in the Bible includes the Rephaim, Emims, and the Zamzumims.

> But the men that went up with him said, We be not able to go up against the people; for they are stronger than we.
>
> And they brought up an evil report of the land which they had searched unto the children of Israel, saying, The land, through which we have gone to search it, is a land that eateth up the inhabitants thereof; and all the people that we saw in it are men of great stature.
>
> And there we saw the giants, the sons of Anak, which come of the giants: and we were

in our own sight as grasshoppers, and so were in their sight. (Numbers 13:31–33)

And there was yet a battle in Gath, where was a man of great stature, that had on every hand six fingers, and on every foot six toes, four and twenty in number; and he also was born to the giant (2 Samuel 21:20).

And Ishbibenob, which was of the sons of the giant, the weight of whose spear weighed three hundred shekels of brass in weight, he being girded with a new sword, thought to have slain David (2 Samuel 21:16).

For only Og king of Bashan remained of the remnant of giants; behold, his bedstead was a bedstead of iron; is it not in Rabbath of the children of Ammon? Nine cubits was the length thereof, and four cubits the breadth of it, after the cubit of a man. (Deuteronomy 3:11)

I would like to bring a couple more pieces of evidence relating to the revelation of who these "Sons of God," really were. I am asking each of you do your own research and come to your own conclusions. My ultimate goal for this book is merely to share the spiritual truths I have learned over the past twenty-five years, and give people the ability to do their own research. One quick comment relating to what Numbers 13:31–33 informs us. Notice the Bible confirms a characteristic of these, "Nephilim," or, "Giants," was they were very evil and literally were cannibals who devoured the inhabitants in the land. The story, "Jack and the Beanstalk," where the giant states, "Fee, Fie, Fo, Fum," I Smell the Blood of an Englishman," may not be such a fictitious story after all.

When reading the Bible you will notice certain scriptures will reference other historical writings that are not considered canon, or a part of the sixty-six books of the Bible we have today. One example of this would be in the book of Jude where a reference is made to, "The Book of Enoch." I have read the entire book of Enoch, as well as other historical writings such as, "The Book of Jasher." If a person can remember their history, a person can recall at least fragments of some biblical books and numerous other writings were found with the, "Dead Sea Scrolls," during the 1940's. It is my understanding parts of, "The Book of Enoch," were also found in caves located in the Judean Desert. Please understand, I am not saying we should take the verses from Enoch as canon, but we can read them as historical texts.

Below is a description from the book of Enoch concerning this event recorded in Genesis 6. Remember Enoch was the great-grandfather of Noah, the son of Jared, and the Bible records him as a righteous man who walked with God. The name, "Enoch," means, "Dedicated and disciplined." It is also interesting the name Jared means, "A Ruling Coming Down." You will discover when many of the ancient historical documents and writings are researched, many of these writings also make reference to this invasion on earth from fallen angels that occurred during the days of Jared and Noah. Speaking of Enoch, we need to remember the Bible mentions two people named Enoch. One of these people named Enoch was righteous and was caught up to heaven by God. The other Enoch the Bible mentions was the son of Cain, and he was known as a builder of cities. It is from the lineage of Cain, Nimrod was born where many of the occult beliefs have originated.

The Book of Enoch
Chapter 6

And it came to pass when the children of men had multiplied that in those days were born unto them beautiful and comely daughters. And the angels, the children of the heaven, saw and lusted after them, and said to one another: Come, let us choose us wives from among the children of men and beget us children. And Semjaza, who was their leader, said unto them: I fear ye will not indeed agree to do this deed, and I alone shall have to pay the penalty of a great sin. And they all answered him and said: Let us all swear an oath, and all bind themselves by mutual imprecations not to abandon this plan but to do this thing. Then sware they all together and bound themselves by mutual imprecations upon it.

And they were in all two hundred; who descended (in the days) of Jared on the summit of Mount Hermon, and they called it Mount Hermon, because they had sworn and bound themselves by mutual imprecations upon it. And these are the names of their leaders: Semiazaz, their leader, Arakiba, Rameel, Kokabiel, Tamiel, Ramiel, Danel, Ezeqeel, Baraqijal, Asael, Armaros, Batarel, Ananel, Zaqiel, Samsapeel, Satarel, Turel, Jomjael, Sariel. These are their chiefs of tens.

Book of Enoch
Chapter 7

And all the others together with them took unto themselves wives, and each chose for himself one, and they began to go in unto them and to defile themselves with them, and they taught them charms and enchantments, and the cutting of roots, and made them acquainted with plants. And they became pregnant, and they bare great giants, whose height was three thousand ells: Who consumed all the acquisitions of men. And when men could no longer sustain them, the giants turned against them and devoured mankind. And they began to sin against birds, and beasts, and reptiles, and fish, and to devour one another's flesh, and drink the blood. Then the earth laid accusation against the lawless ones.

Book of Enoch
Chapter 8

And Azazel taught men to make swords, and knives, and shields, and breastplates, and made known to them the metals (of the earth) and the art of working them, and bracelets, and ornaments, and the use of antimony, and the beautifying of the eyelids, and all kinds of costly stones, and all colouring tinctures. And they arose much god-lessness, and they committed fornication, and they were led astray, and became corrupt in all their ways. Semjaza taught enchantments, and root-cuttings, Armaros the resolving of enchantments, Baraqijal, (taught) astrology, Kokabel the constellations, Ezeqeel the knowledge of the clouds, Araqiel the signs of the earth, Shamsiel the signs of the sun, and Sariel the course of the moon. And the men perished, they cried, and their cry went up to heaven.

Book of Enoch
Chapter 9

And then Michael, Uriel, Raphael, and Gabriel looked down from heaven and saw much blood being shed upon the earth, and all lawlessness being wrought upon the earth. And they said to one another: The earth made without inhabitant cries the voice of their crying upon the gates of heaven. And now to you, the holy ones of heaven, the souls of men make their suit, saying, "Bring our cause before the Most High." And they said to the Lord of the ages: Lord of lords, God of gods, King of kings, (and God of the ages), the throne of Thy Glory (standeth) unto all the generations of the ages, and Thy name holy and glorious and blessed unto all the ages!

Thou hast made all things, and power over all things hast Thou: and all things are naked and open in Thy sight, and Thou seest all things, and nothing can hide itself from Thee. Thou seest what Azazel hath done, who hath taught all unrighteousness on earth and revealed the eternal secrets which were (preserved) in heaven, which men were striving to learn: And Semjaza, to whom Thou hast given authority to bear rule over his associates. And they have defiled themselves, and revealed to them all kinds of sins. And the women have borne giants, and the whole earth has thereby been filled with blood and unrighteousness. And now, behold, the souls of those who have died are crying and making their suit to the gates of heaven, and their lamentations have ascended: and cannot cease because of the lawless deeds which are wrought on the earth. And Thou knowest all things before they come to pass, and Thou seest these things and Thou dost suffer them, and Thou dost not say to us what we are to do to them in regard to these.

Book of Enoch
Chapter 10

Then said the Most High, the Holy and Great One spake, and sent Uriel to the son of Lamech, and said to him: (Go to Noah) and tell him in my name "Hide Thyself!" and reveal to him the end that is approaching: that the whole earth will be destroyed, and a deluge is about to come upon the whole earth, and will destroy all that is on it. And now instruct him that he may escape and his seed may be preserved for all the generations of the world.

And again the Lord said to Raphael: Bind Azazel hand and foot, and cast him into the darkness: and make an opening in the desert, which is in Dudael, and cast him therein. And place upon him rough and jagged rocks, and cover him with darkness, and let him abide there for ever, and cover his face that he may not see light. And on the day of the great judgment he shall be cast into the fire. And heal the earth which the angels have corrupted, and proclaim the healing of the earth, that they may heal the plague, and that all the children of men may not perish through all the secret things that the Watcher have disclosed and have taught their sons. And the whole earth has been corrupted through the works that they were taught by Azazel: to him ascribe all sin. And to Gabriel said the Lord: Proceed against the bastards and the reprobates, and against the children of fornication: and destroy the children of fornication and the children of the Watchers from amongst men and cause them to go forth: send them one against the other that they may destroy each other in battle: for length of days shall they not have.

And no request that they (their fathers) make of thee shall be granted unto their fathers on their behalf; for they hope to live an eternal life, and that each one of them will live five hundred years.

And the Lord said unto Michael: Go bind Semjaza and his associates who have united themselves with women so as to have defiled themselves with them in all their uncleanness. And when their sons have slain one another, and they have seen the destruction of their beloved ones, bind them fast for seventy generations in the valleys of the earth, till the day of their judgment and of their consummation, till the judgment that is for ever and ever is consummated.

In those days they shall be led off to the abyss of fire: (and) to the torment and the prison in which they shall be confined for ever. And whosoever shall be condemned and destroyed will from thenceforth be bound together with them to the end of all generations. And destroy all the spirits of the reprobate and the children of the Watchers, because they have wronged mankind. Destroy all wrong from the face of the earth and let every evil work come to an end: and let the plant of righteousness and truth appear: and it shall prove a blessing; the works of righteousness and truth shall be planted in truth and joy for evermore. And then shall all the righteous escape, and shall live till they beget thousands of children, and all the days of their youth and their old age shall they complete in peace. And then shall the whole earth be tilled in righteousness, and shall all be planted with trees and be full of blessing.

And all desirable trees shall be planted on it, and they shall plant vines on it: and the vine which they plant thereon shall yield wine in abundance, and as for all the seed which is sown thereon shall yield wine in abundance, and as for all the seed which is sown thereon each measure (of it) shall bear a thousand, and each measure of olives shall yield ten presses of oil. And cleanse thou the earth from all oppression, and from all unrighteousness, and from all sin, and from all godlessness: and all the uncleanness that is wrought upon the earth destroy from off the earth. And all the children of men shall become righteous, and all nations shall offer adoration and shall praise Me, and all shall worship Me. And the earth shall be cleansed from all defilement, and from all sin, and from all punishment, and from all torment, and I will never again send (them) upon it from generation to generation and forever.

The book of Enoch: chapter 6, chapter 7, chapter 8, chapter 9, and chapter 10 translated by R. H. Charles (1917, public domain).

Hopefully you have been given enough evidence to make an informed decision on this topic. Believe me, I could go on and on presenting thousands of pages of evidence including historical writings, myths, and legends. We could discuss acres of archaeological evidence also backing up the true biblical cause for the flood.

Another great resource containing thousands of articles and stories concerning artifacts, megalithic structures, burial sites, and bones of people found having great height, would be to search New York Times articles dating back to the late 1800's.

Another interesting read for all you history lovers out there would be the autobiography of a man named William Cody or Buffalo Bill. In his autobiography, Buffalo Bill tells a story where Indians bring some very large bones into the camp, and the camp doctor diagnoses these bones as being that of a human. The problem was, the humans these bones would belong to was a race of people two to three times the height of a normal man. The Indians then tell stories handed down from their elders of, "Star People," who came from the heavens long ago. These, "Star People," coming down from the sky had children who were of great size, and they were very evil. The Indians tell the story these giants were so strong and swift they could run beside a buffalo, tear a leg off, and eat it on the run. The Indians continue with the story stating because these giants were very evil and laughed at the, "Great Spirit," the, "Great Spirit," then sends a great deluge covering up the mountains, killing all these giants off the face of the earth. Of course, this is just another one of many stories and historical coincidences a person can read about. Right?

The bigger question needing to be asked is why has this information been hidden from the world and from the church for that matter. I have believed now for years Satan, "The Father of Lies," has played a major role in this deception. Why would Satan want to cover up this information? I believe it is because if we do not understand what has occurred in the past, we will not understand and will be deceived of what will again take place in the future. This is why I believe the, "antichrist" will literally be as stated in Genesis, the offspring of Satan. This is now not so impossible to believe, since we see Biblical evidence apostasy in the spiritually realm has already taken place on earth. Yes, I truly believe similar events such as these will happen again in the future, and the Bible states the world will be deceived. There is coming a literal manifestation on this earth of the spiritual realm. It will be a time of great deception.

A Question from Abraham

One of the major goals I hope to accomplish in writing this book, is for people to realize the important role history should play in the decisions people make today. The Bible has a lot to say to us as individuals and as a society concerning the subject of history. A remembrance of the past is essential in preventing the same mistakes from being repeated over and over again. I have found many people see the Bible merely as a book crammed full of God's warnings. This idea reminds me of times when I went to a store and purchased an item in a box needing assembled. I would usually load the box up and bring it home thinking to myself, "This project looks easy," and I would then start assembling the item before I read the directions. What usually ends up happening is I get the item almost completely assembled and find out a simple step to the assembly process has been overlooked, because I failed to read the directions. Yes, you guessed it, I then had to disassemble the item, and reassemble it according to the order given in the instructions.

The Bible in many ways is similar to the product assembly instructions we usually believe are a waste of our time. God gives us His word, because He loves us and desires for us to avoid the major mistakes in life that end up having severe lifelong and even eternal consequences. I have found having a basic knowledge of God's word includes many benefits in life most do not realize. Not only does God give us examples of what has happened in the past for our own personal benefit, but He also gives us information relating to future events and prophecies that will one day be fulfilled. The purpose of Bible prophecy is not to cause debate, speculation, and arguing, it is to prove the truth of God's word. Take a look at what Isaiah has to say concerning the purpose of Bible prophecy.

> Remember the former things of old: for I am God, and there is none else; I am God, and there is none like me,
> Declaring the end from the beginning, and from ancient times the things that are not yet done, saying, My counsel shall stand, and I will do all my pleasure. (Isaiah 46:9–10)

I have been shocked during the past several years with the direction I see our society heading. Our world has plummeted into a time of ethnic and moral chaos. We are living in a time where politicians and leaders of our country are regularly caught in actions of extreme immorality. The law of the land, "The Constitution," is trampled on, ridiculed, and isn't any longer seen as a guide for the laws and regulations of government and the rights of the people. We have thrown prayer out of most public places including schools. We are being pressured and instructed not to mention words such as, "Merry Christmas," because statements such as these are not currently seen as being politically correct. We just don't seem to be remembering the mistakes we have made in the past, and the reason why people came to this country in the first place. We are seeing a major shift in the basic moral belief ideology of our world. And guess what, this new age of tolerance and values clarification is even trickling down into the church. There is a growing number of people attending church today who believe the Old Testament scriptures and the entire Bible for that matter is becoming more and more out of touch with our modern world. The Bible is no longer seen as being relevant for this modern age we currently live in.

Not only is the Old Testament relevant to us today, according to the Bible the events of the Old Testament will repeat themselves again. I have always stressed anytime we see evidence of scripture and story patterns in God's word, we need to pay attention to them. We will be addressing a unique question Abraham asks God which

I believe is of great significance to us as believers, and helps to prove the love and concern God has for the righteous. In this chapter, we will be looking at two biblical characters named Abraham and Lot. The Bible records in the book of Romans Abraham was a righteous man because he believed God.

> "For what saith the scripture? Abraham believed God, and it was counted unto him for righteousness." (Romans 4:3)

> And he believed in the Lord; and he counted it to him for righteousness. (Genesis 15:6)

The phrase, "Believed God," implies more than just a realization of the existence of God. This phrase deals with a personal and total reliance upon God. This would be what the Bible would describe as faith. The Bible records even Satan and the demons believe in the existence of God. The Bible teaches us faith is much more than just a belief in the existence of God. Satan and his evil allies will all be judged and thrown into the, "Lake of Fire," because they refuse to worship the very God who created them.

> Thou believest that there is one God; thou doest well: the devils also believe, and tremble. (James 2:19)

> Now faith is the substance of things hoped for, the evidence of things not seen. (Hebrews 11:1)

In order to get to the point of this chapter, we need to take a closer look at the lives of these two Bible characters. In Genesis chapter 11 the Bible informs us these two individuals were relatives, and Lot was the nephew of Abraham. We will later on in the story see Abraham expressing deep concerns to God concerning judgment about to be poured out upon a five city area where Lot and his family lived.

> And Terah took Abram his son, and Lot the son of Haran his son's son, and Sarai his daughter-in-law, his son Abram's wife; and they went forth with them from Ur of the Chaldees, to go into the land of Canaan; and they came unto Haran, and dwelt there. (Genesis 11:31)

Genesis chapter 13 gives us more interesting information concerning a conflict arising between these so-called hired hands of Abraham and Lot. One interesting point is the Bible also informs us in these verses Abraham was very wealthy in cattle, silver, and gold. The Bible also states Lot was evidently quite wealthy himself having many flocks, herds, and tents. The verses below give us information concerning a dispute between the herdsmen of these two relatives, which will set the stage for future drastic consequences taking place with Lot, and his entire family.

> And Abram went up out of Egypt, he, and his wife, and all that he had, and Lot with him, into the south.
> And Abram was very rich in cattle, in silver, and in gold.
> And he went on his journeys from the south even to Bethel, unto the place where his tent had been at the beginning, between Bethel and Hai;
> Unto the place of the altar, which he had make there at the first: and there Abram called on the name of the Lord.
> And Lot also, which went with Abram, had flocks, and herds, and tents.
> And the land was not able to bear them, that they might dwell together: for their substance was great, so that they could not dwell together.
> And there was a strife between the herdmen of Abram's cattle and the herdmen of Lot's cat-

tle: and the Canaanite and the Perizzitte dwelled then in the land.

And Abram said unto Lot, Let there be no strife, I pray thee, between me and thee, and between my herdmen and thy herdmen; for we be brethren.

Is not the whole land before thee? Separate thyself, I pray thee, from me: if thou wilt take the left hand, then I will go to the right; or if thou depart to the right hand, then I will go to the left.

And Lot lifted up his eyes, and beheld all the plain of Jordan, that is was well watered every where, before the Lord destroyed Sodom and Gomorrah, even as the garden of the Lord, like the land of Egypt, as thou comest unto Zoar.

Then Lot chose him all the plain of Jordan; and Lot journeyed east: and they separated themselves the one from the other.

Abram dwelled in the land of Canaan, and Lot dwelled in the cities of the plain, and pitched his tent toward Sodom.

But the men of Sodom were wicked and sinners before the Lord exceedingly. (Genesis 13:1–13)

The Bible gives us a very interesting story describing a conflict between these two relatives. In modern terms, we would say these two individuals were extremely wealthy ranchers. This uncle and his nephew owned so many livestock the land was unable to support the both of them. The tension evidently rises to the level the hired hands from both parties begin arguing and fighting with each other. Before we go further, let me make one comment concerning the name, "Abram," to prevent any confusion. In Genesis chapter 17 God changes the name of, "Abram," to, "Abraham," due to a covenant God makes with him. Abraham's name means, "The father of many."

We notice it is Abraham who acknowledges the conflict between these two livestock owners, and he strives to bring resolution to the problem. Abraham also here confirms he and Lot are brethren. We have already established the fact these two were related, but the word brethren means much more. The Bible is confirming in God's eyes both of these men were righteous. The following verses in the book of 2 Peter also confirm the fact Lot was righteous in the sight of God. We have already viewed evidence in Genesis and Romans informing us Abraham was also a righteous man in God's eyes.

> And delivered just Lot, vexed with the filthy conversation of the wicked:
> For that righteous man dwelling among them, in seeing and hearing, vexed his righteous soul from day to day with their unlawful deeds. (2 Peter 2:7–8)

So according to scriptures, we have confirmed indeed Abraham and Lot were righteous in the sight of God. We will later notice although both men were righteous, poor choices and negative consequences in life are still possible. After Abraham notices the conflict between the workers, he offers a solution. Notice Abraham asks his nephew Lot to choose first concerning the direction he would take. Abraham tells Lot, "Choose from all the land you see, and if you go one direction, I will go the other." The entire land had been given by God to Abraham, but Abraham tells Lot to choose the direction he would go.

The Bible then states Lot lifted up his eyes. These few words offer us clues concerning the spiritual differences between Abraham and Lot most people do not pick up on. Although both men were righteous in the sight of God, Lot makes a decision based not on faith, but by sight. It was greed that was the basis for Lot's decision. It was this decision that would end up costing Lot and his family dearly. We notice in the above verses it states Lot was, "Vexed," while he was living in Sodom being surrounded constantly by such immoral depravity. The word, "Vexed," here literally means "Tormented or

Distressed." Those people who are spiritually awake will understand and see this passage as a spiritual clue. The righteous will know they are living in the, "End Times," when the moral condition in the world around them constantly torments and conflicts their very soul.

The Bible informs us Abraham dwelled in the land of Canaan, and Lot pitched his tent near the city of Sodom. The Bible is trying to tell us Lot was attracted to the city of Sodom, and all the materialism this city had to offer. Another point here in the Bible most people do not recognize is the term, "Cities of the Plain." This term is actually referring to five cities existing in this area. These cities included Sodom, Gomorrah, Zoar, Admah, and Zeboim. Four of these cities are confirmed in the book of Deuteronomy. The city named Zoar is confirmed in Genesis chapter 19, which is the city an angel gives Lot permission to escape too.

> And that the whole land thereof is brimstone, and salt, and burning, that it is not sown, nor beareth, nor any grass groweth therein, like the overthrow of Sodom, and Gamorrah, Admah, and Zeboim, which the Lord overthrew in his anger, and in his wrath. (Deuteronomy 29:23)

A little later in the story we discover the Bible states the Lord and two angels literally appear before Abraham while he is living in the plains of Mamre. The name, "Mamre," means "Bitterness." The Bible goes on to state Abraham literally gives the three visitors water and has a meal prepared for them. Evidently, the Bible is giving us these details to help us understand these visitors were not figures of imagination or spirits, but these three visitors had real physical bodies. I believe this was the literal Christ and two angels who visited Abraham, and I know many in the Church have a real problem with this. I believe the following verses in the book of Colossians solves this issue for us.

> For by him were all things created, that are in heaven, and that in earth, visible, and invisi-

ble, whether they be thrones, or dominions, or principalities, or powers: all things were created by him, and for him:

And he is before all things, and by him all things consist.

And he is the head of the body, the church: who is the beginning, the firstborn from the dead; that in all things he might have the preeminence.

For it pleased the Father that in him should all fullness dwell;

And, having made peace through the blood of his cross, by him to reconcile all things unto himself; by him, I say, whether they be things in earth, or things in heaven. (Colossians 1:16–20)

Christ is before all things, and in Him all things were created. John chapter 1 also informs us Jesus was with God from the beginning, and in Him all things were made and are held together. The Bible tells us during His visit the Lord prophesies to Abraham and his wife Sarah informing they will have a son. We know according to scripture, both Abraham and Sarah considered the prophecy from the Lord to be quite unbelievable and humorous due to their age. We know everything God says does come to pass, because Abraham and Sarah later have a son named, "Isaac," in spite of Sarah being beyond the childbearing years. By the way, the name, "Isaac," means, "Laughter," because Sarah did believe it was quite comical when she heard the news she would one day bear a son. It is when the Lord and the two angels start on their journey toward Sodom, the Lord informs Abraham He has heard the cries coming from Sodom and Gomorrah due to their wickedness, and He was on the way to visit these cities. Yes, God does hear the cries coming from those who are persecuted and killed. Innocent blood that has been shed does literally cry out from the ground, and one of these days all innocent blood shed from the beginning of time will be avenged.

I believe the question Abraham then asks the Lord is one of the most important questions ever asked to God in the entire Bible.

The sad thing is, most people in the church today do not understand this basic biblical truth Abraham clearly understood. The interesting thing is Abraham did not have a clear understanding of the future Church, the bride of Christ. In spite of this, Abraham knew for certain God has a special love for the righteous.

> How that by revelation he made known unto
> me the mystery; (as I wrote afore in few words,
> Whereby, when we read, ye may understand
> my knowledge in the mystery of Christ)
> Which in other ages was not made known
> unto the sons of men, as it is now revealed unto
> his holy apostles and prophets by the Spirit;
> That the Gentiles should be fellowheirs, and
> of the same body, and partakers of his promise in
> Christ by the gospel. (Ephesians 3:3–6)

The Bible then states Abraham drew near to God asking Him a very powerful question. Abraham then asks God, "Wilt thou also destroy the righteous with the wicked?" What a powerful earth-shaking question. What amazing spiritual discernment and faith Abraham displayed concerning his awareness of God's character. One key biblical truth I have realized over the years is a person needs to possess the ability to discern the differences between being persecuted while living in the world, and wrath coming directly from God. Jesus stated we will suffer persecution. Jesus stated the world will hate all believers. The key difference Abraham understood was the wickedness going on in Sodom and Gomorrah would directly result in God's wrath, and this coming wrath was intended for the wicked, not the righteous. The destruction of Sodom and Gomorrah would be a direct result of God's wrath, not due to a random event or a circumstance of life.

When Abraham discovered God's plans for the destruction of Sodom and Gomorrah, he became very concerned. Abraham recognized his relatives would be in serious danger. Abraham understood a loving and merciful God surely wouldn't destroy His own children.

Let's take a look what the Bible has to say concerning this interesting conversation between God and Abraham.

> And Abraham drew near, and said, Wilt thou also destroy the righteous with the wicked?
>
> Peradventure there be fifty righteous within the city: wilt thou also destroy, and not spare the place for the fifty righteous, that are therein?
>
> That be far from thee to do after this manner, to slay the righteous with the wicked: and that the righteous should be as the wicked, that be far from thee: Shall not the Judge of all the earth do right?
>
> And the Lord said, If I find in Sodom fifty righteous within the city, then I will spare all the place for their sakes.
>
> And Abraham answered and said, Behold now, I have taken upon me to speak unto the Lord, which as but dust and ashes:
>
> Peradventure there shall lack five of the fifty righteous: wilt thou destroy all the city for lack of five? And he said, If I find there forty and five, I will not destroy it.
>
> And he spake unto him yet again, and said, Peradventure there shall be forty found there. And he said, I will not do it for forty's sake.
>
> And he said unto him, Oh let not the Lord be angry, and I will speak: Peradventure there shall thirty be found there. And he said, I will not do it, if I find thirty there.
>
> And he said, Behold now, I have taken upon me to speak unto the Lord: Peradventure there shall be twenty found there. And he said, I will not destroy it for twenty's sake.
>
> And he said, Oh let not the Lord be angry, and I will speak yet but this once: Peradventure

ten shall be found there. And he said, I will not destroy it for ten's sake.

And the Lord went his way, as soon as he had left communing with Abraham: and Abraham returned unto his place. (Genesis 18:23–33)

It is very interesting this unique bargaining session between Abraham and God ends with the number ten. It is common archaeological knowledge the city of Sodom had a population numbering in the thousands. Keep in mind this judgment coming from God dealt with more than one city. The Lord promises Abraham if ten righteous souls could be found, just ten of the possible thousands of residents, the city would be spared. Well, we know how the story ends. What a shocking picture for us today. Several years ago, I started to realize many of these stories in the Bible dealing with God's judgment being poured out upon the unrighteous was a prophetic picture of what will one day again take place in the future. Now the verses in the Bible where Jesus states the coming, "Day of the Lord," will be as it was during the days of Noah and Lot makes perfect sense. There is tremendous spiritual revelation gained when people recognize the stories of the Old Testament are still relevant to us today.

When the Lord states Sodom would be spared if ten righteous people were found, Abraham seems to come to peace with the issue. As we've already discussed, Abraham had a nephew and relatives who lived in Sodom. Genesis chapter 19 informs us Lot sat at the gate of Sodom. History tells us city gates were places similar to modern town squares. Important business transactions and public events would take place at the gates of a city.

The Bible informs us Lot had a wife and two daughters who were not married living with them, and he also had more than one son-in-law. Was this the reason Abraham stopped bargaining with God when he was informed Sodom would be spared if just ten righteous people could be found? I believe Abraham had at least ten relatives living in the city of Sodom.

Behold now, I have two daughters which have not known man; let me, I pray you, bring them out unto you, and do ye to them as is good in your eyes: only unto these men do nothing; for therefore came they under the shadow of my roof. (Genesis 19:8)

And Lot went out, and spake unto his sons-in-law, which married his daughters, and said, Up, get you out of this place; for the Lord will destroy this city. But he seemed as one that mocked unto his sons-in-law.

And when the morning arose, then the angels hastened Lot, saying, Arise, take thy wife, and thy two daughters, which are here; lest thou be comsumed in the iniquity of the city. (Genesis 19:14–15)

Earlier we discussed the decision Lot made to pitch his tent near Sodom. There are tremendous life lessons we can learn from reading the Bible. The above verses state Lot pleaded with his sons-in-law to get out of the city and run for their lives. According to the scriptures, Lot was unable to convince them or their wives to leave.

When given a choice Lot looked upon the plains and made a decision based on what he saw, not considering what God's will for his life was. Although the Bible records Lot as being righteous, it appears living several years in Sodom which by the way is a spiritual picture of the world, ends up costing him dearly. Making a decision based upon sight alone ends up causing Lot to lose almost his entire family.

For those who are interested, further research in Genesis chapter 14 reveals Lot had earlier been taken captive while previously living in Sodom and was rescued by Abraham. Evidently Lot did not learn his lesson the first time he resided in Sodom. It seems obvious Lot had a love for the world and the materialism it offered, but it ended up costing him everything.

Love not the world, neither the things that are in the world. If any man love the world, the love of the Father is not in him.

For all that is in the world, the lust of the flesh, and the lust of the eyes, and the pride of life, is not of the Father, but is of the world.

And the world passeth away, and the lust thereof: but he that doeth the will of God abideth forever. (1 John 2:15–17)

Before we conclude this chapter, I would like to discuss a couple points concerning Genesis chapter 19. A book could easily be written on this chapter alone. First, the Bible is clear two angels were sent to the city of Sodom to validate the extent of the wickedness existing in this city. I hear statements all the time people make concerning the limits and capabilities given to angels. There are many biblical examples where angels eat, walk, talk, communicate verbally, and even take people by the hand. I am using the term, "Angels," in a broad sense, but according to scriptures there is an organized order of angels too which each has been given specific duties and abilities. There are spiritual beings known as; seraphim, cherubim, thrones, dominions, strongholds, powers, principalities, archangels, and angels. We know the archangel, "Michael," is known throughout the Bible as the, "Warrior Angel," and he alone has control over an entire company of angels. We know Gabriel is described in the Bible as a, "Messenger angel. We know Satan according to the book of Ezekiel is a mighty, "Cherub," who once was likely second in command in heaven, until he received his pink slip and was relieved of his duties.

It is interesting when Lot meets the angels at the gates of Sodom he realizes there is something unique about these men, because he bowed down before them with his face to the ground. In most biblical cases, when angels interact with humans there is extreme fear. Angels are immortal beings created by God to be His messengers and to carry out His plans. According to the Bible, angels do not die a physical death, and their bodies are not of flesh and blood. We also sense in this chapter Lot is quite stressed over the fact the angels are visiting the city desiring to observe the night life of Sodom. It seems these two angels were drawing a lot of attention from the residents of this city, and Lot couldn't seem to get the two visitors in the house fast enough. Could the Bible through this description of events be giving us a clue to the state of immorality existing in Sodom? I definitely believe so. The Bible records Lot then locked the angels in the house with his family, made supper, and they ate.

Before the household of Lot was able to retire for the evening, the house is surrounded by the men of Sodom, both the young and the old. The men outside the house demanded Lot to bring these two visitors outside so they could, "Know," them. Several Bible interpretations literally state their intentions were sexual in nature. The Bible is quite clear concerning the motives these men of Sodom had with these two angels.

Lot then comes outside his house shutting the door behind him, and pleads with these men not to consider doing such wicked things to his guests. Next we are told something very disturbing takes place. Lot then offers up his two virgin daughters as an exchange for their request to have sexual relations with these two angels. Lot states to the men, "Do whatever you want with my daughters, but please do nothing with these men." Lot, who was a righteous man knew there was something different about his guests, and he knew the sins taking place in this city were an abomination to a holy God. I believe Lot knew these two angels were sent from God, and their purpose was not for a night out on the town.

It's interesting the men of the city want nothing to do with the young daughters of Lot. Instead, these men begin to threaten Lot, and begin to break into his house to seize the guests and have their way with them. What happens next is the Bible confirms these guests are indeed angels because they strike the men breaking into Lot's house with blindness.

The angels then command Lot to gather up his entire family and get them out of the city. God had received his confirmation that indeed the wickedness in Sodom had reached a level that was unredeemable. That's right, the residents of this city were unredeemable. Here again, if a person is able to discern the matter, the Bible is giving us a clue. An interesting concept repeated over and over in the book of Revelation, tells us people during a future time of God's wrath will have the same spiritual condition of wickedness as the men of Sodom. Just like the men of Sodom, those dwelling on the earth during a future time of, "Great Tribulation," will refuse to repent, and turn from their evil ways. You want to know what will take place in the future. All a person needs to do is study the stories in the Old Testament.

We all know how the story ends. Lot is unable to convince most of his family to leave Sodom. Lot loses daughters, his sons-in-law, and even his wife, because he looked upon the plains with a heart filled with greed and stated to his uncle, "I'll go this way." There is tremendous wisdom gained by believing and studying God's word. How sad it is when most professing Christians today state the Bible, especially the Old Testament, cannot be taken literally. The scary thing is, decisions like this will be very costly and they will be mistakes having eternal consequences.

Sodom is a prophetic picture of what the spiritual condition of mankind will be like in the last days. We constantly hear on the local news people committing acts of Sodomy. Sodomy is a word referring to any type of unnatural sexual act. The word, "Sodomy," comes from the word, "Sodom." Below are seven verses in the, "Book of Jasher," giving us historical insight as to the extreme level of wickedness going on in these cities. We should not consider these verses as part of the Bible, but only as factual and historical evidence.

> And the cities of Sodom had four judges to four cities, and these were their names, Serak in the city of Sodom, Sharkad in Gomorrah, Zabnac in Admah, and Menon in Zeboyim.
>
> And Eliezer Abraham's servant applied to them different names, and he converted Serak to Shakra, Sharkad to Shakrura, Zebnac to Kezobim, and Menon to Matzlodin.
>
> And by desire of their four judges the people of Sodom and Gomorrah had beds erected

in the streets of the cities, and if a man came to these places they laid hold of him and brought him to one of their beds, and by force made him to lie in them.

And as he lay down, three men would stand at his head, and three at his feet, and measure him by the length of the bed, and if the man was less than the bed these six men would stretch him at each end, and when he cried out to them they would not answer him.

And if he was longer than the bed they would draw together the two sides of the bed at each end, until the man had reached the gates of death.

And if he continued to cry out to them, they would answer him, saying, Thus shall it be done to a man that cometh into our land.

And when the men heard all these things that the people of the cities of Sodom did, they refrained from coming there. (Jasher 19:1–7)

From the Book of Jasher from the Original Hebrew into English Salt Lake City; published by J. H. Parry and Company (1887).

The above seven verses in the book of Jasher gives us all the information we need to know. Sodom, Gomorrah, and the other cities of the plain were wicked to the extent something had to be done. These verses confirm the cries of torment truly were reaching heaven. When the level of wickedness and sin finally reaches a certain level, God has no choice but to intervene. People have always been committing sins ever since the beginning of time. The book of Jasher as well as the Bible, confirms it is when the leadership of a community or even a nation openly tolerates these types of sins, God brings swift judgment upon these people.

We also see the Lord keeps His promises. God promised Abraham if ten righteous people were found, Sodom would be spared. Just like with the story of Noah, we again see the extent God is willing to go to protect the righteous. The Bible tells us an angel literally had to take Lot by the hand and escorted him out of Sodom before God's destructive wrath would be poured out upon these cities. We need to take the Bible for what it says. The Bible is telling us Sodom was destroyed the, "Same Day," Lot was escorted out of the city. What a picture of God's love and concern for the righteous. What a sober warning this story is for all people who are ungodly and whose lives are characterized by sin. I believe there is more truth to this story than meets the eye. Could it be the righteous will in a similar manner be rescued as Lot was, when they will again be removed from the earth the very day or hour, God pours out His wrath on an unbelieving, sinful world. Didn't Solomon tell us, "What Has Been Done, Will Be Done Again?"

> And while he lingered, the men laid hold upon his hand, and upon the hand of his wife, and upon the hand of his two daughters; the Lord being merciful unto him: and they brought him forth, and set him without the city. (Genesis 19:16)

> Likewise also as it was in the days of Lot; they did eat, they drank, they bought, they sold, they planted, they builded;
> But the same day that Lot went out of Sodom it rained fire and brimstone from heaven, and destroyed them all. (Luke 17:28–29)

Bricks without Straw

Another incredible story in the Bible is the story of the, "Exodus" where God rescues the children of Israel from being held captive in the land of Egypt. Here we have another story teaching us much more than most recognize. The bondage of the children of Israel in Egypt, is more than a story of Israel's history and warnings of consequences relating to disobeying a holy God. This story is a historical picture of what will again happen in the future to the nation of Israel and those dwelling on the earth. It is a story meant to be taken literally, and it is a story intended for the church today.

What concerns me as a Christian is when I hear people state the Bible, specifically the Old Testament, is nothing more than stories filled with half-truths and fairy tales. The Bible is one of the most factually documented historical books ever written by individuals who were under the direction and inspiration of God. The contents of the Bible includes thousands of names, places, dates, and historical events. The Bible is authored by close to forty people, many of whom never knew each other and were not living together during the same time. The ability to compose such a book as the Bible having several authors and covering a several thousand-year timespan, would be a statistical impossibility by mere human effort alone. The Bible gives us multiple examples including the two verses below, proving the fact God was actively involved in the creation of the book we know today as the Bible. We will be digging into a scripture passage later on in Daniel prophesying future events with such pin-point accuracy, many skeptics over the years have denied the timeline of its authorship.

> For the prophecy came not in old time by the
> will of man: but holy men of God spake as they
> were moved by the Holy Ghost. (2 Peter 1:21)

> And he said to Abram, Know of a surety
> that thy seed shall be a stranger in a land that is
> not theirs, and shall serve them; and they shall
> afflict them four hundred years. (Genesis 15:13)

In the book of Genesis, Abraham receives a word of prophecy from God informing his future seed or offspring will be a stranger imprisoned in a foreign land. This verse also informs us the inhabitants of this foreign land will torture or afflict the children of Israel for the duration of four hundred years. It is interesting this verse in Genesis appears to be in conflict with a couple verses we find in the book of Exodus. When people find supposed discrepancies such as these they are quick to conclude the Bible is full of errors, so these people conclude the Bible cannot be taken with credibility. Notice the accounts in Genesis and Exodus seems to give a thirty-year discrepancy relating to the time of Israel's captivity in Egypt.

> Now the sojourning of the children of Israel, who
> dwelt in Egypt, was 430 years.
> And it came to pass at the end of the four
> hundred and thirty years, even the selfsame day it
> came to pass, that all the hosts of the Lord went
> out from the land of Egypt. (Exodus 12:40–41)

The two verses above appear to present a problem with the integrity and validity of the Bible. It appears there is a thirty-year miscalculation in God's word. The answer to this questioned discrepancy can be traced back to the time of Abraham. As already discussed, the Hebrew meaning of the name Abraham is, "The Father of Many." Generally, when most people consider the children of Israel they think of Jacob, his sons, and their descendants. We need to realize in reality the nation of Israel really doesn't begin with Jacob, it began with Abraham, and his son Isaac. When we look at it from this perspective, we see both timelines are actually correct and the once thought discrepancies in the Bible disappear.

I am sure most people are familiar with the statement, "Insanity is defined as doing the same thing over and over again, expecting different results." When an individual or even a nation is unwilling to learn from mistakes made in the past, this should also be defined as insanity or ignorance. I will refer to this principle more than once in this book, but it is very important we remember the past so the same mistakes are not repeated over and over again. The fact is, the children of Israel did not learn from their past mistakes, nor do we seem to today. We are currently witnessing historical monuments being taken down in the United States because they offend certain groups of people. The nation forgetting the mistakes of their past is one day doomed to repeat them.

God was so concerned the nation of Israel would forget their horrible experience in Egypt, He established an eight-day festival which is still celebrated by Israel today. The celebration of Passover deals with the remembrance of Israel being set free from Egyptian bondage by the very hand of God, being allowed to exit the land. The word, "Passover," means, "To Pass Over," referring to God's wrath passing over the homes of the children of Israel, killing all firstborn in the land of Egypt during the evening of the first Passover.

Most people can recall at least parts of the Exodus story. Most remember it was Moses who was called by God completing the task of leading the children of Israel out of Egypt heading toward the, "Promised Land." I can remember as a young boy watching the historic movie, "The Ten Commandments," with Charlton Heston. During this movie, Moses and Aaron would repeatedly come before Pharaoh demanding in the name of God, "Let my people go."

It would take a total of ten plagues poured out by God on the land of Egypt, before Pharaoh would finally agree to let the Children of Israel go. We will discover each of these plagues deals directly with Egypt, and the gods they served. It is also interesting to note the similarities between the plagues of Egypt, and the future coming judgments mentioned in Revelation. Both of these situations deal with wrath being directly poured out by God, and people refusing to repent of their evil deeds and turn to Him. The plagues of Egypt poured out by God are also a futuristic picture of a worldwide wrath being poured out on all people dwelling on the earth during a future time. Below is a list of the plagues God poured out on the land of Egypt along with the Egyptian gods these plagues defeated. These plagues served as an example to prove to the Egyptians and the children of Israel, the God of Israel was superior to the gods of the Egyptians. Keep in mind this is a brief explanation of the, "gods," these plagues represented, since the Egyptians worshipped more than likely hundreds of different spiritual deities. Many of these gods the Egyptians worshipped were not just man-made images, but they were literal fallen angels and demonic spirits.

- The waters of the Nile being turned to blood. Intended for the god Khnum (guardian of the Nile), Hapi (spirit of the Nile), Hatmehit (fish goddess), and Osiris (god of death and resurrection).
- The plague of frogs. Intended for the god Heket (frog goddess, protector of women in childbirth).
- Plague of lice infesting all men and beasts. Intended for the god Geb (earth god).
- Plague of flies. Intended for the god Khepri (solar created god represented by a scarab beetle).
- Plague kills cattle and livestock. Intended for the god Mnevis (a live bull god) and Hesat (a maternal cow god).
- Plague of sores and boils affects the Egyptian people. This plague is intended for the god Imhotep (a healer god) and Sekhmet (a lioness god capable of warding of disease).
- God sends a plague of fiery hail (meteorites). This plague is intended for the god Nut (a sky goddess) and the god Shu (embodiment of wind or air).
- Plague of locusts strip the land of Egypt. Intended for the god Renenutet (goddess of agriculture) and Serapis (a Greco-Egyptian god).

- Plague of darkness that can be felt comes upon the land. Intended for the god Ra (the foremost Egyptian sun god) and Thoth (a moon god).
- Death of all firstborn in Egypt. Intended to show the superiority of the God of the Bible to all Egyptian gods.

(References: Wikipedia, The free encyclopedia: List of Egyptian Deities and Wikipedia, The free encyclopedia: Ancient Egyptian Deities.)

These plagues were designed to hit Egypt where it hurt the most. There is no god like the God of the Bible. It would be the final plague, the death of all firstborn in the land of Egypt, which would finally change the mind of Pharaoh. The Bible tells us Pharaoh literally begs the children of Israel to leave after the effects of this final plague of death. If we can recall our biblical history, it was Joseph who was sold into slavery by his brothers. God's hand was upon Joseph causing him to eventually be promoted to second in command in Egypt answering only to Pharaoh. It was also during this time, a severe drought came upon the land of Israel forcing Joseph's family to move to Egypt. Because of Joseph's obedience to God, the nation of Israel over time became a mighty people filling the land of Egypt. It would be years later after the death of Joseph and his entire family, a new king would rule the land, and he saw this great multitude of people as a threat to Egypt. The following verses in Exodus informs us of this change in attitude involving the children of Israel residing in Egypt.

> And all the souls that came out of the loins of Jacob were seventy souls: for Joseph was in Egypt already.
> And Joseph died, and all his brethren, and all that generation.
> And the children of Israel were fruitful, and increased abundantly, and multiplied, and waxed

exceeding mighty; and the land was filled with them.

Now there arose up a new king over Egypt, which knew not Joseph.

And he said unto his people, Behold, the people of the children of Israel are more and mightier than we:

Come on, let us deal wisely with them; lest they multiply, and it come to pass, that, when there falleth out any war, they join also unto our enemies, and fight against us, and so get them up out of the land.

Therefore they did set over them taskmasters to afflict them with their burdens. And they built for Pharoah treasure cities, Pithom and Raamses. (Exodus 1:5–11)

And so the story begins. There's a new sheriff in town, and he doesn't like what he sees. It's amazing how the attitudes of people change over the years. Years earlier, it would be the wisdom of Joseph who would be responsible for the survival of Egypt. A new Pharaoh arrives on the scene, and he looks at things from a much different perspective. This new ruler in Egypt could only understand there was now a multitude of strangers in the land, and he saw them as a security risk. Pharaoh's solution to the problem would be to control the population of Israel and make them slaves.

So just as God prophesied to Abraham years earlier, the children of Israel are now strangers in a foreign land, and they will be oppressed and enslaved for four hundred years. After hearing the cries from Israel, God sends Moses and his brother Aaron, demanding Pharaoh let God's people go.

We understand God knew all along Pharaoh wouldn't just lie down and agree to every ultimatum given to him by Moses. God informs us in the Bible He will make an example of Pharaoh and will use Pharaoh to carry out His plans. Pharaoh, more than likely the most powerful and prideful man on the earth during this time, will end up bowing to the, "Most High God." Here again the Bible offers great spiritual insight to those having spiritual eyes to see. Egypt in this story is a prophetic picture of the world, and the Pharaoh of Egypt, he is a prophetic picture of the coming antichrist. The gods worshipped by Egypt were not figments of their imagination or just idols made by human hands. These gods were real spiritual deities who literally existed.

One major goal I am hoping to achieve in this book, is to help people to understand there really is such a thing as spiritual warfare. We really do deal with wickedness in high places. There are hundreds of gods being worshipped today through many different religions and belief systems. According to the Bible, these gods people worship today throughout the world can only have two distinct possibilities. These gods can only be fallen angels which includes Satan, or they are demonic spirits. Satan for example, is referred to in the scriptures as the, "God of This World," because he literally has been given control over the affairs of the world for a select period of time. Yes, there are many gods, but there is only one, "Most High God." He is the God of Abraham, Isaac, and Jacob. He does have a Son, and his name is Jesus who the Bible also refers to as the, "Lion of the Tribe of Judah." Let's now take a brief look at these ten plagues being poured out on the land of Egypt.

> **Plague # 1, God Strikes the Nile:** "Thus saith the Lord, In this thou shalt know that I am the Lord: behold, I will smite with the rod that is in mine hand upon the waters which are in the river, and they shall be turned to blood." (Exodus 7:17)

It was no surprise to God Pharaoh would be a very stubborn man to deal with. The heart of this king was filled with pride and arrogance. The first plague hit the Egyptian people where it hurt. God turns the waters of the Nile, all streams, ponds, and even water stored in vessels to blood. As shown earlier, the Nile was worshipped by the people of Egypt. Now all water in Egypt supported no life, smells disgusting, was unfit to drink, and resembles blood. We also see a similar event recorded in Revelation. Although during this future period of time, instead of a regional event, it will be a world-wide event.

> And the second angel poured out his vial upon the sea; and it became as the blood of a dead man: and every living soul died in the sea:
> And the third angel poured out his vial upon the rivers and fountains of waters; and they became blood. (Revelation 16:3–4)

Plague # 2, God Sends Frogs: "And if thou refuse to let them go, behold, I will smite all thy borders with frogs: And the river shall bring forth frogs abundantly, which shall go up and come into thine house, and into thy bedchamber, and upon thy bed, and into the house of thy servants, and upon thy people, and into thine ovens, and into thy kneadingtroughs: And the frogs shall come up both on thee, and upon thy people, and upon all thy servants." (Exodus 8:2–4)

The first plague doesn't change the mind of Pharaoh. Although Pharaoh ultimately had the authority to let the children of Israel go free, the condition of this man's heart affected the entire land and all people dwelling in Egypt. Pharaoh is informed if he refuses to let the people go, frogs will cover the land. The plague of frogs symbolizing one of the gods worshipped by Egypt, caused Pharaoh to temporarily change his mind. Moses and Aaron were summoned by Pharaoh and instructed to take his God, his people, and leave the land. Moses cried out to God, the frogs leave Egypt, and Pharaoh again hardens his heart. The book of Revelation also gives us a similar picture of judgment relating to frogs being released upon the land. In Revelation, these frogs are specifically identified as demonic spirits who deceive the rulers of the nations. The comparison in Revelation also helps us to understand the frogs, lice, and flies were physical representations of literal spiritual entities worshipped in Egypt. Again, these evil spirits and fallen angels being worshipped were not idols made of wood or gold, they were literal spiritual beings.

> And I saw three unclean spirits like frogs come out of the mouth of the dragon, and out of the mouth of the beast, and out of the mouth of the false prophet.
> For they are the spirits of devils, working miracles, which go forth unto the kings of the earth and of the whole world, to gather them to the battle of that great day of God Almighty. (Revelation 16:13–14)

> **Plague # 3, God Sends Lice:** "And the Lord said unto Moses, Say unto Aaron, Stretch out thy rod, and smite the dust of the land, that it may become lice throughout all the land of Egypt. And they did so; for Aaron stretched out his hand with his rod, and smote the dust of the earth, and it became lice in man, and in beast; all the dust of the land became lice throughout all the land of Egypt." (Exodus 8:16–17)

We start to see a pattern here where Pharaoh repeatedly changes his mind and then again hardens his heart. Moses again instructs Aaron to stretch out his rod, strike the ground, and the entire land of Egypt crawls with lice infesting all people and all beasts. The Bible informs us during some of the plagues the magicians and sorcerers of Egypt are able to copy certain elements to these plagues. The Bible informs us the magicians are able to some extent replicate the plague of frogs, but they were unsuccessful in getting rid of them. This is similar to the incident where Aaron cast down his rod before Pharaoh and it turns into a serpent. Pharaoh's magicians then cast down their rods, but their serpents were then swallowed by Aaron's serpent. The magicians attempt to bring about lice on command, but they were unable to do so. The magicians instructed Pharaoh the swarms of lice are from the God of Israel which caused Pharaoh to again harden his heart.

> **Plague # 4, God Sends Flies:** "Else, if thou wilt not let my people go, behold, I will send swarms of flies upon thee, and upon thy servants, and upon thy people, and into thy house: and the houses of the Egyptians shall be full of swarms of flies, and also the ground whereon they are. And I will sever in that day the land of Goshen, in which my people dwell, that no swarms of flies shall be there; to the end thou mayest know that I am the Lord in the midst of the earth. And I will put a division between my people and thy people: tomorrow shall this sign be." (Exodus 8:21–23)

Pharaoh still continues to refuse to let the children of Israel go. Moses informs Pharaoh flies (could be interpreted as insects) will swarm and cover the land. This plague is different because it does not involve Aaron stretching forth his rod. God informs Pharaoh this plague will not involve the children of Israel so he will know the God of Israel is personally responsible for the plague. The flies cause Pharaoh to temporarily soften his heart and change his mind, but when the swarms of flies disappear, his heart is again hardened.

> **Plague # 5, God Sends Pestilence Upon Livestock:** "Behold, the hand of the Lord is upon thy cattle which is in the field, upon the horses, upon the asses, upon the camels, upon the oxen, and upon the sheep: there shall be a very grievous murrain. And the Lord shall sever between the cattle of Israel and the cattle of Egypt: and there shall nothing die of all that is the children's of Israel." (Exodus 9:3–4)

Well I think we know by now how the story goes. Pharaoh again hardens his heart, and God directly sends pestilence upon the livestock in the land of Egypt. With this plague there is again a separation between Pharaoh's livestock and the livestock of Israel. The Bible records all livestock in Egypt die, and not one head of Israel's livestock perishes. The Bible states Pharaoh investigates to see if indeed the livestock belonging to the children of Israel are still alive. In spite of all of this, Pharaoh's heart continues to be hardened.

The condition of Pharaoh's heart reminds me of the condition of those people living on the earth during the future time of, "Daniel's Seventieth Week," recorded in the Bible. According to the Bible, these events recorded here in Exodus are eerie similar to the events coming in the future. Those today who teach and believe the Old Testament does not relate to us today are making a drastic mistake. Revelation gives us an example of this fact. There is a point when a person's heart finally becomes so hard and calloused, it is very unlikely a change in heart is possible. I'm not denying the possibility of miracles because people do change. What I am saying is God knew Pharaoh would not repent of his pride, and so God was going to make an example of him.

> And the rest of the men which were not killed by these plagues yet repented not of the works of their hands, that they should not worship devils, and idols of gold, and silver, and brass, and stone, and of wood: which neither can see, nor hear, nor walk:
>
> Neither repented they of their murders, nor of their sorceries, nor of their fornication, nor of their thefts. (Revelation 9:20–21)

Plague # 6, God Sends Boils: "And the Lord said unto Moses and unto Aaron, Take to you handfuls of ashes of the furnace, and let Moses sprinkle it toward the heaven in the sight of Pharaoh. And it shall become small dust in all the land of Egypt, and shall be a boil breaking forth

with blains upon man, and upon beast, throughout all the land of Egypt." (Exodus 9:8–9)

God instructs Moses to throw the ashes from a furnace into
the air. The ashes would blow across the land of Egypt, causing great
sores and boils to appear upon the people along with their livestock.
The Bible informs us even the magicians were unable to stand before
Moses due to these boils afflicting their bodies. God again hardens
the heart of Pharaoh. God knew Pharaoh would not change his
mind. God will make an example of Pharaoh because of the condition of his heart. We again are reminded of a similar plague recorded
in the book of Revelation.

> And the first (Angel) went, and poured out
> his vial upon the earth; and there fell a noisome
> and grievous sore upon the men which had the
> mark of the beast, and upon them which wor-
> shipped the image. (Revelation 16:2)

> **Plague # 7, God Sends Hail:** "And the
> Lord said unto Moses, Stretch forth thine hand
> toward heaven, that there may be hail in all the
> land of Egypt, upon man, and upon beast, and
> upon every herb of the field, throughout the land
> of Egypt. So there was hail, and fire mingled with
> the hail, very grievous, such as there was none
> like it in all the land of Egypt since it became
> a nation. And the hail smote throughout all the
> land of Egypt all that was in the field, both man
> and beast; and the hail smote every herb of the
> field, and brake every tree of the field. Only in
> the land of Goshen, where the children of Israel
> were, was there no hail." (Exodus 9:23–26)

God then tells Moses to stretch forth his hand towards heaven,
and there will fall hail mingled with fire upon the land of Egypt

unlike there has never been since Egypt existed. This hail will destroy all men and livestock caught out in the field. This hail will destroy all vegetation and trees. But in the land of Goshen where the children of Israel lived, no hail fell from the sky. It is interesting the Bible mentions this hailstorm was mixed with fire. It is quite likely this event would have been a meteor storm where the hail would not be ice, but literal rocks or debris falling from the heavens such as an asteroid. Other possibilities for events such as these could be a comet exploding above the earth, or a volcanic eruption scattering fiery rocks upon the land. The Bible also mentions during this event there is thunder and flashes of lightning. If there were stones impacting the earth, the sounds of the impacts would rumble like thunder and could have literally shook the earth. It is also not uncommon to see lightning and electrical discharges during volcanic eruptions and earthquakes.

These hail, fire, and thunder events caused Pharaoh to again summon Moses and Aaron. Pharaoh confesses to Moses and Aaron he has sinned, the Lord is righteous, and he and the people of Egypt were wicked. Moses states to Pharaoh when he walks out of the city the storm will cease, but I'm sure Moses knew neither Pharaoh nor the people of Egypt would repent of their sins. So as Moses promises, the storm stops. Pharaoh then again hardens his heart, sins against God, and would not let the children of Israel go. Revelation again records a somewhat similar event where those dwelling on the earth will repeatedly refuse to repent, and turn from their sin.

> And there fell upon men a great hail out of heaven, every stone about the weight of a talent: and men blasphemed God because of the plague of the hail; for the plague thereof was exceedingly great. (Revelation 16:21)

Plague # 8, God Sends Locusts: "And Moses and Aaron came in unto Pharaoh, and said unto him, Thus saith the Lord God of the Hebrews, How long wilt thou refuse to humble thyself before me? let my people go, that they may serve me. Else, if thou refuse to let my people go, behold, tomorrow will I bring the locusts into thy coast: And they shall cover the face of the earth, that one cannot be able to see the earth: and they shall eat the residue of that which is escaped, which remaineth unto you out of the field." (Exodus 10:3–5)

After all these repeated judgments from God, Pharaoh still refuses to swallow his pride and humble himself before God. The first verse in Exodus chapter 10 informs us God will again make an example of Egypt's pride and arrogance. The story of Israel's captivity in Egypt will be recorded in God's word. It will remind Israel's children for generations to come, of God's signs, His mighty power, and to know He is their God.

Moses and Aaron again approach Pharaoh informing him if he again refuses to let the people go, a plague of locusts will come upon the land. There will be such a severe plague of locusts a person will not be able to see the ground. The locusts will eat every green thing left from the previous hailstorm. The locusts will strip away all living vegetation. Moses informs Pharaoh the plague of locusts will be unlike any plague the earth has ever seen. The locusts will fill the houses of all Egyptians. After this, the servants of Pharaoh tried to convince him to let the people go due to the devastation Egypt has already suffered.

Again, Pharaoh refuses to let God's people go. Pharaoh was willing to make exceptions by permitting the men to go serve their God, but refused to let the women and children of Israel leave Egypt. So Moses stretched forth his rod over Egypt, the locusts cover the land, and the devastation described earlier by Moses indeed does take place. The Bible states there was no green vegetation left of any kind in the entire land of Egypt.

Pharaoh now in haste calls for Moses and Aaron. Pharaoh again verbally asks for forgiveness, and for Moses to ask his God to send away the locusts from the land. The Lord then sends a mighty west wind taking away the locusts causing them to perish in the Red Sea. Not one locust was found in all the coasts of Egypt. Over and over again Pharaoh continues to verbally acknowledge God, but his heart continues to be hard. Pharaoh definitely wants the plagues to cease, but he refuses to fall down on his face and worship God. No, not the Pharaoh of Egypt, his heart is filled with far too much pride to worship the God of Israel. Pharaoh's heart was still far from God.

A literal locust plague devoured all vegetation from the land of Egypt. Not one green leaf could be found. The plague of locusts God sent upon Egypt is a prophetic picture of what will again happen in the future. Revelation chapter 9 tells us another locust plague is one day coming during a future event known as, "The Day of the Lord." This future event is also referred to as a time of, "Jacob's Trouble." It is interesting the name, "Jacob," is a literal biblical reference to the nation and children of Israel. Many Christians today are confused concerning this truth, but this future wrath that will be poured out upon those who dwell upon the earth is for those rejecting the truth and salvation of a loving God. This future time of God's wrath will be felt worldwide, and it will again be a time of, "Great Tribulation," for Israel similar to the time of their captivity in Egypt. This is why Jeremiah describes this future event as a time of, "Jacob's trouble."

I believed years ago the locust plague spoken of in Revelation, was a prophetic reference to apache helicopters or other advanced military equipment. During the past five to seven years I've become firmly convinced this event needs to be taken literally. In the same way the flood of Noah was a literal event resulting from angels leaving their first estate, descending upon the earth, and ultimately corrupting all flesh on earth. The future, "Day of the Lord," will again involve the physical manifestations of demonic and angelic beings on this earth. Yes, just as Jesus stated, it will be like the days of Noah. I will go into more detail concerning this event described in Revelation chapter 9 later on in the book.

It is interesting the book of Joel in the first couple chapters, gives us a picture of what will take place during this future time of, "Great Tribulation," coming upon those dwelling on the earth. We see here the prophet Joel describing in every way he knows how what he sees coming in the future to those who reject God. We notice the prophet Joel describes this future demonic army coming upon the earth, comparing them to a literal locust army stripping the land, devouring all vegetation in their path. A person needs to pay close attention to the way Joel describes these demonic creatures invading the land and tormenting those on the earth. A person needs to do their homework to understand Joel is comparing a literal locust plague to future demonic creatures coming out of the earth. I believe the words spoken by the prophet Joel directly relate to what John has to say to us in Revelation chapter 9, because I believe they are references to the same event.

> A fire devoureth before them; and behind them a flame burneth: the land is as the garden of Eden before them, and behind them a desolate wilderness; yea, and nothing shall escape them.
>
> The appearance of them is as the appearance of horses; and as horsemen, so shall they run.
>
> Like the noise of chariots on the tops of mountains shall they leap, like the noise of a flame of fire that devoureth the stubble, as a strong people set in battle array.
>
> Before their face the people shall be much pained: all faces shall gather blackness.
>
> The earth shall quake before them; the heavens shall tremble: the sun and the moon shall be dark, and the stars shall withdraw their shining:
>
> And the Lord shall utter his voice before his army: for his camp is very great: for he is strong that executeth his word: for the day of the Lord is great and very terrible; and who can abide it? (Joel 2:3–6, 10–11)

This great plague of locusts coming upon Egypt stripping the land of all vegetation and covering the earth was a literal event. I believe this event is symbolic of a much worse invasion one day coming upon the earth during the time known as, "Daniel's 70th week." Whether people want to believe it or not, the plagues of Egypt although they literally took place, are a picture of a future wrath coming upon the world.

> **Plague # 9, God Sends Darkness:** "And the Lord said unto Moses, Stretch out thine hand toward heaven, that there may be darkness over the land of Egypt, even darkness which may be felt. And Moses stretched forth his hand toward heaven; and there was a thick darkness in all the land of Egypt three days: They saw not one another, neither rose any from his place for three days: but all the children of Israel had light in their dwellings." (Exodus 10:21–23)

The Egyptians worshipped the sun god, "Ra," but now even the sun refuses to shine. This was not a normal solar eclipse. This was darkness so heavy it could literally be felt. This was an evil darkness lasting for a period of three days. It is also interesting the events of Revelation include darkness taking place on the entire earth. I have always believed the solar and lunar eclipses we see on the earth are reminders to us God is in complete control of His creation. I also believe these events are pointing to future cataclysmic events, when again the sun will literally be darkened and refuse to shine on the entire earth possibly for days.

> Blow ye the trumpet in Zion, and sound an alarm in my holy mountain: let all the inhabitants of the land tremble: for the day of the Lord cometh, for it is nigh at hand:
> A day of darkness and of gloominess, a day of clouds and of thick darkness, as the morning spread upon the mountains: a great people and a strong; there hath not been ever the like, neither shall be any more after it, even to the years of many generations. (Joel 2:1–2)

The sun shall be turned into darkness, and the moon into blood, before the great and terrible day of the Lord come. (Joel 2:32)

Immediately after the tribulation of those days shall the sun be darkened, and the moon shall not give her light, and the stars shall fall from heaven, and the powers of the heavens shall be shaken. (Matthew 24:29)

For the stars of heaven and the constellations thereof shall not give their light: the sun shall be darkened in his going forth, and the moon shall not cause her light to shine. (Isaiah 13:10)

The Egyptian people were intelligent. They studied the heavens and recognized the order in God's creation. When darkness covered their land for three days, no doubt it scared the living daylights out of them. Pharaoh again calls for Moses telling him to go and serve the Lord, but the livestock must stay. Moses states to Pharaoh, "Our livestock goes with us." So again, the Lord hardens the heart of Pharaoh. Pharaoh then instructs Moses to leave his presence, or he will die.

Plague # 10, God Kills all Firstborn in Egypt: "And the Lord said unto Moses, Yet will I bring one plague more upon Pharaoh, and upon Egypt; afterward he will let you go hence: when he shall let you go, he shall surely thrust you out hence altogether. And Moses said, Thus saith the Lord, About midnight will I go out into the midst of Egypt: And all the firstborn in the land of Egypt shall die, from the firstborn of the maidservant that is behind the mill; and all the firstborn of beasts. And there shall be a cry throughout all the land of Egypt, such as there was none like it any more. But against any of the children

of Israel not a dog move his tongue, against man
or beast: that ye may know how that the Lord
doth put a difference between the Egyptians and
Israel." (Exodus 11:1, 4–7)

God sends one last plague upon the land of Egypt. God has
given Egypt many chances to repent of their evil ways and let the
children of Israel go. God knew the condition of Pharaoh's heart, and
He knew it would take such a devastating event as this to break him.
Not only should this be a lesson for us as individuals, but this story
should be a lesson for the nations.

Notice in the above verses the contrast in the ways this judgment affected the people of Israel and Egypt. Egypt loses all firstborn
as the result of this plague, both man and beast. The firstborn of
Israel and all livestock were spared from God's wrath. Yes, the Lord
does make a distinction between Egypt and Israel. A concept most
churches and even Christians today fail to recognize, is God does not
deal with all groups of people in the same way. Pharaoh and Egypt is
a prophetic picture of the future antichrist and the world. Egypt is a
picture of what will happen to those who trust and serve other gods.
The Bible consistently gives us a picture of the spiritual separation
between the righteous and the unrighteous. We see illustrations of
light and darkness, wheat and tares, and those who have been sealed
and marked by the Holy Spirit, contrasted with those people who
will one day receive the mark of the Beast.

Israel is a picture of those who love and serve God. God has
always and always will have a special love for Israel. Israel has repeatedly been disciplined by God, and they will again be harshly disciplined in the future. God again, will one day come to their rescue.
We will later on be discussing this truth in more detail.

God informs Moses ahead of time this last plague would convince Pharaoh to let Israel go. God informed Moses He was establishing this final plague of death as a memorial to the children of Israel.
God commanded all Israel to remember this event and tell it to their
children from now on. The Lord informed Moses and Aaron the
current month will now be called the first month of the year. From

now on, annually on the tenth day of the month a lamb is taken for each household, and it will be sacrificed on the fourteenth day of the month. This lamb was to be without spot or blemish, a male of the first year. Here the Bible records the very first Passover celebration, the day the wrath of God passed over the children of Israel when He saw the blood of a lamb.

Entire books have been written on this one chapter alone in the book of Exodus. The one concept I really want to drive home is the symbolic and prophetic meanings of the lamb and the blood. It seems most churches today stray away from talking and singing about the blood of Christ. The old hymn, "The Old Rugged Cross," doesn't seem to be as popular in churches today as it once was. The Bible informs us the shedding of blood is required for the forgiveness of sin.

> But if we walk in the light, as he is in the light, we have fellowship one with another, and the blood of Jesus Christ his Son cleanseth us from all sin. (1 John 1:7)

> Then Moses called for all the elders of Israel, and said unto them, Draw out and take you a lamb according to your families, and kill the Passover.
> And ye shall take a bunch of hyssop, and dip it in the blood that is in the bason, and strike the lintel and the two side posts with the blood that is in the bason; and none of you shall go out at the door of his house until the morning. (Exodus 12:21–22)

> And the blood shall be to you for a token upon the houses where ye are: and when I see the blood, I will pass over you, and the plague shall not be upon you to destroy you, when I smite the land of Egypt. (Exodus 12:13)

In memory of this historical event about to take place, God commands the children of Israel to do several things. God commanded a lamb without spot or blemish was to be sacrificed. Yes, there was a Lamb who was without spot or blemish. He was perfect, and His blood was offered as a payment for the sins of the world. This reminds me of the following verse in the New Testament.

> The next day John seeth Jesus coming unto him, and saith, Behold the lamb of God, which taketh away the sin of the world. (John 1:29)

The blood of the lamb was to be collected in a basin. Hyssop branches being symbolic for cleansing and purification were then dipped in the blood, and the blood was smeared on the exterior doorframes of each house. Notice the people of Israel were commanded not to go outside their homes until the next morning after the blood was applied to the doorframes.

God warned His children He would pass through that night killing all firstborn, both man and beast in the land of Egypt. God killed all firstborn that night no matter if they were rich, poor, free, or in chains. God states He will pass over all homes of Israel having applied the blood of the lamb on their doorframes. Those Israelite families whose home was covered by the blood of the lamb would see no wrath from God.

What a promise this is for us today. It is my hope the patterns we see in the Bible such as in this story, is teaching us lessons concerning the character of God. God's wrath passed over Noah and his family when God shut the door to the ark. God's wrath passed over Lot when he was literally drug out of Sodom by an angel. God's wrath passed over the children of Israel when the blood of the Lamb was applied to the doorframes of their homes. God will again in the future protect the children of Israel, and His wrath will again pass over His bride, when He brings wrath upon an unbelieving, unrepentant world.

There is therefore now no condemnation to them which are in Christ Jesus, who walk not after the flesh, but after the Spirit. (Romans 8:1)

For the wrath of God is revealed from heaven against all ungodliness and unrighteousness of men, who hold the truth in unrighteousness;

Because that which may be known of God is manifest in them; for God hath shewed it unto them.

For the invisible things of him from the creation of the world are clearly seen, being understood by the things that are made, even his eternal power and Godhead; so that they are without excuse:

Because that, when they knew God, they glorified him not as God, neither were thankful; but became vain in their imaginations, and their foolish heart was darkened.

Professing themselves to be wise, they became fools. (Romans 1:18–22)

The Bible informs us we all are without excuse. Pharaoh had no excuse, and Egypt had no excuse. It has always amazed me science is constantly proving to us the complexity of our entire solar system, our planet, and how fragile and beautiful life really is. Take one dead skin cell and place it under a microscope. The more it is magnified, the more complex it appears. Nobody denies the watch on our wrist has a creator due to its evidence of design, but millions of people deny the universe the watch keeps time with has a creator. Spend some time in the great outdoors with nature, and stare up into the heavens on a starry night. Look at the order and complexity in all God's creation, and all people should come to the conclusion we really truly are without excuse.

Nothing New under the Sun

Studying the Bible gives us answers to handling many of life's difficult situations. Sometimes I have discovered Bible study does a better job of creating questions rather than providing answers to various subjects. I always have liked to compare studying the Bible with digging for gold. Many people in the beginning are excited with the thought of finding gold. In most cases, after digging and sweating a few hours, the thrill of the hunt usually fizzles out causing people to lose interest and abandon the search. I believe this is what happens to many Christians today. It is shocking when a person realizes how little time most professing Christians spend reading and studying the Bible. I have read many articles stating most people attending church on a regular basis may sometimes go weeks and even months, without consistently spending time in God's word.

In my earlier years as a Christian, I must confess I did not take Bible study and the privilege of teaching in the church setting serious enough. During my earlier years it seemed studying and teaching the Bible became more like a job or a task I felt I had to complete. Yes, I was at church most Sunday mornings and even most Sunday evenings. I listened to the pastor give his message, but there was very little personal time being spent studying the Bible and spending time with God.

As I got a little older and hopefully a little more mature, I began to realize the call to teach was a gift and privilege from God, and was something I needed to take more seriously. After all, the Bible tells us those in positions of leadership in the church will be one day held to a higher standard. I believe the gradual increased interest to spend more time studying and digging for answers in the Bible, was just me growing up and maturing in Christ.

Over a period of years, my desire to study the Bible continued to increase taking on a new level of enthusiasm. I always loved the subject of eschatology and was fascinated about what the Bible not only teaches us about history, but also what it has to say concerning future events. During the next ten years or so, I steadily developed an increased desire to study anything I could having to do with the Bible and history. I spent thousands of hours listening and watching any type of audio or video presentation I could get my hands on. Any show on television I could find relating to good Bible study or prophecy, I would enjoy watching. On a daily basis I began to pay attention to current events taking place worldwide, and would try to figure out where these events fell on God's prophetic timetable. As I continued to study and mature as a Christian, I began to see some of the questions I once had with certain scriptural passages were being answered. It's kind of like putting together a puzzle. The first few pieces reveals little of the big picture, but as more pieces came together, patterns would start to emerge and questions concerning Bible subjects would be answered.

A certain Bible verse stated by Solomon in the book of Ecclesiastes would end up being one of those major pieces to the puzzle, opening my eyes to spiritual and prophetic truths unlike any other verse I have read. Sometimes Bible study creates more questions, but just like with prospecting for gold, continuing to dig eventually brings rewards. The way to gain biblical wisdom, is to keep on praying, digging, and God will eventually reveal truth and light on various subjects. The verses below makes reference to this biblical truth.

> Give therefore thy servant an understanding heart to judge thy people, that I may discern between good and bad: for who is able to judge this thy so great a people?

And the speech pleased the Lord, that Solomon had asked this thing.

And God said unto him, Because thou hast asked this thing, and hast not asked for thyself long life; neither hast asked riches for thyself, nor hast asked the life of thine enemies; but has asked for thyself understanding to discern judgment;

Behold, I have done according to thy words: lo, I have given thee a wise and an understanding heart; so that there was none like thee before thee, neither after thee shall any arise like unto thee (1 Kings 3:9–12).

The Bible informs us Solomon loved the Lord and walked in the ways of his father David. The Lord appeared to Solomon in a dream and asked him if there was anything he desired from Him. Let's imagine for a minute the Creator of the universe coming to us and asking if there was anything we needed from Him. Sure God, a couple million bucks and everything would probably be fine for now. Maybe a person would ask for a job or how about, "Hey God, you know this person who has really wronged me, one simple lightning strike would be fine." Well, let's hope a request to do harm to someone would not be on the list.

Solomon asked God for wisdom. Solomon asked God for the gift of discernment allowing him to be a better leader of the people. There is a difference between being intelligent and having common sense. God answers Solomon's prayer by giving him a wise and understanding heart. The Bible states there would be no other person or king whose wisdom would ever compare to him. There never has been and never would be a wiser man than Solomon.

But this isn't the end to the story. God goes on to let Solomon know if he continued to walk with God keeping His laws and commandments, his days would be lengthened. The Bible goes on to state the entire nation of Israel feared and respected Solomon as their king, because of his wisdom in leading the people. The Bible provides more information detailing the wisdom God gave Solomon:

> And God gave Solomon wisdom and understanding exceeding much, and largeness of heart, even as the sand that is on the sea shore.
>
> And Solomon's wisdom excelled the wisdom of all the children of the east country, and all the wisdom of Egypt.
>
> For he was wiser than all men; than Ethan the Ezrahite, and Heman, and Chalcol, and Darda, the sons of Mahol: and his fame was in all nations round about.
>
> And he spake three thousand proverbs: and his songs were a thousand and five.
>
> And he spake of trees, from the cedar tree that is in Lebanon even unto the hyssop that springeth out of the wall: he spake also of beasts, and of fowl, and of creeping things, and of fishes.
>
> And there came of all people to hear the wisdom of Solomon, from all kings of the earth, which had heard of his wisdom. (1 Kings 4:29–34)

According to the Bible, Solomon was wiser than any other man who lived or was yet to live. The Bible tells us Solomon memorized more than a thousand songs and could recite three thousand proverbs. Any subject a person could discuss, Solomon was more informed on it than anyone else. The above Bible verses prove the fact Solomon's wisdom did not come from man, it came from God. An important truth most people today fail to realize is when people who are daily seeking wisdom from God, and He provides discernment concerning a matter, the wisdom God gives a person, group, or even a nation will be correct, honest, and truthful.

There is a verse in Ecclesiastes containing a quote from Solomon most are familiar with and have read many times. Most people including myself, really had no spiritual idea as to the true meaning of this verse. I have read this verse over and over for years really not grasping what Solomon was really telling us. When I finally came to understand the meaning of this one verse, my perspective on much of the Bible changed drastically. I now understand this verse given to us by Solomon is crucial in understanding many of the biblical events of the Old Testament. This verse is also crucial for understanding the prophetic events that will take place in the future. The verse I am referring to is referenced below.

> The thing that hath been, it is that which
> shall be; and that which is done is that which
> shall be done: and there is no new thing under
> the sun. (Ecclesiastes 1:9)

This verse in Ecclesiastes is packed with many layers of truth. At the surface, Solomon is informing us the heart of man has really never changed over time and never will change. In reality, mankind throughout history has struggled with the same issues Adam and Eve struggled with in the garden. Man has always insisted in doing things his own way. Humanity has always held to the idea God is not qualified to tell people how to live, and what decisions should be made concerning life. Man desires to believe they are their own god, and no one has the right to interfere in their own personal decisions and choices. People want to live life according to their own desires where they alone will be in charge of their destiny. God does give people the free will to choose their own destiny. Everyone needs to realize they individually will be held accountable by a holy and just God concerning the consequences of their decisions. God did not send the flood primarily because man was becoming more and more sinful. God knew the mistakes man would continue to make, and he would continue to sin. Satan instructed Eve if she would eat of the tree of knowledge of good and evil, her eyes would be opened. In a sense, Satan told Eve a half truth. When Adam and Eve disobeyed God and sinned in the garden, for the first time in their lives their eyes were opened. Immediately they experienced emotions of guilt, shame, separation from God, and recognized their relationship with God had changed drastically.

Satan convinced Adam and Eve they were missing out on life. The grass always seems greener on the other side of the fence. Adam and Eve traded immortality for mortality. I believe the genetic makeup of their bodies literally did change immediately when the decision to disobey God was made. Now, for the first time in their lives they realized they were naked and were spiritually and physically dying. The Bible informs us the blood of animals was shed in order to make garments to cover up their nakedness. We find the term nakedness in the Bible such as in this case is usually symbolic for sin and unrighteousness. The idea that man would sin was no surprise to God. From the beginning of time, God had already made plans to send an unblemished Lamb to pay the sin debt of all people who freely accept Him.

Another spiritual truth this verse is trying to tell us is history truly does repeat itself. Kingdoms, societies, nations, and even individuals seem to learn nothing from the past. The same mistakes have been and will continue to be repeated over and over again. There really isn't such a thing as a new problem. Similar historical and social issues continue to repeat themselves over and over again, although they may be packaged or presented in a different way.

We really need to understand Satan really never changes his schemes. Yes, they may come in a different colored package and have a different name, but in reality false teaching and false doctrine will always come with the same underlying theme. Spiritual deception will always involve the denial of the deity of Christ. One of the most interesting questions I've been asked deals with the origins of religion. The question relates to, "If it is true only one God exists, why are so many different religions and religious beliefs in the world today?" The Bible as well as archaeology informs us man has worshiped many gods throughout history. If we will just learn to take the Bible for what it says, we are given the answers to this question. The Bible informs us in the past there was an invasion upon earth by fallen angels who left their first estate or habitation, descended on the earth and were worshipped as gods. I believe this manifestation of fallen angels to earth during the days of Noah was the reason and purpose for God destroying all flesh on this earth. All flesh on earth including the animals was genetically corrupted by these spirit beings. Yes, there are many gods one can serve, but there is only one, "Most High God," who is the God of the Bible. There is a, "god of this world," and his name is Satan. Millions of people have been and will continue to be deceived by him. Satan's goal in life is to lie, to deceive, and to prevent as many people as possible from coming to a personal saving relationship with Christ. The Bible warns us Satan is like a roaring lion continually roaming the earth, seeking someone to devour.

It was an amazing moment in my life when I realized this verse in Ecclesiastes is attempting to inform the reader similar events to what took place in the stories of the Old Testament, will one day be repeated again. Although these events were real and literally took place, the stories in the Old Testament such as the flood of Noah, the Exodus, and the destruction of Sodom and Gomorrah are also meant to be prophetic pictures of future events. This would also explain the reasoning behind Satan having the world including a large percentage of churches deceived into believing the Old Testament stories were allegorical in nature and were not literal events. Have you also noticed all the deception in the world today concerning the subject of climate change? Climate change has taken place since the beginning of time, and individuals need to understand in the big picture, people have a minimal impact on climate change. History and science informs us there were cataclysmic life-changing events that have taken place in the past. According to the Bible, there will be severe cataclysmic events coming again in the future. All a person needs to do is access the internet and look at the evidence. Many megalithic structures and entire civilizations once existing on dry land, now can be seen at the bottom of the ocean. We've already discussed some of these events such as the, "Exodus," in great detail, where catastrophic sudden events prophesied by God took place. One can find over five hundred stories telling of a worldwide flood event covering the earth ending all life.

According to the Bible, not only was there tremendous flooding rainfall taking place during the flood of Noah, but the Bible also informs us the fountains of the deep also burst forth. The reality is the stories of the Old Testament really did take place. The cities of Sodom and Gomorrah did once exist and were completely destroyed by God. Extreme climate change occurred in the past, and extreme climate change is coming again. I would like to stress in no way am I stating we as people are relieved of our responsibility of being good stewards with God's creation.

The Bible in the book of Joshua tells us of a very interesting event where the sun stood still in the sky. I have heard people make the comment this story is just proof the Bible cannot be trusted as being historically accurate. If one is willing to do a little homework, you will find the Egyptians, various Indian tribes, and the Chinese supposedly tell stories of a, "Long Night," and a day, "When the sun became confused," corresponding to this same period of time. History also confirms the ancient calendars of past civilizations such as the Egyptians, the Chinese, and the Mayans were once based on a 360-day year. It is also interesting around 700 BC, many of these ancient calendars for some reason changed from a 360-day calendar year to a 365-day calendar year. Let's take a look at a few verses in Joshua chapter 10 describing this incident.

> And the Lord discomfited them before Israel, and slew them with a great slaughter at Gibeon, and chased them along the way that goeth up to Bethhoron, and smote them to Azekah, and unto Makkedah.
>
> And it came to pass, as they fled from before Israel, and were in the going down to Bethhoron, that the Lord cast down great stones from heaven upon them unto Azekah, and they died: they were more which died with hailstones than they whom the children of Israel slew with the sword.
>
> Then spake Joshua to the Lord in the day when the Lord delivered up the Amorites before

the children of Israel, and he said in the sight of
Israel, Sun, stand thou still upon Gibeon; and
thou, Moon, in the valley of Ajalon.

And the sun stood still, and the moon stayed,
until the people had avenged themselves upon their
enemies. Is not this written in the book of Jasher?
So the sun stood still in the midst of heaven, and
hasted not to go down about a whole day.

And there was no day like that before it
or after it, that the Lord hearkened unto the
voice of a man: for the Lord fought for Israel.
(Joshua 10:10–14)

People today are so quick to come to conclusions when they
read stories such as these in the Bible. People are quick to state events
occurring such as these are scientifically impossible, so these individuals conclude the Bible cannot be trusted. The Bible makes it clear
in these verses God was supernaturally involved in the protection of
Israel. I believe the Bible is giving us a hint in verse 11 of Joshua 10,
informing us God may have sent a great meteorite storm to kill the
enemies of Israel. I believe it is very possible a large heavenly object
coming close or striking the earth could affect the tilt and rotation
of the earth. If a close pass by from a heavenly body would somehow
tilt or slow down the rotation of the earth, the day literally could be
prolonged, and the sun would appear to literally stand still in the sky.
Those who believe this is impossible, the Japan earthquake in March
of 2011 according to scientists slightly shifted the earth's axis and
shortened each day.

The Bible is full of many other stories where God supernaturally
intervenes in the affairs of man. The story of Sodom and Gomorrah is
a prime example of this. God could have directed an asteroid or comet
to impact the area located near Sodom, causing total sudden destruction to these cities. I believe these were all literal events occurring in
the past. But more importantly, I believe these events are prophetic
pictures of what is coming in the future. For all people believing events
such as these are impossible, I would recommend you spend a little

time looking at the historical data. Here are just a few other Bible verses warning us of future cataclysms coming upon the earth.

> And I beheld when he had opened the sixth seal, and, lo, there was a great earthquake; and the sun became black as sackcloth of hair, and the moon became as blood;
>
> And the stars of heaven fell unto the earth, even as a fig tree casteth her untimely figs, when she is shaken of a mighty wind.
>
> And the heaven departed as a scroll when it is rolled together; and every mountain and island were moved out of their places.
>
> And the kings of the earth, and the great men, and the rich men, and the chief captains, and the mighty men, and every bondman, and every free man, hid themselves in the dens and in the rocks of the mountains. (Revelation 6:12–15)

> The earth shall reel to and fro like a drunkard, and shall be removed like a cottage; and the transgression thereof shall be heavy upon it; and it shall fall, and not rise again. (Isaiah 24:20)

As previously stated, there were once cities existing on dry land now located under the ocean. According to the Bible, similar cataclysmic events are coming again. People need to be spiritually preparing for events such as these. What has been done, will be done again. I understand this is a hard message to deal with, and it sure is a lot easier to just not discuss it. Jesus informs us there is coming a time when people will have the same spiritual condition as during the days of Noah. People heard the preaching of Noah, watched the ark being built, but refused the message and the signs of the times.

According to the Bible, there is another worldwide period of, "Great Tribulation," coming. The Bible informs us this time will be worse than during the days of Noah. This coming event will not take place with a flood, it will involve fire. The Bible informs us it will also be as it was in the days of Sodom. The days when Lot lived in Sodom was a time when people living in these cities became so wicked, rebellious, and unrepentant God had no other choice but to intervene.

It's amazing how many questions one verse can answer. People ask me what events are coming in the future. It's simple, the same types of events that have occurred in the past. The first issue people today should be concerned with is making sure they are secure in Christ and clothed in His righteousness. The second issue people should be concerned with is where we are on God's prophetic time-table. Fallen angels have literally manifested themselves on the earth in the past. Fallen angels will in the future literally again walk on this earth. It is interesting the increasing numbers of articles and TV shows telling us it appears extraterrestrials visited our planet in the past. In a sense, this coming event will be extraterrestrial in nature. A better word describing this event occurring during the coming tribulation period, would be to refer to it as an extradimensional event. Satan, his fallen angels, and demonic spirits are extradimensional beings. Yes, we really do not wrestle against flesh and blood, but against spiritual wickedness in high places.

> And the great dragon was cast out, that old serpent, called the Devil, and Satan, which deceiveth the whole world: he was cast out into the earth, and his angels were cast out with him.
>
> And I heard a loud voice saying in heaven, Now is come salvation, and strength, and the kingdom of our God, and the power of his Christ: for the accuser of our brethren is cast down, which accused them before our God day and night.
>
> And they overcame him by the blood of the Lamb, and by the word of their testimony; and they loved not their lives unto the death.
>
> Therefore rejoice, ye heavens, and ye that dwell in them. Woe to the inhabiters of the earth and of the sea! for the devil is come down unto

you, having great wrath, because he knoweth that
he hath but a short time. (Revelation 12:9–12)

So why would Satan want to deceive us and lie about the past?
It is because having knowledge of the past is the key to understanding the future. I will later on in the book spend an entire chapter
discussing events the Bible warns us are coming in the future. It is
crucial for all people to understand the events taking place in the Old
Testament were real literal events, meant as prophetic warnings for
future judgments coming from God.

In 2013, I conducted a study through the entire book of
Revelation. I then completed a Bible study on the book of Jude.
During both of the studies I gave opinions on who I believe will be
the coming antichrist. According to Revelation, this man of sin will
be one of seven great Gentile kings that once ruled the world. The
Bible tells us he is one of these seven kings, but he is the, "Eight,"
king. I believe the Bible is informing us the coming of the antichrist
will somehow involve a resurrection. You might recall in the book of
Genesis, God informs us the Serpent will have seed which I believe
is referring to offspring. The antichrist will literally fulfill the seed of
the serpent prophecy. I believe the literal interpretation of the Bible
is telling us the antichrist once walked the earth, was killed and now
is dead, and he will be allowed during God's appointed time to rise
again. In the same way Christ will return again coming from heaven,
this man is coming again, but he will ascend out of the bottomless pit.

In the book of Revelation we are given the name of, "the antichrist." His Hebrew name is, "Abaddon," and his Greek name is,
"Apollyon." It is of my opinion the antichrist very well could be a
resurrected Nimrod. Nimrod was the first great leader who rebelled
against God. The name Nimrod means "Rebellion." The tower of
Babel Nimrod was constructing I believe was an attempt to overthrow God, and sit on His throne. The name Babel means, "Gate to
God." The following verses in Isaiah informs us of Satan's goals.

For thou hast said in thine heart, I will
ascend into heaven, I will exalt my throne above

the stars of God: I will sit also upon the mount of
the congregation, in the sides of the north:
    I will ascend above the heights of the clouds;
I will be like the most High. (Isaiah 14:13–14)

So where will all of these prophetic events end up taking us? I believe the story could possibly end where it all began. It is possible the first great man of rebellion named Nimrod could be the last great king leading the kingdoms of the earth. He will attempt to destroy the nation of Israel, and overthrow the plans of God. We know how the story ends. Revelation tells us Satan, the false prophet, and the Beast will be thrown into the, "Lake of Fire," for eternity.

We can see this one verse given to us from Solomon provides a tremendous amount of wisdom to those who are spiritually awake. We will be discussing this in more detail later as we move on in the book. Understanding the spiritual meaning of this one verse stated by Solomon is a major goal of the entire book. When we begin to understand history and prophecy repeats itself, we gain tremendous spiritual insight concerning the truths of the scriptures. What has been done, will truly be done again. There really is nothing new under the sun.

And They Became Fools

People always ask me how we will know we are getting close to the return of Jesus Christ and the end of the world. First of all, I don't see any verse in the Bible informing us the world is about to end. According to my years of study, the Bible informs we will first come to the end of this current age. When this current age of grace we are now living comes to a close, the world will then go through a seven-year period of time described in the book of Jeremiah as the time of, "Jacob's Trouble." The Bible in several places makes it clear, the final 3.5 years of this seven-year event will be referred as a time of, "Great Tribulation." It is interesting the Bible seems to always link this coming time of tribulation as being a time specifically intended for Israel and those dwelling on the earth during this time.

During the end of this seven-year period of tribulation, Jesus Christ will literally return to this earth to rescue Israel from annihilation and set up His kingdom on earth. This future period of time is referred to as the millennial reign of Christ, and will last for one thousand years. So as we can see, according to the Bible the world will not end in the near future. Although this coming time of Tribulation will include unthinkable death and destruction being far worse than the flood of Noah, the end of the earth will not come during this time. A verse in Daniel chapter 12 gives us evidence as to how devastating this time of God's wrath will be.

> And at that time shall Michael stand up, the
> great prince which standeth for the children of
> thy people: and there shall be a time of trouble,

such as never was since there was a nation even
to that same time: and at that time thy people
shall be delivered, every one that shall be found
written in the book. (Daniel 12:1)

The Bible refers to the age we are currently living in as the church
age, or the age of grace. I believe the Bible teaches us the church age
will end when the true church, those people who the Holy Spirit
indwells, will be suddenly removed from the earth. I believe the Bible
in the book of Thessalonians refers to the Holy Spirit who indwells
all who are, "In Christ," as the restraining force of evil being one day
removed from the earth. The Bible tells us the Holy Spirit arrived
during Pentecost, and there will be a day in the future when His
convicting and restraining power will be removed from the earth.
When this restraining force of evil, the true bride of Christ is in the
twinkling of an eye removed, Satan will then be permitted to have his
time on earth characterized by death, horror, and deception.

When the bride of Christ is suddenly caught up to meet Christ
in the air, I believe a sudden spiritual darkness and a possible temporary literal darkness will come upon the world. It will be a time
when Satan will be allowed by God to deceive those dwelling on the
earth, who have rejected the truth of God's word. Although we are
currently living in a time of deception, the Bible refers to this event
as a time of, "Great Deception." One of the major events happening
prior to the end of this age will be churches falling away from sound
doctrine. A major clue to discerning the times we are living in will
be churches falling away from sound doctrine. This spiritual falling
away will eventually climax to the point where churches operating
during the tribulation will completely refuse sound doctrine. These
churches more than likely will outlaw the Bible due to its intolerance
with worshipping false gods and false doctrines. I believe the church
of Laodicea is a spiritual picture of the collective church during the
end of the age.

We will in this chapter be dealing with the characteristics and
spiritual conditions of two groups of people living on the earth
during the end of the age. This book is about discerning the times

which we are living and understanding where we are at prophetically speaking. The Bible warns us more than once not to be ignorant of the times we are living in. We will be taking a closer look dealing with the spiritual condition of the church during this coming period of deception. The other group of people we will be addressing will be the spiritual condition of the world in general. We will find as we draw closer to the end of this age, the spiritual condition of the church will become more tolerant and similar to that of the world. The verses below in 2 Thessalonians warns all those who are spiritually awake of this fact.

> Now we beseech you, brethren, by the coming of our Lord Jesus Christ, and by our gathering together unto him,
>
> That ye be not shaken in mind, or be troubled, neither by spirit, nor by word, nor be letter as from us, as that the day of Christ is at hand.
>
> Let no man deceive you by any means: for that day shall not come, except there come a falling away first, and that man of sin be revealed, the son of perdition;
>
> Who opposeth and exalteth himself above all that is called God, or that is worshipped; so that he as God sitteth in the temple of God, shewing himself that he is God.
>
> Remember ye not, that, when I was yet with you, I told you these things?
>
> And now ye know what withholdeth that he might be revealed in his time.
>
> For the mystery of iniquity doth already work: only he who now letteth will let, until he be taken out of the way.
>
> And then shall that Wicked be revealed, whom the Lord shall consume with the spirit of his mouth, and shall destroy with the brightness of his coming:

Even him, whose coming is after the working of Satan with all power and signs and lying
wonders,

And with all deceivableness of unrighteousness in them that perish; because they received
not the love of the truth, that they might be
saved.

And for this cause God shall send them
strong delusion, that they should believe a lie:

That they all might be damned who believed
not the truth, but had pleasure in unrighteousness (2 Thessalonians 2:1–12).

It is extremely essential today for an individual to have the
ability to discern the differences between what is truth and what is
deception. The ability to establish what is truth is directly related to
a person's knowledge of the Bible. If we do not study God's word
daily, and we only rely on what someone else tells us even though
they may hold a position of leadership in the church, a person may
be making a big mistake. I know there are still many sound doctrinal
churches and many good pastors out there, but as time marches on,
the preaching and teaching of sound doctrine will become the exception instead of the rule.

One example of a false doctrine in the church includes teaching there's more than one way or path to heaven. Another example
would include, "if you live a good enough life or if your good karma
outweighs your bad karma, you'll go to heaven." Another common
false teaching informs people it makes no difference what god people
serve, since they are all equal.

It blows my mind how many people even in the church today
share these types of doctrinal beliefs. The Bible clearly tells us works
alone will not save anyone. The worship of any other gods besides
Jesus Christ, the Son of the, "Most High God," will not save a person from their sins. The Bible gives very clear instructions concerning how a person obtains righteousness. The Bible commands us to
test the spirits. We have already discussed the fact fallen angels and

demonic spirits exist and are very real spiritual beings. These fallen angels and demonic spirits have deceived millions in the past and are deceiving many in the churches today.

Millions of people today are literally unaware they are worshipping demons and fallen angels. If we take the Genesis flood account as a literal event it is not hard to understand where the many religions of the world came from, since fallen angels literally descended upon the earth during this time. We need to realize Satan really doesn't care how or who you worship, as long as it's any other god besides Jesus Christ.

Let's take a closer look at the previous verses in Thessalonians. The first point to bring out would be to understand Paul is addressing the brethren or those, "In Christ." Paul is addressing the Thessalonian church on what appears to be a misunderstanding in the body concerning when, "The Day of the Lord," and the second coming of Christ will take place. It appears many members in this church were very worried about their faith in Christ, quite possibly due to false doctrine creeping into the church. Paul commands the church to stand firm in their faith and encourages them, by stating the righteous will one day be counted worthy to inherit the kingdom of God. Paul confirms with this church, "The Day of the Lord," had not yet taken place. This event will only take place after a great falling away or rebellion occurs in the church and the, "Man of Sin," is revealed. Then Jesus would one day descend from heaven with great power and glory.

Paul warns this church not to let any man deceive them. This warning from Paul to the Thessalonians concerning deception in the church is important for the church today to remember. Jesus also warned several times deception would play a huge role during the last days. Those who are not well grounded in God's word will be deceived. Paul tells this church to remember what he had taught them, to stand firm, and hold to the traditions and teachings which they had been taught. The traditions and doctrines of the early church are fast becoming thought of as intolerant and no longer politically correct in most churches today.

Paul gives this church some very important advice. He informs this church of a sign that must take place before, "The Day of the Lord," can occur. This key event will be a worldwide falling away from sound biblical doctrine. Another major prophetic event that must occur before, "The Day of the Lord," will be the revealing of the man the Bible refers to as the antichrist. The antichrist or the, "Son of Perdition," is the man we previously discussed in Genesis, who I believe is from the literal seed of the serpent. Make no mistake, Paul is informing the church this man of sin must be revealed and allowed to deceive the world, before Jesus Christ literally descends to earth and walks on earth a second time. Paul is not referring to the event known as the catching away of the church where the bride literally meets Christ in the air. These two events are greatly confused by the church, because I believe the Bible is discussing two separate events. A spiritual concept taught throughout the Bible is there are several different types of harvests addressed in the scriptures, each with their own unique characteristics.

It really is shocking what I see going on in a lot of churches today. When these verses are brought up in Bible studies, most people have no idea what the Bible is telling them. The second coming of Jesus Christ where He literally sets His feet on this earth, will not occur until the seven year tribulation or what is also called, "The 70th Week of Daniel," runs its course. Before the second coming of Christ, the antichrist must be revealed and be given complete authority over the entire earth for forty-two months.

Paul goes on to give the church two other key prophetical events that must take place before the literal second coming of Christ to this earth. One of these events we have already touched on, which is a worldwide spiritual falling away from sound doctrine. The Bible warns us during the latter times the church will digress to the point of refusal of sound doctrine. What's a sign letting us know we are getting close to the end of the age? It will be the spiritual condition of the church. The verses below in 2 Timothy warn us of this coming apostasy taking place in the church.

I charge thee therefore before God, and the
Lord Jesus Christ, who shall judge the quick and
the dead at his appearing and his kingdom;
Preach the word; be instant in season, out
of season; reprove, rebuke, exhort with all long
suffering and doctrine.
For the time will come when they will not
endure sound doctrine; but after their own lusts
shall they heap to themselves teachers, having
itching ears;
And they shall turn away their ears from
the truth, and shall be turned unto fables.
(2 Timothy 4:1–4)

When the collective church refuses to teach sound doctrine and
will not put up with anyone who tries to preach or teach sound doctrine, we will know we are living in the end of the age.

There is one other key prophetical event Paul informs us in
2 Thessalonians that must take place before Jesus returns to earth.
Paul informs us this event involves the removal of a restraining force
currently preventing evil to completely overtake the earth. I believe
this, "Restrainer," is the Holy Spirit residing in all who have made
a profession of faith in Christ. The Holy Spirit is the, "Comforter,"
Jesus referred to who came to earth when the church was established. In order words, God is literally holding back the appearance
of the antichrist along with Satan's evil agenda, until their appointed
time.

We need to remember as powerful as Satan and all his allies are,
they are created beings and under the authority of God. Just as it was
during the days of Noah, a future time is coming which will close
the door of opportunity to be saved by grace, in a similar way God
closed the door to the ark. During this time God will say to His Son,
go get your bride.

Paul clearly informs all who are listening, when this restraining
force of good is removed from this earth then wickedness or this,
"Man of Sin," will be revealed. It is during His second coming to

earth, the Lord will destroy this wickedness with the spirit of His mouth and the brightness of His coming.

One last key element is Paul informs the brethren God will send those dwelling on the earth during this time a, "Strong Delusion." Why does God send these people a strong delusion? Paul gives us the answer to this question. It will be because, "They," received not the love of the truth and had pleasure in unrighteousness. Paul goes on to state it is because of this, "They," perish and are eternally damned. It is very important when looking at scripture, a person determines what group of individuals are being addressed. Paul here is not referring to the brethren, but to those who reject Christ and His truth. Sadly this truth is widely misunderstood, but people do need to realize the rejection of God's gift of salvation will have eternal consequences.

All those rejecting the truth of the scriptures even in the churches, will one day have a heavy price to pay. We need to accept Jesus Christ and the truth of the Bible while the opportunity still exists. I see the church today becoming more and more like the world. Later on we will be taking a more in depth look at the seven churches of Revelation. We will discover one of the churches named, "Pergamum," literally describes a church of compromise who is married to the world. As we draw closer to the end of this age, it will become harder and harder to tell the differences between the church and the world.

Let's review quickly what Paul tells the Thessalonians concerning what events must take place before the second coming of Christ will occur. The second coming of Christ is also confirmed in Revelation chapter 1. During this time Jesus Christ will come with the clouds, and every eye will see Him, even those who pierced Him. The Bible goes on to tell us the nations will mourn when they see Him, because they will truly know He is the, "King of Kings," and, "Lord of Lords." Jesus came to this earth the first time as an unblemished Lamb. Jesus is coming to earth the second time as, "The Lion of the Tribe of Judah." One should also notice the event discussed in Revelation does not involve Jesus Himself, does not occur in the twinkling of an eye, but does occur when every eye will see Him coming with the clouds. The reason being, is the Bible is not here referring to the catching away of the bride. We will be addressing this subject later on in the book.

According to 2 Thessalonians 2, here is a list of events that must take place before the second coming of Christ will occur.

- A general worldwide falling away from sound doctrine in the churches.
- The Holy Spirit and all those He indwells, "The Bride," are taken out of the way.
- The Man of Sin, "antichrist," is then revealed.
- The Man of Sin, "antichrist," signs a seven-year peace agreement, or covenant with Israel. This seven-year period of time is known as the Seven-Year Tribulation, The Day of Jacob's Trouble, or the Seventieth Week of Daniel. (Daniel 9:27) The two witnesses, who will be given power for 1,260 days to withstand the, "antichrist," will arrive in Jerusalem during this time.
- The Man of Sin, "antichrist," breaks this Covenant Agreement with Israel at the 3.5-year timeline, and He desecrates an operational Jewish Temple, exalting himself as god. The two witnesses will be overcome and killed by the antichrist during this time. After 3.5 days, their bodies will be resurrected and caught up to heaven.
- The Man of Sin, "antichrist," will be given worldwide power for a period of forty-two months or 3.5 years. He will be given power to kill the saints and persecute Israel during this time. These saints are the tribulation saints that refuse the mark.
- All those who have believed not the truth and received the mark, will make a spiritual profession of faith to Satan eternally damning their souls.
- Jesus Christ destroys the, "antichrist," and the, "false prophet," with the power and glory of His coming.

Isn't it incredible the spiritual wisdom we receive from just reading a few verses in God's word? Amazingly, these spiritual truths are not being taught in most churches today. Believe it or not, we are experiencing many of the same problems in the church today which occurred during the time of Paul's ministry. We seem to be living in a time where churches are more concerned about attendance, money, and offending the feelings of others. Yes, the church needs to be telling the truth of scripture in a spirit of love and humility, but we need to be boldly proclaiming the gospel message and the truth of the Bible. The church today needs to understand the urgency of this matter. The most important goal of a church is not how many programs a church has, or how much money is in their bank account. The church should be more concerned in sharing the truth of the gospel message and adding souls to the kingdom.

We will now take a look at the overall spiritual condition of the world during this time. One of the many things concerning me, is the steady moral deterioration of the world I've witnessed over the past twenty years. I am especially concerned about the consistent moral decay in the family I see. The percentage of single-parent families due to divorce has risen considerably over the past couple decades. When we lose the family unit, we lose our societies. If we can recall the verse we discussed earlier by Solomon, we have learned those who forget the mistakes of the past are doomed to repeat them.

It's not rocket science. In the last ten years we have witnessed a major shift in society dealing with a several thousand-year tradition, defining marriage as the union between a man and a woman. Marriage was not man's idea, it was God's idea. Marriage is intended to be a holy covenant between a man and a woman for life. God knew mankind would not be perfect, therefore God set up guidelines where a divorce between a man and a woman would be allowed. God's original intention for the marriage covenant was a lifelong commitment between a man and a woman. The book of Ephesians gives us some interesting insight concerning the covenant of marriage.

Wives, submit yourselves unto your own husbands, as unto the Lord.

> For the husband is the head of the wife, even as Christ is the head of the church: and he is the saviour of the body.
>
> Therefore as the church is subject unto Christ, so let the wives be to their own husbands in everything.
>
> Husbands, love your wives, even as Christ also loved the church, and gave himself for it;
>
> That he might sanctify and cleanse it with the washing of water by the word,
>
> That he might present it to himself a glorious church, not having spot, or wrinkle, or any such thing; but that it should be holy and without blemish.
>
> So ought men to love their wives as their own bodies. He that loveth his wife loveth himself.
>
> For no man ever hated his own flesh; but nourisheth and cherisheth it, even as the Lord the church:
>
> For we are members of his body, of his flesh, and of his bones.
>
> For this cause shall a man leave his father and mother, and shall be joined unto his wife, and they two shall be one flesh.
>
> This is a great mystery: but I speak concerning Christ and the Church. (Ephesians 5:22–32)

These verses in Ephesians give us spiritual insight relating to the importance of marriage. The marriage covenant represents much more than a relationship between a man and a woman. The marriage covenant is a picture of God's love for His bride, the church. This spiritual truth explains why marriage and the family are under such an attack today. We need to realize Satan hates anything having to do with God's creation including the family. If the family, or the belief of what a family represents can be destroyed or even corrupted, society as a whole can be changed or destroyed. Within a 70 year period of time, no human life would exist on this planet if men and women were not getting married and giving birth to children.

Everywhere a person looks, there is evidence for design and order in God's creation. Husbands are commanded in the Bible to love their wives in the same way Christ loves His bride, the church. In the same way Christ literally laid down His life for His bride, husbands are commanded to love their wives in such a way. Wives are commanded to love their husbands submitting themselves to them in the same way the church submits to Christ, who is the head of the church. We find no statements in the Bible relating to the wife being a slave to her husband, nor is any wife expected to stay in an abusive marriage relationship.

In God's eyes, the joining together of a man and a woman is a sacred lifelong covenant. Marriage is actually not only a physical union, but it is a spiritual union where a man and a woman literally become one flesh. As stated earlier, the earthly picture of marriage is symbolic with Christ's spiritual marriage to His bride, the church. People who have entered into a personal relationship with Him. It is for this reason Christ is referred to many times as, "The Bridegroom," and the true church, those who personally know Him, "His Bride." And by the way, Jesus Christ is the husband of one wife who is the "Church," being made up of one body with many parts.

The Bible refers to this eternal marriage relationship Christ has with His bride as a, "Great Mystery." There is a wedding ceremony and feast coming one day taking place in heaven, between Christ and His bride, the church. There is a tremendous amount of confusion in the churches today concerning this spiritual union. The bride of Christ is not the Old Testament saints and it is not the tribulation saints. The bride of Christ is those who have placed their faith in Christ accepting Him as Lord and Savior. The bride of Christ is made up of those who are, "In Christ," and have trusted in Him during the church age, the age of grace. The verses in Revelation below deal with this issue.

> And I heard as it were the voice of a great
> multitude, and as a voice of many waters, and as
> the voice of mighty thunderings, saying, Alleluia:
> for the Lord God omnipotent reigneth.
>
> Let us be glad and rejoice, and give honour
> to him: for the marriage of the Lamb is come,
> and his wife hath made herself ready.
>
> And to her was granted that she should be
> arrayed in fine linen, clean and white: for the fine
> linen is the righteousness of saints.
>
> And he saith unto me, Write, Blessed are
> they which are called unto the marriage supper
> of the Lamb. And he saith unto me, These are the
> true sayings of God. (Revelation 19:6–9)

Yes, there is a great wedding celebration coming. Notice the verse above states the wife has made herself ready. Time and time again, the Bible commands us to be waiting, watching, and to be looking for His appearing. The bride of Christ is dressed in white linen, a symbol of righteousness. This righteousness cannot be obtained by any self-righteous act of works, but only through trusting in the shed blood of Christ.

Notice there is a blessing for those who are called or invited to the marriage supper of the Lamb. The bride does not receive an invitation to her own wedding. The bride is the purpose for the wedding. The wedding guests are the saints throughout the ages such as Noah, Abraham, and Lot who through faith were credited as righteous. It also includes all those who during the tribulation refuse the mark and refuse to worship the antichrist. These saints who are martyred during the tribulation because they refuse to make a spiritual profession of faith to the antichrist, are given white robes and are counted as righteous. The following verses in Revelation give us more information concerning these people.

> After this I beheld, and lo, a great multi-
> tude, which no man could count, of all nations,

and kindreds, and people, and tongues, stood before the throne, and before the Lamb, clothed with white robes, and palms in their hands;

And cried with a loud voice, saying, Salvation to our God which sitteth upon the throne, and unto the Lamb.

And all the angels stood round about the throne, and about the elders and the four beasts, and fell before the throne on their faces, and worshipped God,

Saying, Amen: Blessing, and glory, and wisdom, and thanksgiving, and honour, and power, and might, be unto our God for ever and ever. Amen.

And one of the elders answered, saying unto me, What are these which are arrayed in white robes? And whence came they?

And I said unto him, Sir, thou knowest. And he said to me, These are they which came out of great tribulation, and have washed their robes, and made them white in the blood of the Lamb.

Therefore are they before the throne of God, and serve him day and night in his temple: and he that sitteth on the throne shall dwell among them.

They shall hunger no more, neither thirst, any more; neither shall the sun light on them, nor any heat.

For the Lamb which is in the midst of the throne shall feed them, and shall lead them unto living fountains of waters: and God shall wipe away all tears from their eyes. (Revelation 7:9–17)

So who is this multitude of people made up of all nationalities, clothed in white robes? It is those who have come out of,

"Great Tribulation," who are made righteous through the blood of the Lamb. Notice this group of saints is before the throne of God, serving Him day and night in the temple. The Bible is not referring to the bride of Christ here in this passage. The verses above are not referencing the Old Testament saints. This group of saints comes out of the tribulation period.

One concept many do not understand is the Bible makes references to more than one type of harvest. For example, the Bible mentions barley, wheat, and grape harvests. This is a difficult concept for most people to understand, but the Bible suggests in many places the righteous and the unrighteous will not be rewarded, judged, gathered together, or harvested in the same manner.

The scripture tells us all people will reap what they sow. All people, the righteous and unrighteous, will give an account for their lives according to their works. Although salvation or righteousness is not obtained by works, everyone will be rewarded or shown mercy according to their works. The righteous will receive rewards relating to their works, and the unrighteous will be eternally punished based on their works during their time on earth. We will discuss this in more detail later on.

There are specific instances in the Bible where God chooses to deal with certain groups of people in different ways. Israel has always had a special place in God's heart. Although Israel rejected God and is even referred to as an unfaithful spouse, God will again specifically deal with Israel during the coming, "Tribulation." This event is also referred to as a time of, "Jacob's trouble." It is interesting in the book of Hosea, God tells Hosea to marry an adulterous wife symbolizing the unfaithful relationship Israel had with God. Israel was unfaithful to God because they worshipped Canaanite gods instead of the God of Israel. Israel eventually was judged by God because of their spiritual adultery, just as in the case of Hosea whose wife was also unfaithful to him. Despite Israel's unfaithfulness, God never stopped loving them as His chosen people.

For now in a sense, God has put Israel on the back burner, but a time is coming when God will again directly deal with His chosen people. This event will occur when this current age of grace, the

church age, comes to a close. We will discuss this seven-year period of
time in more detail in an upcoming chapter. These few verses below
in Romans informs us because Israel rejected Christ, their hearts have
now been hardened. Israel has been spiritually blinded allowing the
Gentile nations to be given a time for salvation.

> According as it is written, God hath given
> them the spirit of slumber, eyes that they should
> not see, and ears that they should not hear; unto
> this day.
> And David saith, Let their table be made a
> snare, and a trap, and a stumblingblock, and a
> recompence unto them:
> Let their eyes be darkened, that they may
> not see, and bow down their back always.
> I say then, Have they stumbled that they
> should fall? God forbid: but rather through their
> fall salvation is come unto the Gentiles, for to
> provoke them to jealousy. (Romans 11:8–11)

God hasn't forgot about Israel, and no the church has not
replaced Israel. There is coming a time in the future when the cur-
tains will close, and the world will enter a new dispensation of time.
Israel will be placed in an, "Old Testament Exodus," experience forcing them to repent of their sins, and cry out to God to save them.

So as we continue to draw closer to the end of this current
age, we will continue to see a worldwide steady increase in moral
and ethnic chaos. I know this seems crazy, but most in the churches
today and for sure in the world, do not realize we are steadily sliding
down a slippery slope where it will soon be similar to the days of
Noah and Lot. I like to stay aware of the spiritual condition of the
world by watching the local and world news to gain understanding
where we are from a prophetic perspective. Twenty years ago, it was a
major news story when the local news reported a shooting, a murder,
or someone committing some sort of serious crime. Today, violent
crimes including murder are reported almost every day, and on many

days we are now talking multiple events. Yes, during the past fifty or sixty years we've continued on a moral downward spiral. During the last ten to twenty years, it seems violent crimes are increasing exponentially.

A purpose for this book is to stop people in their tracks so they can slow down long enough to open their eyes, and see what is going on around them. It is interesting the Bible informs us the characteristics of people living during the days before the flood will be similar to those living in the last days. People today are so busy running to and fro living life and going nowhere fast. People today are so caught up with life's daily drama, they have very little time to dwell on what is really important in life. If Satan can keep your mind constantly on life, materialism, and keeping up with the next-door neighbors, he is doing his job well.

The verses below in 2 Timothy shed some light on what the characteristics of people will be like during the last days. People are always looking for signs. All you have to do is stop, open your eyes, and look around. These signs are everywhere.

> This know also, that in the last days perilous times shall come.
>
> For men shall be lovers of their own selves, covetous, boasters, proud, blasphemers, disobedient to parents, unthankful, unholy,
>
> Without natural affection, trucebreakers, false accusers, incontinent, fierce, despisers of those that are good,
>
> Traitors, heady, highminded, lovers of pleasures more than lovers of God;
>
> Having a form of godliness, but denying the power thereof: from such turn away.
>
> For of this sort are they which creep into houses, and lead captive silly women laden with sins, led away with divers lusts,
>
> Ever learning, and never able to come to the knowledge of the truth. (2 Timothy 3:1–7)

The last days will be very dangerous times. The reason times will be so dangerous is because of people's spiritual condition. One title I was considering for this chapter is "It's All about Me." When people live only caring about themselves and what benefits them, the world becomes a cold and dark place. The condition of the world will continue to grow colder and colder, and become darker and darker. Doesn't the scripture warn us in the last days, the hearts of many will grow cold.

It shocks me how much the hearts of people have changed over the past thirty years. People use to treat one another with respect and common courtesy. Now we see young people walking up to the elderly and punching them in the face, or knock them to the ground just for kicks. I have never seen a time as this when children are so disrespectful to their parents. Now, drive-by shootings are becoming very common, where people are being shot and sometimes killed for no apparent reason, except for the hatred and evil in a person's heart. People are killed because of greed, anger, drug addictions, and even peer pressure.

In the current time we live, it is becoming more difficult to find employees who can pass a background check. It seems like everyone has committed a crime or has a drug problem. It is interesting the meaning of the word, "Sorceries," in the Bible is very similar to the meaning of the word, "Pharmacy," used today, which is a reference to drug addiction. When I was a young man thirty years ago, it was a disgrace for a man not to have a job. Now the attitude of many people is to see how much they can take advantage of the system. The idea today has become work is for fools when money is handed out for free. I realize there are those who fall on bad times and need a hand up, but I am not referring to situations such as these.

Notice the Bible tells us during the latter times people will be without natural affection. The term, "Natural Affection," is referring to a young man being naturally attracted toward a young woman and a young woman being attracted to a man. The Bible is telling us in the latter times, there will be a dramatic shift in these types of normal affections between males and females.

As a young man living in a rural area, I've seen many a deal made between two individuals with a handshake. Today you'd better have a contract and a lawyer. In these current times, the rules are you do whatever it takes to come out on top. People just don't take care of others like they use to years ago. Churches will outwardly present themselves as being godly, but these churches will deny the deity of Christ, and the sanctity of God's word. Many churches will become places of traditionalism and tolerance. Churches will become no more than a name on a door, and a place to socialize.

The Bible states in the last days people will have a form of godliness, but they will deny the power of God and the authenticity of the Bible. Quite honestly, the world will be characterized by unbelief and unfaithfulness. It's interesting the book of Jude also mentions what people will be like during the end times. Jude states people will be grumblers. People will constantly be trying to find faults in others, and they will be conceited and full of arrogance. These people will live by their own evil desires, and their goal in life will be to take advantage and abuse others.

Concerning the spiritual condition of the church, we will know we are living in the last days when churches are characterized by apostasy. Jude goes on to state apostates and false teachers will creep into churches teaching false doctrines. These teachings will include such things as Jesus is not the Son of God, Jesus is not the only way to salvation, and the Bible cannot be taken literally. At best, these false teachers will state the Bible is full of allegorical stories for the sole purpose of moral instruction. These false teachers will state heaven and hell are not literal places. Apostates will always deny Jesus Christ is, "The Son of God." In the last days, these types of characteristics in people and churches will be the norm, and anything related to sound doctrine will not be tolerated.

I will in a following chapter be dealing more specifically with the characteristics of the church during the end of the age. We will be looking at what Jesus had to say to seven specific churches. I also want to make it clear I am in no way, "Antichurch." I have been raised in church all my life. I am very thankful my parents took me to church as a young boy, and I am thankful for all the committed teachers and pastors who have taught me God's word. I have come to believe one major sign pointing to where we are in God's timetable is to be able to discern the spiritual condition of the church. Apostasy, tolerance, and an outright hatred for anything pointing to Christ such as the cross, is becoming the norm these days. I also want to restate there are many godly churches, pastors, and teachers who are desperately trying to seek God's will, spreading the, "Good News," of the gospel of Jesus Christ to all willing to listen.

We are now living in a time of tremendous knowledge and technology. I have heard we have reached a point where advancements in technology are doubling now every couple months. Science and technology tells us our solar system, the plant and animal kingdom, and the human body are all extremely complex creations. It is amazing we can create electronic clocks that keep time with the precise accuracy of one second per billion years, yet we deny the accuracy of our solar system too which these clocks keep time with has a designer. Our entire solar system, the sun, the earth, day after day, year after year runs with the efficiency of a finely tuned machine. Yet we deny the existence of a creator. The Bible states in Psalms, it is the fool who says in his heart, there is no God.

The Bible says we are all without excuse. If you have ever witnessed the birth of a child, a sunrise, sunset, or looked into the heavens at the stars on a clear night, the Bible states you are without excuse. Today with all of our achievements and wisdom, man continues to deny a creator exists. People state we are in the process of evolving. Even with all the world's money and all the modern technology we have today, the world is a more dangerous place and in a more chaotic time than it has ever been. The problem is man wants to be in control of his own destiny. Man wants to be in charge and be their own boss. Man wants to be accountable to no one including God.

Faith in God is leaving this earth. Jesus made a statement relating to people's faith when He returns to earth again. Jesus asked a rhetorical question relating to His second coming dealing with whether or not He would find faith on the earth. Jesus knew the answer to the question. Jesus was giving those who would hear a sign of what the

144

spiritual condition of people would be like, during a future time of tribulation coming upon the earth. Let's take a look at a few verses in Romans chapter 1, to further explore the spiritual condition of men's hearts during the end of the age.

> For the wrath of God is revealed from heaven against all ungodliness and unrighteousness of men, who hold the truth in unrighteousness;
>
> Because that which may be known of God is manifest in them; for God hath shewed it unto them.
>
> For the invisible things of him from the creation of the world are clearly seen, being understood by the things that are made, even his eternal power and Godhead; so that they are without excuse:
>
> Because, that when they knew God, they glorified him not as God, neither were thankful; but became vain in their imaginations, and their foolish heart was darkened.
>
> Professing themselves to be wise, they became fools,
>
> And changed the glory of the uncorruptible God into an image made like to corruptible man, and to birds, and fourfooted beasts, and creeping things.
>
> Wherefore God also gave them up to uncleanness through the lusts of their own hearts, to dishonour their own bodies between themselves:
>
> Who changed the truth of God into a lie, and worshipped and served the creature more than the Creator, who is blessed forever. Amen.
>
> For this cause God gave them up unto vile affections: for even their women did change the natural use into that which is against nature:

And likewise also the men, leaving the natural use of the woman, burned in their lust one toward another; men with men working that which is unseemly, and receiving in themselves that recompence of their error which was meet.

And even as they did not like to retain God in their knowledge, God gave them over to a reprobate mind, to do those things which are not convenient;

Being filled with all unrighteousness, fornication, wickedness, covetousness, maliciousness; full of envy, murder, debate, deceit, malignity; whisperers,

Backbiters, haters of God, despiteful, proud, boasters, inventors of evil things, disobedient to parents,

Without understanding, covenantbreakers, without natural affection, implacable, unmerciful:

Who knowing the judgment of God, that they which commit such things are worthy of death, not only do the same, but have pleasure in them that do them. (Romans 1:18–32)

I hear people constantly asking how perilous and evil will times be in the future. The Bible gives us the answer to this question. It will be as it was during the days of Noah and the days of Lot. How many righteous people existed on earth when God shut the door to the ark? The answer is one person, and his name was Noah. How many righteous people existed in the city of Sodom before it was destroyed? The Bible tells us God promised Abraham Sodom would be spared if ten righteous people could be found. Sodom was a large city that more than likely had several thousand residents. It is evident ten righteous people could not be found in this city. Lot and his daughters ended up being the only survivors.

I am always shocked by the number of people who believe the Old Testament stories of the Bible are fairy tales. The church is warned more than once stories such as the flood and the destruction of the cities of the plain were examples of what is coming again. History and prophecy do repeat themselves. One of the main reasons I feel compelled to write this book is to attempt to wake people up while there is still time to make a spiritual decision to accept Christ.

We always need to keep in mind when interpreting the scriptures, what groups of people are being addressed in the Bible. Paul is addressing here in the book of Romans, the saints who are called of Jesus Christ. Paul is reminding the brethren God's wrath is coming. Paul goes on to give us the answer to whom God's wrath is intended. It is for those people who are seen as unrighteous and ungodly. These words here from Paul give each of us a homework assignment. The question needing to be answered is what groups of people are being identified as ungodly and unrighteous. We see God using patterns such as these running throughout the entire Bible. The reason God reveals certain truths in the Bible through patterns is because we have a God who loves all people desiring not one person to perish. God gives us Bible patterns to get our attention because He loves us in the same way a parent loves his or her children. Parents will go out of their way warning their children repeatedly to keep them from danger.

Paul doesn't pull any punches making it clear people are without excuse. As we live our daily lives experiencing the order of things we are constantly being surrounded with, we are without excuse. We see the order of all life. We see order when we look into the heavens. We are all without excuse. Where there is order, there is a designer.

The Bible informs us even though men down deep in their soul know there must be a God, they failed to glorify God and deny Him as creator. Men became foolish in their thinking, and their hearts became dark. Because of this outright disobedience and denial of God's existence, the Bible states these men became fools.

So because of man's disobedience, the descent down the slippery slope of rejecting God continues. This is not God's will, but it is of man's own choosing. One thing always amazing me is how a person can make an image of something, and bow down and worship that image. Instead of worshipping a God who has always existed, is all knowing, all seeing, and creator of all things, these people worship an image created by their own hands. I understand to some degree how people can worship many things. People worship their cars, their homes, and money, but to literally fall down and worship an image made by human hands has always amazed me.

People need to understand there comes a point where God just gives people over to live and worship how they please. The issue people need to realize is there will be consequences for the actions they take. We truly do reap what we sow. It's like the old saying, "You play with fire, you're going to get burned."

Another sign informing us we are coming to the end of this age, will be when people refuse to worship the very God who created and loves them. During this time people will be consumed with the evil desires of their own hearts. People will dishonor and devalue their own bodies which were created in the very image of God. People will have no care or concern for others, and their lives will be characterized with wickedness and immorality. Do behaviors such as these describe what is seen every day on the local news? When we look back to the days of Noah and the times of Sodom, we need to understand there finally comes a point where God says enough is enough.

In the book of Genesis, the Lord states He would allow those people living on the earth during that time 120 more years to turn from their evil ways. Just like with the story of Sodom, its oblivious there was no change of heart, because God did bring a flood upon the earth. There was a time in the past when people were no longer receptive to God's message and refused to repent of their evil ways. These same types of events as recorded in the Old Testament where individuals completely refused to turn from their evil ways, will repeat themselves again.

Notice again, the Bible states people finally reach a level of wickedness where they digress to the point of dishonoring their own bodies. This is what we see happening today. I know this is not politically correct, and I know most churches will not speak out against this type of lifestyle, but in God's eyes it is sin and it is an abomination. God's word is very clear. In Revelation chapter 21, the Bible confirms absolutely no form of sexual immorality will be allowed in heaven. The Bible informs us those whose lives are characterized by sexual immorality will be thrown into the, "Lake of Fire," and will suffer the second death. The Bible is not a message of hate. The Bible clearly states it is God's will none should perish and that all people would repent, and trust in Him. God is warning us of what will take place in the future, because He loves all people.

So if people continue in their sin and refuse to turn from their evil ways, God finally gives people over to be consumed and destroyed by their evil desires. Paul tells us these people morally reach a point where God gives them over to unrighteous and ungodly affections for one another which ends in their own destruction. The Bible is telling us people finally reach a point if they refuse to repent of their sins, their minds become depraved and dysfunctional to the point they are incapable of rational thought. If one studies their history, any society experiencing serious social problems relating to all forms of immorality ceases to exist. God in a sense finally has no choice but to remove His hedge of protection from these people or these nations, turning them over to their own destruction.

If a person denies this spiritual truth, I would suggest taking a look at Israel's history. The children of Israel although warned by God, reached a level of spiritual depravity where they were literally burning their own children alive, believing they were appeasing the Canaanite god, "Molech." Molech was a Canaanite god associated with child sacrifice. The altar of Molech was a large statue looking somewhat like a bull. A fire would be built either inside or at the bottom of this godlike statue. The children of Israel stooped to a level of such depravity, they ended up sacrificing their own children on the altar of this god.

Paul goes on to explain the level of depravity these affections end up taking a person. The Bible tells us sexual immorality finally reaches a point where women and men end up living in contrast to the very laws of nature. Lifestyles develop where women are lusting after other women. Likewise men will no longer have natural affections for women, but they will burn with lust after other men.

Because of this steady progression of ungodliness, God finally gives people over to a reprobate mind. In other words, people finally reach the state where their hearts are eternally incapable of obtaining righteousness. People become so filled with all types of ungodliness and unrighteousness to the level it becomes impossible for them to repent. This is a picture of how morally corrupt the men of Sodom became. God is His infinite wisdom knew these men had no intentions in repenting from their sins, so God had no choice but to intervene.

The cities of the plain including Sodom were not destroyed because God hated these people. God destroyed these cities because He was tired of the innocent blood being shed, and the cries of torture coming from those being tormented. More than once the Bible confirms God hears the cries of those whose blood has been needlessly spilt. We will find a major purpose of the coming future, "Day of the Lord," will be to avenge the blood of all innocent people throughout the centuries that has been needlessly spilled.

I would like to bring one more scriptural reference from 2 Peter which also gives confirmation to the condition of men's hearts during the last days. I have stated this before, but it is crucial to understand the Bible validates itself in many places by using several scriptural texts and witnesses. Most answers to biblical questions will be backed up in multiple books or texts in the Bible. One quick example of this would be in 2 Timothy 3:8, where the Bible informs us Jannes and Jambres were the names of the two magicians who withstood Moses during the time of Israel's captivity in Egypt. These two magicians were examples of spiritual counterfeits to Moses and Aaron, and are pictures of Satanic deception repeating itself in the last days.

As we look at these verses in 2 Peter, it is again important to be mindful of the intended audience. Paul is speaking to the beloved, the church saints. One pattern we see from Paul over and over again is a continual plea of remembrance. If there is one thing the church today needs, it is instruction from the pulpit on the validity of God's word and a rekindled belief in the scriptures. To understand what will happen in the future, we must believe what the Bible tells us about the past.

> This second epistle, beloved, I now write unto you; in both which I stir up your pure minds by way of remembrance:
>
> That ye may be mindful of the words which were spoken before by the holy prophets, and of the commandment of us the apostles of the Lord and Saviour:
>
> Knowing this first, that there shall come in the last days scoffers, walking after their own lusts,
>
> And saying, Where is the promise of his coming? for since the fathers fell asleep, all things continue as they were from the beginning of the creation.
>
> For this they willingly are ignorant of, that by the word of God the heavens were of old, and the earth standing out of the water and in the water:
>
> Whereby the world that then was, being overflowed with water, perished:
>
> But the heavens and the earth, which are now, by the same word are kept in store, reserved unto fire against the day of judgment and perdition of ungodly men.
>
> But, beloved, be not ignorant of this one thing, that one day is with the Lord as a thousand years, and a thousand years as one day.
>
> The Lord is not slack concerning his promise, as some men count slackness; but is longsuffering to us-ward, not willing that any should perish, but that all should come to repentance.
>
> But the day of the Lord will come as a thief in the night; in the which the heavens shall pass

away with a great noise, and the elements shall
melt with fervent heat, the earth also and the
works that are therein shall be burned up.

Seeing then that all these things shall be dissolved, what manner of persons ought ye to be in
all holy conversation and godliness,

Looking for and hasting unto the coming
of the day of God, wherein the heavens being on
fire shall be dissolved, and the elements shall melt
with fervent heat?

Nevertheless we, according to his promise,
look for new heavens and a new earth, wherein
dwelleth righteousness. (2 Peter 3:1–13)

Peter writes this second epistle to the various churches in Asia
Minor. The purpose of the Epistle seems to be due to Peter becoming
alarmed by the number of false teachers creeping into the church.
Peter strongly proclaimed the inspiration of the word of God, and
the need for Christians to become strong in their faith. Peter warned
the saints of their need to remember the teachings in the Old and
New Testaments as the basis for their faith.

Peter warned the church saints not to be surprised when false
teachers come into the church mocking the promise of the second
coming of Christ one day to earth. The apparent reason for mocking
the second coming of Christ would be to fulfill the selfish desires of
these false teachers. If the illusion can be created the Bible is just a
fairy tale, heaven and hell really don't exist, and Christ will not come
to earth a second time, the promise of coming judgment and personal accountability is not taken seriously.

Notice the basis for the mockery coming from these false teachers. These false teachers present their case based upon the idea things
have continued on and on for hundreds perhaps thousands of years,
and nothing has changed. These false teachers ridicule the saints for
their supposedly false hope Christ is coming to rescue them and
will one day pour His wrath upon an unbelieving world. These false
teachers state the sun comes up and goes back down, and things have

continued as they always have. The promises in the word of God are mocked, and an atmosphere of disbelief is created.

I hear statements relating to people doubting the truth of God's word all the time. I am amazed how much I hear a professed doubt of the second coming of Christ expressed in the church today. I hear comments stating Christ is not going to rescue and snatch His bride away. These false teachers state the entire church is all going through the tribulation, and we are all going to die. I am seeing a tremendous amount of confusion and a whole lot of false teaching in the churches today. Maybe the church today needs to heed the words of Peter where he warns the church over and over again to remember what they had been taught. Maybe we should remember the words of Abraham in the book of Genesis.

> And the Lord said, Because the cry of Sodom and Gomorrah is great, and because their sin is very grievous;
>
> I will go down now, and see whether they have done altogether according to the cry of it, which is come unto me; and if not, I will know.
>
> And the men turned their faces from thence, and went toward Sodom: but Abraham stood before the Lord.
>
> And Abraham drew near, and said, Wilt thou also destroy the righteous with the wicked?
>
> Peradventure there be fifty righteous within the city: wilt thou also destroy and not spare the place for the fifty righteous that are therein?
>
> That be far from thee to do after this manner, to slay the righteous with the wicked: and that the righteous should be as the wicked, that be far from thee: Shall not the Judge of all the earth do right? (Genesis 18:20–26)

So we see a reason why the brethren are called in several places to remember God's word. It was shocking when I realized Abraham had a better understanding of God's character than most of the churches today. Yes, we are living in a fallen world. Yes, we as Christians are subject to persecution and even death, but we have not been appointed to God's wrath. Abraham understood this basic spiritual concept, although most people in the church today do not. God's wrath is coming again, this is a biblical fact. This coming wrath is not for the bride, it is for the ungodly and the unrighteous dwelling on the earth during a future time.

So these false teachers will base their teachings on the fact nothing has changed from generation to generation, and really nothing has changed since the beginning of time. Notice Peter refers to these false teachers as being ignorant. A good Bible study to conduct sometime would be to look at every instance in the Bible the brethren are warned not to be ignorant concerning biblical issues.

Another issue that has always shocked me is the number of so-called Christians that doubt God created everything and accept evolution as fact. There is some truth all life does change with respect to time, but to state factually we know for certain all life evolved from lower life forms is just not true according to the Bible. We definitely can see variations within species. Think of all the many different dog breeds we have today. All these different dog breeds originated from one male and one female dog. There probably wasn't as many animals on the ark as one would believe. One needs to pay close attention to what the Bible tells us. God informed Noah two of every kind of animal would be placed on the ark.

It is interesting the second law of thermodynamics states things tend to go from order to disorder. Nothing really gets better with time. I know I'm sure not. My joints and muscles ache more today than they did twenty years ago. Go install a new bearing on your lawn mower. Yes, it changes with respect to time, it flies to pieces.

If we are so much more evolved and smarter today, how come we still can't explain how structures were built thousands of years ago, where engineering and construction techniques were used which cannot be duplicated even today? We today with current equipment and technology, cannot build a replica of the Giza pyramid to its original specifications.

These false teachers come into the churches speaking out against the deity and second coming of Christ as fact, because they also deny God as creator. Of course, these teachers also speak falsely against other truths relating to the sovereignty of God. The main goal of the false teacher is to bring a spirit of confusion and doubt into the body of Christ. If Satan can get a person to doubt God as creator and the truth of God's word, that person will doubt the saving power of Christ and definitely will doubt the truth of prophecy.

Why do we see so many in the church today doubting the events relating to the catching away of the bride and the second coming of Christ? Because many in the church today doubt the validity of God's word and the fact God literally created all things. Many doubt Satan is a literal being, they doubt the flood of Noah took place, so why wouldn't they also doubt Jesus is literally coming to earth a second time.

Peter goes on to explain why these false teachers are so ignorant. It is because they refuse to accept the fact the world was once covered with a great deluge of water, and the purpose of this great flood was judgment from God. I have stated before, the subject of the flood is not worth arguing. There are at least five hundred ancient stories and legends all speaking of a worldwide flood event. The Indians tell stories of a race of people existing on the earth before them. Many of these ancient stories speak of gods coming from the stars who became so evil, "The Great Spirit," had to destroy them with a flood. Sounds a lot like the Genesis chapter 6 event to me. We have the stories of Greek mythology telling us about gods having relationships with mortal women and even animals for that matter. The fact the Bible tells us the flood event took place is enough evidence for me.

Well, if a person does not believe the earth was once destroyed by a flood, there is also a good possibility a person will not believe God will one day again pour out His wrath upon all those dwelling on the earth. Peter warns all people who are listening, this future worldwide wrath event will involve not water, but fire. So all those who hold to the belief in global warming I guess they have part of it right. Peter informs us the earth is reserved for fire and will be burned up. Peter even tells us to what group of people this judgment is reserved. It is reserved for the ungodly. Dealing with the subject of global warming, the earth may be changing and it may even be warming, but the deception taking place is blaming the citizens of the world as the cause. Maybe if all the tax paying citizens of the world would each send me five hundred dollars per year, maybe I could solve global warming.

Peter again warns the brethren not to be ignorant. He also warns God keeps His promises. Peter informs the brethren one day to God is like a thousand years to us. God is patiently waiting and is being merciful to all those living on the earth, because it is not His will any should perish, but all should come to repentance. If you are still breathing and your heart is still beating, God is showing His mercy to you. God is giving you another day to repent, and turn to Him. We need to remember, God does keep His promises.

Just like there was a day when God shut the door to the ark, there is coming a day when God's patience and mercy with those living on this earth will end. The Bible warns us this time will come like a thief in the night. A time when it is least expected.

Peter goes on to tell the brethren since we know and trust as believers these events will surely one day take place, we need to be concerned with living holy and godly lives. We as believers are informed not to be caught up in the desires of the world, but to be busy laying up treasures in heaven too which we will be eternally rewarded. Since we know as believers in Christ what wrath is being stored up for those who currently reject the truth, we should be living our lives in such a way that shines a light so others can see the truth.

Peter closes out these verses again warning the brethren to not be led astray with false teachings that come from the wicked. We need to continually be growing in grace and in the knowledge of Jesus Christ found only in the scriptures.

We have discussed the characteristics people will exhibit during the latter days. Looking at the level of evil and ungodliness I see in the world today, I firmly believe we are coming to the end of this age. This is the major reason I am writing this book. We will later on be discussing the signs in the heavens and on the earth occurring during a future time known as the time of, "Jacob's trouble."

Another amazing thing to me, is the fact we are all being fore-warned in the Bible hundreds of years before these events will actually take place. Because God loves all people and wishes none would perish, He precisely lays out events taking place in the future and gives us warning signs so we can know the signs of the times. I know some of the words and stories in the Bible coming from God are tough to read and think upon. A person needs to remember God wants no person to spiritually perish, but desires all people to receive the life He alone offers.

Who Receives a Reward

One of the purposes of this book is to hopefully clear up confusion people have by answering questions about the Bible many struggle with. One of the main doctrinal issues people and churches struggle with today deals with questions relating to the differences between doing good works and being considered righteous in God's eyes. I believe the major reason for this confusion is many people struggle with the idea righteousness is obtained by meeting certain moral standards accomplished through individual effort. A huge breakthrough is realized when people understand righteousness is not obtained by something we have accomplished. Righteousness is obtained only through a belief and faith in what Christ has already accomplished for us on the cross. In other words, righteousness is not so much about us, it's about Him. The following verses in Ephesians relates to this truth.

> For by grace are ye saved through faith; and that not of yourselves: it is the gift of God:
> Not of works, lest any man should boast.
> For we are his workmanship, created in Christ Jesus unto good works, which God hath before ordained that we should walk in them. (Ephesians 2:8–10)

One thing I'm continuing to realize is the Christian life is much simpler if we just take the Bible for what it says. Several times we have discussed the issue of what it means to be counted as righteous in God's eyes. This is one of the most important issues in life to be concerned with since our eternity depends upon it. I have also mentioned several times in the scriptures, the Bible refers to God's wrath being poured out upon those who are ungodly, unrighteous, naked, and blind. These are characteristics given to those who have rejected the salvation Christ offers to all people who believe and accept Him.

Notice a requirement the Bible reveals concerning the issue of salvation. First of all, grace is involved. I have always heard grace defined as unmerited favor. I have always loved the way Dr. Chuck Missler worded it, stating, "Grace is getting something, we do not deserve." When a person realizes on their best day their righteousness is incapable of saving them, that person is well on their way to receiving the saving grace Christ offers them.

One requirement for an individual to obtain righteousness is faith. We must have faith God will do what He says and will keep His promises. We need to understand faith involves much more than just believing in somebody or something. Many people state they believe in God. The Bible states even the demons believe there is one God, and they shudder at the thought of standing before Him. Even Satan believes there is a, "Most High God," and according to scriptures his ultimate goal is to somehow overthrow God and seat himself on His throne. The Bible informs us of Satan's ultimate goal, recorded in the following verses.

> How art thou fallen from heaven, O Lucifer, son of the morning! How art thou cut down to the ground, which didst weaken the nations!
> For thou hast said in thine heart, I will ascend into heaven, I will exalt my throne above the stars of God: I will sit also upon the mount of the congregation, in the sides of the north:
> I will ascend above the heights of the clouds; I will be like the most High. (Isaiah 14:12–14)

Satan's ultimate goal in life is to somehow try to overthrow God, take His place, and seat himself on God's throne. Those who believe there is no God. Satan, who the Bible describes as a, "Mighty Cherub," evidently believes in the existence of God, since his goal is to defeat Him. I know there are people who tend to believe Satan has equal authority and standing with God. Satan is a created being who according to the Bible may have been at one time God's second in command, but because of pride he and a third of the angels were thrown out of heaven. Satan will one day be cast into the, "Lake of Fire," along with the antichrist and the false prophet. People need to understand faith requires much more than a belief in God. It involves a complete reliance in God's ability to keep His promises.

So we see righteousness involves both grace and faith. Another issue Ephesians makes clear is other than a required faith of the individual, there is no work we can do on our own to receive this gift of salvation from God. Salvation is a gift freely given from God to all people willing to accept it. The Bible states for this reason we as sinners saved by grace have nothing to brag or boast about. Our only response should be to give all honor and glory to God.

So we really have no reason to boast. It is because when it is all said and done, nobody can really claim to have accomplished anything on their own. It is God who has created all things. It is God who gives us life, breath, and the ability to reason. It is God who gives us free will, the ability to make choices, and the ability to think for ourselves. When we begin to understand this spiritual truth it is very humbling, and it changes our perspectives on life. We are His workmanship and have been created in His image. The reason we were created in the first place is to ultimately give glory to God.

The most important thing is not the works and deeds a person accomplishes during a lifetime. The most important thing in life is having a relationship with God. Our relationship with God is a lot like marriage. If a husband and wife truly love and care for each other, the desire to be faithful and please one another will come naturally. Our relationship with Christ should be the same. Paul told the church brethren to work out their salvation. Paul was saying when people become new creatures in Christ, doing good works and producing fruit should be a desire that comes naturally. Jesus also made the reference a tree should be known by the fruit it produces. Righteous people produce good fruit.

Before we go deeper into the subject of works and rewards, I want to make clear we understand the difference between being, "Saved," and, "In Christ," and being rewarded for works while living here on earth. The doctrines of salvation and works are two entirely different subjects. According to the Bible, one day every human being will either be rewarded, or they will be judged by their works. Those "In Christ," will be rewarded for their works in heaven. Those who are lost, who the Bible refers to as the, "Spiritually Dead," will be eternally condemned by their works. I see a tremendous amount of confusion dealing with this subject in the churches today. This spiritual truth is tough for some people to swallow, but the Bible tells us all people will not be treated equally and will not all be rewarded in the same way. It is God who saves us from our sins. It is then our responsibility to grow and produce good fruit. Yes, people will one day truly reap what they have sown.

> But this I say, He which soweth sparingly shall reap also sparingly; and he which soweth bountifully shall reap also bountifully.
>
> Every man according as he purposeth in his heart, so let him give; not grudgingly, or of necessity: for God loveth a cheerful giver.
>
> And God is able to make all grace abound toward you; that ye, always having all sufficiency in all things, may abound to every good work:
>
> As it is written, He hath dispersed abroad; he hath given to the poor: his righteousness remaineth for ever (2 Corinthians 9:6–9).

I would like to nail down another issue I see a lot of confusion with today, and this deals with the subject referred to as, "Eternal Security." If a person comes from the doctrinal belief salvation is something one can lose, it is almost always based on the belief salvation or justification is obtained or maintained by something a person is required to do. In other words, if a person is capable of earning salvation through works, a person then is also capable of losing his or her salvation through some sort of sin or disobedience. This is the reason we need to understand it isn't about us, it's about Him. The verses below in John deals with these various doctrinal issues we have been discussing.

> Then came the Jews round about him, and said unto him, How long dost thou make us to doubt? If thou be the Christ, tell us plainly.
>
> Jesus answered them, I told you, and ye believed not: the works that I do in my Father's name, they bear witness of me.
>
> But ye believe not, because ye are not of my sheep, as I said unto you.
>
> My sheep hear my voice, and I know them, and they follow me:
>
> And I give unto them eternal life; and they shall never perish, neither shall any man pluck them out of my hand.
>
> My Father, which gave them to me, is greater than all; and no man is able to pluck them out of my Father's hand.
>
> I and the Father are one. (John 10:24–30)

John chapter 10 is a great chapter answering many questions related to salvation and eternal security. Notice Jesus makes statements here in John that would definitely not be considered politically correct today. Jesus in this same chapter refers to Himself as, "The Door," and, "The Good Shepherd." The Bible in several verses makes reference to Jesus being the only way to obtain salvation. The lie most people believe today is there are many roads to heaven. Yes, there are many spiritual beings that have been worshipped throughout history as gods, but according to the Bible there is only one, "Most High God," and His Son is named Jesus.

We also notice in these verses one of the many times the Bible records the Jewish people denying Jesus as their Messiah, and His equality with God. It is because of this outright rejection of Christ, the nation of Israel will be allowed to go through a future time of, "Great Tribulation," where they will repent of their sins calling upon Jesus their Messiah to save them. Actually most don't understand this concept, but this is one of the main purposes for their future tribulation and the reason why Jeremiah calls it a time of, "Jacob's Trouble." The prophet Hosea gives us insight on this future time of tribulation in the following verse.

> I will go and return to my place, till they acknowledge their offence, and seek my face: in their affliction they will seek me early. (Hosea 5:15)

This verse in Hosea gives tremendous spiritual insight to a major prerequisite for the second coming of Christ to earth. Hosea states Christ will not literally return to earth again until the nation of Israel acknowledges their sins, and seeks His face. It will be then and only then during a time of great affliction, Israel will seek God. So we see here there are things that must take place before Christ returns to earth a second time to fight for Israel and sets up His earthly kingdom here on earth.

Jesus goes on to explain to these Jewish people in the book of John the reason for their unbelief is because they do not know Him as Messiah, and they are not His sheep. Jesus goes on in John 10:27 informing all people His sheep hear and listen to His voice, they follow Him, and they are known by Him. Jesus Christ personally knows His children, and He alone gives them eternal life. It is Jesus Christ only who is the way, the truth, and the life.

Jesus then makes a very powerful statement concerning salvation and eternal life. Jesus tells us His sheep who are His children, "Never," perish, and no one can snatch these sheep out of His hand. This statement from Jesus is about as straight forward as it can get.

As if the issue of eternal security hasn't already been dealt with, Jesus goes on to say His Father who has given these sheep to Him is greater than all, and nobody can snatch His sheep out of God the Father's hand either. Jesus then closes by stating, "He and the Father are one."

It always comes back to an understanding it's not about us, it's about Him. Christ knows His sheep, He gives them eternal life, and He promises they will never perish. People need to understand those who are, "In Christ," your eternity is one hundred percent safe and secure in Christ. Salvation is a free gift given to those who freely accept Christ as Savior and Lord.

The subject of eternal security reminds me of a sermon I heard years ago concerning the prodigal son. There was a father whose son became rebellious and demanded his inheritance. The father gave him what was rightfully his, so the son went on his way ending up blowing his inheritance, living in extreme immorality, poverty, and ended up eating food fed to pigs. When the son came to his right mind, he had a moment of brilliance realizing his father's servants were living better than he was, so he decided to move back home and work for his father. The story goes on to say the son's father was watching, praying, and hoping his son would one day return home. When the father sees his son returning home, the father runs out to meet him welcoming him back into the family. This biblical story is a symbolic picture of God's love for His children. If we are one of His sheep, we will always be one of His sons or daughters, and God will always be our Father no matter what happens in life. A child of God may lose their inheritance or their rewards, but they will always be one of God's children, and He will always be their Father.

Before we dive further into the subject dealing with salvation and works, I want to nail down another issue of confusion in the churches today. This issue deals with a verse in the book of Revelation, and goes along with the beliefs of many in the church today. Many people in the church will attempt to use the verse below in Revelation chapter 3 as a scriptural reference the Bible is stating a person can lose their salvation. The problem here is this is clearly not what the Bible is teaching us in this verse.

> Behold, I come quickly: hold that fast
> which thou hast, that no man take thy crown.
> (Revelation 3:11)

The context of the above verse deals with John in the book of Revelation addressing the church in Philadelphia. Jesus is giving this church along with other churches a spiritual score relating to their level of spiritual maturity. Jesus informs this Church He is aware of their works, they have kept God's word, they have not denied His name, and they have kept God's command to endure patiently. Jesus promises this church He will keep them from, "The hour of trial," coming upon the whole earth, testing those people living on the earth during this time. Notice first, Jesus makes reference to this trial coming upon the entire earth. This is not a regional trial. This is a worldwide testing. I believe this is a direct reference from Jesus of a deception coming so great and powerful it would deceive the very elect if possible. The good news is this coming deception is not intended for those, "In Christ." This deception is intended for those who reject the truth of God's word.

Jesus then warns this Church to hold on to what they have. Jesus commands this church to hold on to their faith, keep doing good deeds, keep God's word, and don't deny His name. Jesus promises this church if they continue to hold on to their faith and endure, no man will be able to take their crowns. The mentioning of crowns in the Bible are not dealing with the subject of salvation. Crowns are given as rewards for various types of service. Jesus was warning this church to not let any person cause them to stumble, resulting in them one day losing their heavenly rewards.

The people living during the time of the early church understood the concept and purpose for crowns. Winners of ancient athletic events many times received an honorary wreath of leaves placed upon the victor's head. The Bible promises the faithful believers who endure to the end, remain steadfast in their faith, and finish the race will also receive a crown. However, this crown will be an eternal imperishable crown. Notice Jesus did not tell us to hold fast so no one would steal your salvation. No, afraid not, our salvation is secure in the hand of Christ.

According to scripture, it is possible for a person due to greed, the pursuit of materialism, or just the inability to faithfully endure to someday miss out on receiving a crown. This is why Jesus is warning all in the church to be careful not to let any man's actions cause a believer to stumble, losing the crown or rewards intended for them. Believe me, this will happen. Because many people today have been led astray by false teachers and are caught up in the cares of this world, they will one day miss out on eternal blessings. What does the Bible tells us? It warns the righteous to not be consumed storing up treasures here on earth which can rust and be stolen, but to store up treasures in heaven which are incorruptible and are eternal. How is this accomplished? It is accomplished through works and good deeds. We will all reap what we sow. Let's look at a couple verses in 1 Corinthians of what Paul is reminding the believer concerning the game of life.

> Know ye not that they which run in a race run all, but one receiveth the prize? So run, that ye may obtain.
> And every man that striveth for the mastery is temperate in all things. Now they do it to obtain a corruptible crown; but we are incorruptible.
> "I therefore so run, not as uncertainly; so fight I, not as one that beateth the air."
> (1 Corinthians 9:24–26)

I have mentioned at the beginning of this book I was involved in competitive sports for a good part of my life, including four years in college. I understand what Paul is telling us here in these verses. I put my body through years and years of rigorous training to better be able to compete in sports. I have no regrets for the many years of extreme physical conditioning, the literal hundreds of miles of running, and the tons of weight lifted.

I now realize at the age of fifty-six, although it does bring back some good memories, most things in life considered as accomplishments are nothing more than corruptible crowns. According to the Bible, there are at least five crowns I am aware of the believer has the potential to one day receive. These crowns are eternal incorruptible crowns that will never rust and cannot be stolen. The Bible identifies these different types of crowns as the following:

- Imperishable crown–For those living disciplined lives for Christ denying self.
- Crown of rejoicing–For those who were faithful soul winners.
- Crown of righteousness–For those looking for Christ's appearing.
- Crown of glory–For those who were faithful shepherds over the flock.
- Crown of life–For those who were faithful through trials, suffering, and even death.

Let's now continue dealing with the subject of what groups of people will one day receive eternal rewards. During the past few years I'm realizing more and more the importance of making every day count spiritually. Every day on this earth God has given us is another opportunity to plan for a heavenly retirement. Jesus made an interesting comment in the book of Matthew relating to giving to those in need. Jesus stated those who give with the motive of impressing others might indeed impress people on earth, but they will receive no reward in heaven for deeds such as these. Those people on earth who help others with a heart filled with genuine love and compassion will one day be rewarded for their works. There is coming a day when everything done in secret will be brought to light. It will be a sad day for some people when they stand before God, realizing all the projects, promotions, and concerns of life they thought were important are now meaningless. It will be a very humiliating time filled with great sorrow for many people, but there will be a great award ceremony and a time of rejoicing for those whose hearts are filled with love and compassion for their neighbor.

Jesus informs us in the book of Matthew, those who have made great sacrifices for His sake during their lives will one day be rewarded one hundred times over for their work. Jesus also informs us a time is coming when those who have been first will be last, and those who were always last will be first. It will be a glorious time for those who have worked hard and have finished the race sowing seed for the kingdom. People will truly reap what they have sown. Let's now take a look at some very crucial verses in 1 Corinthians dealing with the importance of producing good fruit. These verses also include a very strict warning from Paul.

> Now he that planteth and he that watereth are one: and every man shall receive his own reward according to his own labour.
>
> For we are labourers together with God: ye are God's husbandry, ye are God's building.
>
> According to the grace of God which is given unto me, as a wise masterbuilder, I have laid the foundation, and another buildeth thereon. But let every man take heed how he buildeth thereupon.
>
> For other foundation can no man lay than that is laid, which is Jesus Christ.
>
> Now if any man build upon this foundation gold, silver, precious stones, wood, hay, stubble;
>
> Every man's work shall be made manifest: for the day shall declare it, because it shall be revealed by fire; and the fire shall try every man's work of what sort it is.
>
> If any man's work abide which he hath built thereupon, he shall receive a reward.
>
> If any man's work shall be burned, he shall suffer loss: but he himself shall be saved; yet so as by fire.

> Know ye not that ye are the temple of God,
> and that the Spirit of God dwelleth in you?
> (1 Corinthians 3:8–16)

Continuing to deal with the subject of who will one day receive rewards, the Bible gives us very clear answers to all these questions. The Bible gives us a clear picture concerning the differences between being counted righteous and doing good works. The verses above in Corinthians do a great job in nailing these issues down. Those individuals who spend their time on this earth producing fruit for the kingdom will be the people who will receive eternal rewards.

We are made righteous because we by faith receive the sacrificial gift Jesus made for us on the cross. Salvation is a free gift to those who accept it, but salvation was not free. The gift of salvation is only available to us because Jesus, "The Son of God," was willing to lay down His life for all people. Eternal rewards are earned through a person's service and labor. In the same way an athlete receives a medal because of commitment and training, those who are, "In Christ," also will receive heavenly rewards because of hard work and service. Even though the Bible is so clear on this issue, millions of people have believed and continue to believe they can work their way to heaven. This is serious stuff, and the belief works can save a person will be mistakes possibly millions will end up making. If people were able to obtain salvation through works alone, the death of Christ on the cross was in vain. The verses below in Matthew give us this warning.

> Not every one that saith unto me, Lord, Lord, shall enter into the kingdom of heaven; but he that doeth the will of my Father which is in heaven.
>
> Many will say to me in that day, Lord, Lord, have we not prophesied in thy name? and in thy name have cast out devils? And in thy name done many wonderful works?

169

> And then will I profess unto them, I never
> knew you: depart from me, ye that work iniquity.
> (Matthew 7:21–23)

Those who believe eternal salvation can be obtained through works will one day be in for a rude awakening. We of ourselves have no righteousness. We must to be clothed in, "His Righteousness." It is Christ who makes us worthy. This spiritual truth goes all the way back to Israel's time of Egyptian captivity. God was trying to show the children of Israel it would only be through the blood of an unblemished lamb symbolizing Jesus the true Lamb of God, the forgiveness of sins could be obtained. We also need to remember Jesus informed Nicodemus one must be born of spirit or born again to be worthy of the kingdom of God. I know this is not politically correct today, but it is what Jesus said. The choice is up to you.

Paul then goes on to give all people who will listen a very disturbing warning. This warning is also similar to the warning given to us by Jesus. If works accomplished during a lifetime are not based on the foundation of Jesus Christ, these works are all in vain. Jesus is our foundation, and He is the, "Chief Cornerstone." Jesus was the living water offered to the woman of Samaria promising her if she would drink from the water He offered, she would never thirst again. Jesus was the symbolic rock struck by Moses providing living water for the children of Israel. He is the way, the truth, and the life. All that come to Him will never perish, they will never thirst, and no man will be able to pluck them out of His hand.

Paul goes on to list for us examples of corruptible and incorruptible works accomplished by the righteous during a lifetime. To aid us in our understanding, Paul compares works which will one day result in eternal rewards to precious stones and precious metals. Corruptible works, works that will bring no eternal rewards, are compared to wood, hay, and stubble.

These verses in 1 Corinthians show God is just, and He is holy. People will reap what they have sown. Those who work hard and produce much fruit will be rewarded for their work. The Bible is very clear, informing us every man's work will one day be made known.

According to the Bible, fire will be put to every man's works. An interesting fact to know about gold and silver is the more times these precious metals are melted, more impurities rise to the top and the more purified the metal becomes. This process is an earthly picture of how our works will be one day put to the test. The incorruptible works accomplished during our lifetime will stand the test of fire, and the appropriate rewards will be distributed. The corruptible works which the Bible compares to as wood, hay, and stubble will be burned up, and those people having such works will suffer loss.

So we see the Bible is giving us an interesting picture of an awards ceremony for those who are righteous, one day taking place in heaven. Some righteous people will be rewarded greatly for their works done here on earth. Some people who are counted righteous will suffer great losses, although the Bible makes very clear they personally will be saved from God's wrath. This biblical concept goes all the way back to the story of the prodigal son. Although the disobedient son squandered his inheritance, his father never stopped loving him and never disowned him as a son.

Just a few chapters back we took an interesting look at two different men named Abraham and Lot. Although the Bible makes it very clear both men were righteous in the sight of God, we are given two very different examples in the way these two people chose to live their lives. Abraham throughout the scriptures is a type or a picture of God. It is also interesting Abraham's son Isaac is a prophetic picture of Christ who was also an only Son offered as a sacrifice by His Father. We find Abraham is a biblical example of a man who literally walks by faith. Lot although righteous is a biblical picture of a man who walks by sight. The Bible states Lot looked upon the plains and based his decisions in life by what he saw, or what was determined by his fleshly nature. Because Lot did not walk by faith, it cost him very dearly. Although Lot and his two daughters were saved from God's wrath, Lot lost most of his family because he had given in to his earthly desires.

The story of Abraham and Lot is a reminder of what it will be like for many of the righteous. This is why the Bible warns us not to be caught up in the cares and the desires of the world, but to be concerned with laying up treasures in heaven which will not rust and cannot be stolen. Yes, one day every man's work will be made known. Would you like to receive a reward in heaven one day? If you are still breathing, you still have time.

> I have fought a good fight, I have finished my course, I have kept the faith:
> Henceforth there is laid up for me a crown of righteousness, which the Lord, the righteous judge, shall give me at that day: and not to me only, but unto all them also that love his appearing. (2 Timothy 4:7–8)

Twice Dead

I have lived in Northwestern Oklahoma my entire life. Oklahoma is a state which is nationally known for severe weather outbreaks including very large damaging tornadoes. It is not uncommon for local news and radio stations to be warning people days ahead of possible coming severe weather events. The purpose of these warnings is to save lives. Several thousand storm shelters have been purchased since the historic tornado devastated Moore, Oklahoma several years ago. Most people living in this area believe it would be considered essential for any person owning a home or property to have insurance to protect their assets. Most people purchase insurance for their automobiles, homes, crops, health, and even their lives. We spend most of our time here on earth protecting the material things in our lives, but spend very little time preparing for eternity. The Bible warns us not to be so caught up in the affairs of life and all it involves, since the world in its present form will one day pass away.

I believe the events prophesied in the Bible that will occur in the future, need to be taken more seriously than a tornado warning. The Bible has been given to us by a loving God who desires we live life to our fullest potential. A major purpose of the Bible is to warn those willing to listen, informing them of future events coming upon all people dwelling upon the earth. God has made a way of hope and salvation through His Son Jesus Christ for all who believe. Every human being is given the free will to make moral and spiritual decisions concerning their belief or unbelief in God. Because of this free will God gives to all mankind, each individual will one day ultimately be held accountable for decisions they make during their time living on this earth.

Just like with a tornado warning where people choose not to take shelter and suffer the consequences, those who do not heed the warnings of the Bible will also suffer the consequences. It is a horrible thing to hear of someone needlessly dying in a severe storm or any type of disaster such as a house fire, but it is much more catastrophic when a person dies denying the eternal salvation and grace freely given to them by God. One major spiritual truth I am trying to get across to people is the need to understand the wisdom the Bible gives us concerning the future, and what is defined as eternity. Subjects such as these should be discussed regularly in the church setting, but surprisingly they are scarcely mentioned in most churches today. The subject in this chapter I will be providing answers to is what the Bible refers to as the, "Second Death."

Jesus informed a person named Nicodemus a man must be born again to see the kingdom of God. Jesus was not referring to a physical rebirth. Jesus was referring to a spiritual rebirth. We all live in physical bodies and have a soul. If the Lord does not return during one's lifetime a physical death will one day take place. The Bible uses the analogy comparing the body we live in to a tent. A tent is a very fragile and temporary structure, and in many ways is very similar to our human bodies. The Bible promises those who trust in Christ will one day receive an immortal body which will not wear out, suffering a spiritual or second death. The, "Second Death," describes an eternal separation from God, and one day being cast into a, "Lake of Fire."

Another primary reason I am writing this book is because it truly is my desire all who read this book will choose Christ, and the life He offers. Ultimately the choice is ours, and no one including God will force anybody to make any decision they refuse. It always blows my mind when people ask the question how a loving God could send people to hell condemning them eternally. The answer to the question is God simply doesn't send anyone to hell. This is not the answer many like to hear, but the Bible states people send themselves to hell by denying the gift of eternal life Christ offers to all people.

A person can simply deny the law of gravity exists, but when a person jumps off a bridge or building they will have to suffer the consequences. A truth I have realized over the years is the spiritual laws which have been put in place by God are just as real as the laws of physics most people do not deny exist. God went to great lengths to give all people who are willing to trust and believe in Him eternal life. God sent His Son, His only Son so we might have life and have it more abundantly. Jesus, who was the literal, "Son of God," freely laid down His life paying the debt for our sins. God gave us the Holy Bible to reveal His character, will, prophetic message, and His ministry on this earth. God also displays Himself throughout His creation bearing witness to His existence. God desires all people will come to Him, and freely drink from the water of life provided to all who will accept Him.

The sin debt of all people has already been purchased through the shed blood of Christ, and ultimately the choice to accept or reject the free gift of salvation is up to each individual. There is an interesting parable in the Bible concerning a king who gave invitations to a wedding banquet. A parable is a story used to teach spiritual truth. Many people would want to make us believe parables in the Bible are there just for moral and ethical guidance, and these parables really have no other meaning or purpose. Nothing could be further from the truth. When the Bible makes the statement, "The Kingdom of Heaven is Like," this is exactly what the Bible means, and we need to take the Bible for what it says. A biblical illustration may be given to us in story form, but the spiritual truth behind the story needs to be taken literally. One such example is found in Matthew chapter 22.

> And Jesus answered and spake unto them again by parables, and said,
> The kingdom of heaven is like unto a certain king, which made a marriage for his son,
> And sent forth his servants to call them that were bidden to the wedding: and they would not come.
> Again, he sent forth other servants, saying, Tell them which are bidden, Behold, I have pre-

pared my dinner: my oxen and my fatlings are killed, and all things are ready: come unto the marriage.

But they made light of it, and went their ways, one to his farm, another to his merchandise:

And the remnant took his servants, and entreated them spitefully, and slew them.

But when the king heard thereof, he was wroth: and he sent forth his armies, and destroyed those murderers, and burned up their city.

Then saith he to his servants, The wedding is ready, but they which were bidden were not worthy.

Go ye therefore into the highways, and as many as ye shall find, bid to the marriage.

So those servants went out into the highways, and gathered together all as many as they found, both bad and good: and the wedding was furnished with guests.

And when the king came in to see the guests, he saw there a man which had not on a wedding garment:

And he saith unto him, Friend, how camest thou in hither not having a wedding garment? And he was speechless.

Then said the king to the servants, Bind him hand and foot, and take him away, and cast him into outer darkness, there shall be weeping and gnashing of teeth.

For many are called, but few are chosen. (Matthew 22:1–14)

An interesting fact I have discovered concerning the Bible, is the entire book is not required to make an educated decision concerning a person's spiritual condition before a Holy God. For instance, if a person was shipwrecked on an island, and while walking along the beach they found a torn and mangled portion of a Bible. After picking up the partial Bible, the survivor noticed it contained a dozen pages of Luke and John. If this person was to read the remaining portions of these two books, they would more than likely be given enough information to make an educated decision concerning his or her relationship with God. Likewise, it is amazing the amount of information Jesus gives us here in just these fourteen verses. In these fourteen verses a person comes to understand the need for salvation, the eternal celebration for those counted righteous, and the coming future judgment for all who God determines are unrighteous. But this is just the beginning to the wealth of information Jesus is telling us in this parable.

So why did Jesus speak in parables? Why didn't Jesus always make things simple, and tell it like it is? Well the truth is, Jesus does tell it like it is, but there are some people who deny and will not accept the truth. One thing to always consider when a person is reading the Bible is to understand the context of the subject matter, and what group of people are being addressed. Jesus spoke to the Jewish people in parables, because of their unwillingness to accept Him as Messiah, Lord, and the Son of God. If we are willing to search, the Bible gives us the answers to many of the questions we have. We find the answer for one of the reasons Jesus spoke in parables in the book of Luke. Notice the comments Jesus shares secretly with His disciples concerning the true reason He would many times speak to people in parables.

> And his disciples asked him, saying, What might this parable be?
> And he said, Unto you it is given to know the mysteries of the kingdom of God: but to others in parables; that seeing they might not see, and hearing they might not understand. (Luke 8:9–10)

So who are these groups of people to whom Jesus would only speak using parables? Jesus informs the reader the use of parables is not for the purpose of keeping people from understanding spiritual truth. Jesus spoke in parables to those who refused to accept the truth of who He was and refused to accept His message of salvation. A more thorough response concerning the issue of parables is given by Jesus in Matthew chapter 13.

> And the disciples came, and said unto him, Why speakest thou unto them in parables?
>
> He answered and said unto them, Because it is given unto you to know the mysteries of the kingdom of heaven, but to them it is not given.
>
> For whosoever hath, to him shall be given, and he shall have more abundance: but whosoever hath not, from him shall be taken away even that he hath.
>
> Therefore speak I to them in parables: because they seeing see not; and hearing they hear not, neither do they understand.
>
> And in them is fulfilled the prophecy of Esaias, which saith, By hearing ye shall hear, and shall not understand; and seeing ye shall see, and shall not perceive:
>
> For this people's heart is waxed gross, and their ears are dull of hearing, and their eyes they have closed; lest at any time they should see with their eyes and hear with their ears, and should understand with their heart, and should be converted, and I should heal them.
>
> But blessed are your eyes, for they see: and your ears, for they hear. (Matthew 13:10–16)

I have taught the Bible for over twenty five years, and it has always amazed me the different interpretations people will have concerning various scriptural texts and stories in the bible. The problem is the misinterpretation of scripture occurs often in the church setting, and deals with people who should know the answers to these basic biblical truths. On several occasions I would hear people stating the parables in the Bible were just stories and should be taken as no more than moral guidance. One thing I have learned through the years is Jesus didn't waste His time telling stories. Every word coming out of the mouth of Christ had spiritual meaning and purpose and was meant to be taken very seriously.

As we continue to address the reasons Jesus spoke in parables, Jesus tells us in Matthew parables were given to the Jewish people and all unbelievers whose hearts are hardened to conceal truth from them. Jesus quotes from Isaiah informing people of the historical spiritual condition of the children of Israel, as well as giving us prophetic insight of a future time when Israel will again turn back to Him.

> And he said, Go, and tell this people, Hear ye indeed, but understand not; and see ye indeed, but perceive not.
> Make the heart of this people fat, and make their ears heavy, and shut their eyes; lest they see with their eyes, and hear with their ears, and understand with their heart, and convert, and be healed.
> Then I said, Lord how long? And he answered, Until the cities be wasted without inhabitant, and the houses without man, and the land be utterly desolate. (Isaiah 6:9–11)

Jesus spoke in parables to the Jewish people because they refused to accept Him as their Messiah. How long would it be before the nation of Israel will again turn back to God? Isaiah gives us the answer to this question. Israel will acknowledge Jesus as their Messiah when their cities and fields will again one day be destroyed, and their houses will again not be inhabited. A person needs to prophetically understand the children of Israel have now once again been reestablished as a nation since 1948. The Bible is informing us the nation of Israel will again one day be made desolate, and their cities will one day again be uninhabitable. This event will occur during the future, "Day of Jacob's Trouble." I have discovered the words of Solomon have been and will again be fulfilled over and over again. That which has been done, will most certainly be done again.

Most people in the church today fail to realize what one of the major purposes for the, "Tribulation Period," will be. Through great persecution, God will bring the nation of Israel back to Him. In a sense, it will be a repeat experience of Israel's captivity in Egypt, and the time Israel spent in the wilderness. There truly is nothing new under the sun. Yes, both history and prophecy will continue to repeat themselves.

There is one crucial point we need to realize concerning the use of parables before we move on. The Bible records an event referred to as the, "Triumphal Entry," of Christ which was a key prophetical turning point for Israel. This event would result in catastrophic repercussions for Israel lasting thousands of years, climaxing during a future time of, "Great Tribulation," for Israel. We will now look what Luke has to say concerning the, "Triumphal Entry," of Christ.

> And when he was come nigh, even now at the descent of the mount of Olives, the whole multitude of the disciples began to rejoice and praise God with a loud voice for all the mighty works that they had seen;
>
> Saying, Blessed be the King that cometh in the name of the Lord: peace in heaven, and glory in the highest.
>
> And some of the Pharisees from among the multitude said unto him, Master, rebuke thy disciples.
>
> And he answered and said unto them, I tell you that, if these should hold their peace, the stones would immediately cry out.
>
> And when he was come near, he beheld the city, and wept over it,

Saying, If thou hadst known, even thou, at least in this thy day, the things, which belong unto thy peace! but now they are hid from thine eyes.

For the days shall come upon thee, that thine enemies shall cast a trench about thee, and compass thee round, and keep thee in on every side,

And shall lay thee even with the ground, and thy children within thee; and they shall not leave in the one stone upon another; because thou knewest not the time of thy visitation. (Luke 19:37–44)

We are told Jesus wept for the city of Jerusalem because He knew Israel would ultimately reject Him as Messiah. Jesus also makes a shocking prophetic statement in these verses regarding future events coming to Jerusalem, and the people of Israel. Jesus was able to literally see the futuristic events coming upon Jerusalem because of their rejection of Him as Messiah. The most shocking comment Jesus makes we find is during the conclusion of Luke 19:44, which most people do not pick up on. All future events happening to Jerusalem and Israel including the time of, "Jacob's Trouble," will be because they failed to recognize Jesus as Messiah during His triumphal entry into Jerusalem. It is because of this denial of Jesus, from this moment on we see Jesus speaking to the people of Israel by way of parables. It would be only a few years later, the Romans would besiege the city of Jerusalem taking it captive in, "70 AD," and because of this many Jewish men, women, and children would lose their lives. Israel's spiritual blindness and continued rejection in Jesus their Messiah is the reason a future time of persecution and tribulation will come upon Israel referred to as, "The 70th Week of Daniel." These are the reasons Jesus wept over Jerusalem and the children of Israel.

Now that we have a basic understanding as to the reason Jesus spoke in parables, I would like to work back and deal with the parable in Matthew chapter 22. Jesus here again is speaking in parables to the Jewish people because He knew they would not accept the truth of who He was, so He uses a parable to describe their spiritual unbelief. Here in this story Jesus is referring to Himself and His Father, but the Jewish unbelievers lack the spiritual wisdom and insight to understand the meaning of the story, or the role they play in the parable itself.

We need to understand Jesus perfectly understood the spiritual condition of the chief priests, the Pharisees, and all the other religious leaders. These people were trying to trap Jesus in His own words, because they hated His message and denied Him as the, "Son of God." The religious leaders had been holding meetings for the very purpose of destroying Christ and His ministry, and quite frankly they wanted Him killed. From their perspective, Jesus was a great teacher, possibly a prophet, but the, "Son of God," that was impossible. In their eyes this was blasphemy for Jesus to consider Himself equal to God. The sad thing is, Jesus was the literal, "Son of God," standing right in front of them, and they failed to recognize who He was. Jesus knew the heart of these religious leaders, just like He knows the hearts of all people. This is why Jesus spoke to these people in parables. Jesus also makes an interesting comment in Matthew chapter 7, dealing with the spiritual condition of people's hearts.

> Give not that which is holy unto the dogs, neither cast ye your pearls before swine, lest they trample them under their feet, and turn again and rend you.
> Ask, and it shall be given you; seek, and ye shall find; knock, and it shall be opened unto you:
> For every one that asketh receiveth; and he that seeketh findeth; and to him that knocketh it shall be opened. (Matthew 7:6–8)

The three verses above in Matthew chapter 7 give us further evidence as to the reason Jesus spoke in parables to the Jewish people, as well as all people who refused to believe in Him. Notice the instructions given by Jesus in these verses. Jesus stated, "Do not give that which is holy, to the dogs." What Jesus was referring to as being holy was the gospel message. The gospel message is being compared here in these verses to pearls. The use of the words, "Dogs and Swine," is used many times in the scriptures describing those who scoff or completely reject the gospel message. Dogs return to their vomit, and pigs return to the mud. There is a very interesting chapter found in the book of Psalms. When a person reads this chapter a very clear picture of the crucifixion of Jesus is portrayed. The interesting thing concerning these verses is they were written hundreds of years before Jesus Christ was born and walked the earth. A person needs to pay close attention to the wording contained in these verses. A person will notice the terms, "Dog, Bulls, and Lion," are used in these verses. Here is a few of the verses given to us in Psalms 22.

> But I am a worm, and no man; a reproach of men, and despised of the people.
>
> All they that see me laugh me to scorn: they shoot out the lip, they shake the head, saying,
>
> He trusted on the Lord that he would deliver him: let him deliver him, seeing he delighted in him.
>
> But thou are he that took me out of the womb: thou didst make me hope when I was upon my mother's breasts.
>
> I was cast upon thee from the womb: thou are my God from my mother's belly.
>
> Be not far from me; for trouble is near; for there is none to help.
>
> Many bulls have compassed me: strong bulls of Bashan have beset me round.
>
> They gaped upon me with their mouths, as a ravening and a roaring lion.
>
> I am poured out like water, and all my bones are out of joint: my heart is like wax; it is melted in the midst of my bowels.

My strength is dried up like a potsherd; and my tongue cleaveth to my jaws; and thou hast brought me into the dust of death.

For dogs have compassed me: the assembly of the wicked have inclosed me: they pierced my hands and my feet.

I may tell all my bones: they look and stare upon me.

They part my garments among them, and cast lots upon my vesture. (Psalms 22:6–18)

An entire book could be written on Psalm chapter 22 alone. I believe without a shadow of doubt these verses are referencing events occurring during the crucifixion of Christ. The statement is made in these verses relating to dogs closing in and encompassing Christ, even identifying these people as those who pierced His hands and His feet. I believe there was much more going on during this horrible event than most realize. The mention of, "Lions and Bulls," I believe is referencing the spiritual warfare taking place during this time. Satan believed he would finally be victorious when Christ was hung on the cross, but what Satan believed would be a great achievement, became his worst nightmare. The Bible literally describes Satan as a, "Roaring Lion," in 1 Peter.

A person needs to notice the way this chapter in Psalms begins. The comment, "My God, My God, Why Hast Thou Forsaken Me?" are identical words to what Jesus stated when He was on the cross. A person also needs to notice the descriptive details relating to Christ's bones being pulled out of joint, the piercing of the hands and feet, and the Roman soldiers casting lots for His clothing. A person can just keep going on and on concerning the hundreds of prophetic implications the Bible gives us including here in these verses. After a while, scriptures such as these just becomes so far beyond the possibilities of coincidence, it becomes absurd to think the Bible is a book written by human effort alone.

The Bible is informing those who reject, mock, or refuse to listen to the gospel message, repeated sharing is not required. It is interesting Jesus states anyone who is not receptive or refuses the presentation of the gospel message, the person presenting the gospel message is instructed to dust off their feet, and leave the place immediately.

Hopefully now we are beginning to understand the reason Jesus spoke to certain groups of people using parables. A person also needs to keep in mind although Israel or any other group of people may reject the gospel message, Jesus never stops loving and desiring people to repent, and turn towards Him. Jesus also spoke to the Jewish people in parables, because He knew one day far into the future the children of Israel would discern the words of Christ and truly understand who He was. Since one of the major purposes of this book is to equip people to discern the times, the Bible informs us in 2 Timothy even those in the church will not put up with sound doctrine as we draw closer to the end of the age. There are many people in the church today who do not take the Bible from a literal perspective, so in their eyes the parables taught by Jesus are no more than allegorical stories with little more than a moral lesson.

So for those who have spiritual eyes and ears, what is Jesus teaching us in this parable? Jesus informs us the kingdom of heaven is like a king who prepared a wedding banquet. First of all just as in this parable, the Bible informs us in many places heaven is a literal place. Heaven is a place ruled by a King setting on a literal throne who is the, "Most High God." A literal wedding banquet is being prepared to occur during a future time only known by the Father. This coming wedding ceremony and banquet is for a Groom, His bride, and the wedding guests who are the saints throughout the ages given white robes. The Groom is Jesus, God's only Son. The bride includes those, "In Christ," who are dressed in white, counted as being righteous. The bride is the true church, those who have been washed in the precious blood of Christ which was shed on the cross.

The invitation to the wedding banquet was first sent to the children of Israel personally by God, but they refused the invitation. God even sends servants to compel the children of Israel to attend the banquet, but still they refused.

So out of continued compassion and love for His people, God sends more servants and prophets pleading with them to come to this banquet. The call rings out from the king, the table is prepared, the food is ready, come to the banquet. The parable goes on to explain the children of Israel continued to ignore and outright reject the invitation from the king. Even worse, the children of Israel become angry with these servants or prophets inviting people to attend the banquet, and end up abusing and killing many of them.

The murdering and abusing of the king's servants made the king extremely angry. The king then sends an army to kill those people who murdered the king's servants, then burned the city. This is more than likely a picture of Jerusalem being taken captive by the Romans in 70 AD where many people were killed, and the city was burned.

So because of the refusal of Israel to accept the invitation to the wedding banquet, the invitation was then sent out to all people. Those who received the first invitation now no longer deserve to attend the banquet. So now all people who are willing to attend are offered an invitation to the wedding banquet. The Bible says it is God's will that none should perish, but that all people should have everlasting life. The table has been made ready, the sacrifice has been made, and the choice is up to us. Who will accept the invitation of the King? This parable brings to mind words stated by Paul in Romans 11.

> What then? Israel hath not obtained that which he seeketh for; but the election hath obtained it, and the rest were blinded.
>
> According as it is written, God hath given them the spirit of slumber, eyes that they should not see, and ears that they should not hear; unto this day.
>
> And David saith, Let their table be made a snare, and a trap, and a stumblingblock, and a recompence unto them:
>
> Let their eyes be darkened, that they may not see, and bow down their back alway.
>
> I say then, Have they stumbled that they should fall? God forbid: but rather through their

fall salvation is come unto the Gentiles, for to
provoke them to jealousy. (Romans 11:7–11)

The reason Jesus spoke to the children of Israel in parables was
because they had eyes that refused to see the truth and ears that
would not hear. Paul goes on to state because of Israel's condition
of spiritual blindness, salvation has now come to all people and all
nations. Let's be clear, God has not forgotten or given up on Israel.
And no, the church has not replaced Israel. God will again through
means of tribulation and persecution turn Israel's heart back towards
Him. This will happen during a future event known as, "Daniel's
70th Week." This period of time is also referred to in the book of
Jeremiah as the time of, "Jacob's Trouble." It will be during this
future time of tribulation, the nation of Israel will once again just
like in the days of Egyptian captivity, turn back to their Messiah and
confess their sins. God will then descend from heaven and rescue
His chosen people.

So because of Israel's blindness, salvation has been offered to all
people. So now according to this parable, because of God's invitation
to all people the wedding hall is now filled with guests. Jesus continues on in this parable explaining a very unusual event taking place
while the king is making his rounds, admiring the number of guests
present during this banquet. During his observation, the king notices
a guest who is not wearing wedding clothes. The king then asks the
guest how he got into the banquet without the appropriate wedding clothes. According to the parable, the improperly dressed guest
is speechless. The king then gives orders for the man to be bound
and thrown outside into outer darkness where there was weeping
and gnashing of teeth. Jesus then ends the parable with a statement
informing all who will listen that many people receive invitations to
the banquet, but few are chosen.

The last three or four verses of this parable are extremely
important and very shocking. Although this is a story, this is a literal
picture of what will happen to those who reject Christ. This is much
more than an allegorical message designed to bring moral insight to
those who read it. This is a warning from the, "Most High God,"

of what will happen to those who refuse Christ. It is interesting, it may very well have been a custom during this time for the host of the party to provide the guests with the appropriate garments. The wedding garment is throughout the Bible a picture of righteousness. The Bible as well as Jesus was making this spiritual truth very clear for us. Only those who are clothed in the righteousness of Christ will be allowed into heaven and will then be allowed to participate in the wedding ceremony. Notice this guest was bound and thrown into outer darkness where there was weeping and gnashing of teeth. This is a prophetic picture of the horrible future for those who choose to reject Christ.

There will be unspeakable sorrow, eternal weeping, and gnashing of teeth for those who are eternally condemned and eternally separated from Christ. I know this subject is not politically correct today, and this spiritual truth is not taught in many churches. We need to understand the Bible is the ultimate source for truth, not the church. We will later on take a very interesting look what Jesus had to say to seven specific churches. The statements Christ gives to these seven churches includes compliments for their endurance and perseverance, but it also includes very serious warnings. The offer from Jesus still stands for all who will listen. There is a great wedding banquet, feast, and ceremony scheduled to one day take place in heaven. You have been invited. Please accept Him while there is still time.

Of all the verses in the Bible, there are a few verses given in the book of Revelation which I believe all people should take extremely serious. These verses deal with the subject of being called, "Twice Dead." If there ever was a picture of hopelessness, this is it. The wonderful thing is, if a person is still breathing and their heart is still beating, there is still hope. We all are given one chance at life here on this earth, and we are given the free will to make our own decisions. It's kind of like the first time I was given the keys to drive a car. My father warned me driving a vehicle too fast and in a reckless manner could have deadly circumstances. I really can't say I listened much to the warnings my father had to say concerning speeding, since I would drive everywhere as fast as the vehicle would go. But you know, I could never say I wasn't warned. This is what churches need to be doing today. Churches need to be warning people to the reality of what lies ahead spiritually.

According to my years of reading the Bible, it very clearly tells us all people who have ever lived and are currently living on this planet, will end up in one of two places. Every person will one day end up spending eternity in the presence of God, or they will end up spending eternity eternally separated from God. This eternal separation from God is what the Bible refers to as hell and ultimately is the second death. This eternal separation from God is not for a hundred, a thousand, or even a million years. The second death will be for an eternity, and it is a picture of utter hopelessness. God is a loving and just God. He has done everything possible making a way through His Son Jesus Christ for all people to accept Him, and the eternal life He offers.

One of the many reasons for me writing this book is to stress the finality and the reality of this spiritual truth. We will all stand before God one of these days. God in His word is warning all people, judgment day is coming. We have been given warnings in the Old Testament as well as warnings in the New Testament concerning this fact. I would like to close out this chapter defining what the Bible has to say concerning the, "Second Death," using examples in Revelation dealing with this spiritual certainty. The Bible tells us the book of Revelation is given to the church by Jesus Christ primarily for the purpose of warning the church saints of what will take place in the future. The first example of scripture we will look at comes from Revelations 21.

> And he said unto me, It is done. I am the Alpha and Omega, the beginning and the end. I will give unto him that is athirst of the fountain of the water of life freely.
>
> He that overcometh shall inherit all things; and I will be his God, and he shall be my son.
>
> But the fearful, and unbelieving, and the abominable, and murderers, and whoremongers, and sorcerers, and idolaters, and all liars, shall

have their part in the lake which burneth with
fire and brimstone: which is the second death.
(Revelation 21:6–8)

The Bible makes it very clear the different types of sins charac-
terizing those people suffering the second death. These verses inform
us those who seek Christ and the life He offers will freely drink from
the water of life, who is Jesus Christ. Jesus instructed the woman He
met at the well, all who would drink the water He offered would
never thirst again. Of course, we understand this story took place at
a well, and the water Jesus was referring to was symbolic to the living
water, He alone offers.

We notice in the second verse the word, "Overcomer," is used.
The term, "Overcomer," describes those who are counted worthy and
are clothed in righteousness. The man discussed in the parable of the
wedding banquet not wearing the appropriate garments was not an
overcomer. This man was not clothed in the righteousness offered by,
"The King." Because this man was not wearing the appropriate garments although he was invited to the banquet, this man was bound
and thrown into outer darkness. This is a subject all people should
take very seriously. One has to wonder how many churches today
even discuss this spiritual truth. Do you have eternal life insurance?
Are you clothed in the garments offered by the, "King of Kings?"

So what groups of people will suffer the second death? The
answer is all people rejecting Christ who have been born of the
seed of Adam, born of sin at birth who continues to sin, and are
called unrighteous. The Bible continues by giving us examples of
sins which will commit people to an everlasting spiritual death. The
list includes, unbelievers, murderers, liars, the sexually immoral, and
those involved in sorcery and idolatry. The Bible states all people
found guilty of these types of sins will be thrown into the fiery lake
of burning sulfur. The Bible is trying to tell us being clothed in the
righteousness of Jesus Christ is our only hope. No human being born
of Adam can be called righteous on their own merits, due to the fact
all people are sinners at birth. This is what the Bible refers to as the,
"Second Death."

The parable told by Jesus concerning the wedding banquet states those found not wearing wedding garments or righteousness of the, "King," will be thrown into the, "Lake of Fire." Notice the list includes liars. How about those people who state they have only told one lie in their life? Well guess what, now they have told two lies. According to the Bible, they will be found guilty. Notice the Bible states the sexually immoral will be thrown into the, "Lake of Fire." Those found guilty of adultery, fornication, homosexuality, and any other type of sexual immorality will be thrown into the, "Lake of Fire." No unrighteousness whatsoever will be allowed into heaven. I understand the Bible in the book of Romans takes a tough stance on homosexuality, but in reality the Bible has zero tolerance for any form of sexual immorality. Because of this zero tolerance stance with all sin, one may ask the question regarding how any person is found worthy to get into heaven. The answer to this question is really very simple. It's all because of Jesus and what He accomplished for all mankind when He went to the cross. The positive news is it matters not what sins you have committed in the past. When a person truly repents and turns from their sins they are considered worthy, and they will one day be given white robes to wear. Remember, it's not about us, it's about Him.

The Bible tells us Jesus is currently seated at God's right hand making intercession for the saints. Jesus is our advocate. Jesus in a sense becomes our criminal defense attorney, because we are all guilty of sinning against a holy God. This spiritual truth goes all the way back to Israel's captivity in Egypt. During Passover an unblemished lamb was sacrificed, and God's wrath passed over all people covered by the blood of the Lamb.

For me, the subject of the, "Second Death," is one of the most sobering subjects to discuss in the Bible. It is a literal picture of eternal hopelessness. For the most part, I believe the days of hellfire and brimstone preaching are over. We are living in a time where people are more concerned about being seen as tolerant, politically correct, and sensitive to hurting the feelings of others. I myself have never been one to force my beliefs upon others, but I do believe Christians should take a stand for their beliefs, always ready to speak truth to anyone who may ask.

The final example I would like to discuss dealing with the second death can be found in Revelation chapter 20. These verses deal with the, "Great White Throne Judgment," which takes place after, "Daniel's 70th Week," also known as the time of, "Jacob's Trouble." "The Great White Throne Judgment," will also follow the thousand year, "Millennial Reign," of Christ on earth.

> And I saw a great white throne, and him that sat on it, from whose face the earth and the heaven fled away; and there was found no place for them.
>
> And I saw the dead, small and great, stand before God; and the books were opened: and another book was opened, which is the book of life: and the dead were judged out of those things which were written in the books, according to their works.
>
> And the sea gave up the dead which were in it; and death and hell delivered up the dead which were in them: and they were judged every man according to their works.
>
> And death and hell were cast into the lake of fire. This is the second death.
>
> And whosoever was not found written in the book of life was cast into the lake of fire. (Revelation 20:11–15)

The above verses give us a futuristic glimpse of what will happen during an event known as the, "Great White Throne Judgment." This is not a fictitious story. This is a realistic picture of a real event coming to all people who reject Jesus Christ, the Son of the, "Most High God." It is not hard to understand why most teachers and preachers do not discuss this subject. It is not easy to look someone in the eye informing them they will be one of those people in attendance during this time of judgment, if they have not trusted Christ as their Lord and Savior. I know this subject it greatly shunned today in most churches, but it deals with some of the most important information people need to hear.

The reality people need to face is this event is coming to those who reject Christ. The Bible goes on to say it is the dead and only the dead who will be present for this judgment. The Bible here is not referring to those who have died a physical death. No one will be judged for dying a physical death. Solomon stated there is a time to be born as well as a time to die. The group of individuals participating in this judgment are those who are spiritually dead. We are not referring to those people who the blood of the Lamb has redeemed. This judgment is not intended for those called, "Righteous," and are, "Overcomers." This judgment is for those who are spiritually eternally dead.

Notice the Bible tells us these dead are standing before God. We are not talking about ghosts or spirits here. We are talking about literal people who are spiritually dead standing before a holy God. We know this fact because the Bible literally tells us the seas will give up the dead in them, and even hell will give up its dead. Every living soul that has lived since the beginning of time choosing to reject God will be present during this coming judgment. Every person who ever fell overboard while on a ship, died during a shipwreck, or drowned at sea who has rejected God will be present during this time of judgment. God is making this very clear to all who will listen. Every unrighteous soul from the time of Adam and Eve until the end of time, will be standing before God during this judgment.

I have grown up most of my life believing hell was the eternal final place of punishment for those who reject God. John informs us here in Revelation, hell is not the final place of punishment for those who are perishing. During this, "Great White Throne Judgment," hell will literally deliver up those who have rejected God throughout all time. During this time of judgment, a person's eternal soul will be reunited with their body, and they will stand before God. During this time the sea literally will give up the dead to be reunited with their soul for the purpose of being condemned eternally. These spiritually dead souls will be once again reunited with their bodies, and they will eternally be in a state of death, but never able to die. This is the most horrible picture of anything I can ever imagine. The great news is, if you are alive when you read this information there is still hope.

Another important statement the Bible makes concerning this time of judgment, is even the spiritually dead will be judged according to their works. Notice the Bible states books will be opened during this judgment. Records are being kept in heaven relating to the works a person does during their life here on earth. Every sin and every good work a person has done during their entire life is being recorded in books and will be made known. I personally hold to the belief everyone will truly reap what they have sown. A person attending, "The Great White Throne Judgment," will not be declared righteous by his or her works, these people will be punished and held accountable based on the works they have done during their life on earth.

I believe just as the Bible gives us evidence the righteous will be rewarded for their works, the unrighteous will be judged according to their works. The Bible declares God is just, and He judges people according to their works. The Bible tells us men will one day give an account for every idle word spoken and every idle deed committed while living. Jesus gives us some interesting insight relating to this truth in Matthew chapter 12.

> A good man out of the good treasure of the heart bringeth forth good things: and an evil man out of the evil treasure bringeth forth evil things.
>
> But I say unto you, That every idle word that men shall speak, they shall give account thereof in the day of judgment.
>
> For by the words thou shalt be justified, and by the words thou shalt be condemned. (Matthew 12:35–37)

So when the Bible says books will be opened during this time of judgment, I believe we need to take this literally. Jesus stated in the above verses in Matthew people will one day give an account for every idle word that has come out of their mouth at the, "Great White Throne Judgment." Make no mistake about it, the spiritually dead will be judged according to their works while living on earth from the things which are written in these books. The Bible also makes it clear there will be no special considerations given due to a person's earthly status, his or her church membership, or the political party they belong to. The small and great, the rich and the poor, and members of all religious denominations who have not been considered righteous in the sight of God, will be standing before God during this time waiting to be judged.

John in Revelation gives us further clarification as to what group of people will stand before God during this time. This group will include all people who have not been found written in the book of life. If there was one Bible verse everyone should memorize, I would say verse 15 of Revelation chapter 20 would be an important verse to include on the list. If you desire to escape this future horrible time of judgment the answer is simple. Make sure your name is written down in the book of life. God is going to great lengths to warn all who will listen and has made a way through His Son for all who believe.

There is coming a time in the future when all things recorded in the Bible will be completed. This present age, the coming seven-year tribulation, and the millennial (one thousand year) reign of Christ will all come to pass just as the Bible states. A time is coming when death and hell will be cast into the, "Lake of Fire." Yes, hell will one day give up its dead, but not for the purpose of receiving a second chance at righteousness. It will be for the purpose of eternal sentencing and being cast into the, "Lake of Fire." This is the second death. This second death is final and it is eternal. The wonderful thing is this judgment can be avoided. All a person has to do is choose Christ and choose life. Choose Jesus, the Son of the, "Most High God." When Jesus stated today is the day of salvation, He wasn't kidding. We have today, but no one is guaranteed tomorrow.

One last thought concerning the, "Great White Throne Judgment." Those people the Bible refers to as the, "Dead," who are standing before God will not be judged in the same manner as those who are counted righteous through the grace offered by Jesus Christ. These spiritually dead will be judged by every word spoken, and every deed they have done during their entire lifetime. These people will be held accountable for every sin they have personally committed. Those found unworthy will be treated far differently than those counted as righteous. These people here will literally be judged by their works. The Bible makes this very clear.

> When the Son of man shall come in his glory, and all the holy angels with him, then shall he sit upon the throne of his glory:
> And before him shall be gathered all nations: and he shall separate them one from another, as a shepherd divideth his sheep from the goats:
> And he shall set the sheep on his right hand, but the goats on his left. (Matthew 25:31–33)

> Then shall he say also unto them on the left hand, Depart from me, ye cursed, into everlasting fire, prepared for the devil and his angels:
> For I was hungered, and ye gave me no meat: I was thirsty, and ye gave me no drink:
> I was a stranger, and ye took me not in: naked, and ye clothed me not: sick, and in prison, and ye visited me not.
> Then shall they answer him, saying, Lord, when saw we thee an hungred, or athirst, or a stranger, or naked, or sick, or in prison, and did not minister unto thee?

> Then shall he answer them, saying, Verily I
> say unto you, In as much as ye did it not to one
> of the least of these, ye did it not to me.
>
> And these shall go away into everlasting
> punishment: but the righteous into life eternal.
> (Matthew 25:41–46)

Yes, there will be no excuses for those who reject Christ. Their own words and deeds will condemn them. The righteous however, will not be condemned by the sins they have committed. Their sins have been paid for, washed by the blood of Christ, and thrown into a sea of forgetfulness. The Bible tells us in several places there is now no condemnation for those who are in Christ Jesus, and we have not been appointed unto wrath, but unto salvation. The Bible informs us we should comfort one another with these words.

> And when ye spread forth your hands, I
> will hide mine eyes from you: yea, when ye make
> many prayers, I will not hear: your hands are full
> of blood.
>
> Wash you, make you clean; put away the
> evil of your doings from before mine eyes; cease
> to do evil;
>
> Learn to do well; seek judgment, relieve
> the oppressed, judge the fatherless, plead for the
> widow.
>
> Come now, and let us reason together, saith
> the Lord: though your sins be as scarlet, they
> shall be white as snow; though they be red like
> crimson, they shall be as wool. (Isaiah 1:15–18)

The righteous will not be judged according to the sins committed during their time here on earth. They have been forgiven of their sins and trespasses. Those who are righteous have been washed white as snow and will be given white raiment. Yes, the, "King," has given all who are righteous a wedding garment. Christ has also given them a personal invitation to a future wedding banquet and wedding ceremony in heaven. It is my hope and prayer every person reading this book will accept this invitation, and put on the wedding garments of righteousness offered by the, "King of Kings." We have all been given the free will to choose our own path in life. The offer still stands. Jesus informs all who will listen to freely drink from the water of life He offers, promising they will never spiritually thirst again. Jesus stated He is the way, the truth, and the life. Choose Christ today and live.

A Form of Godliness

I will never forget a statement I heard the wife of a missionary family make years ago. This family had spent years in Papua New Guinea doing missionary work sharing the, "Good News," of the gospel to tribes living in the jungle. While this family was on leave visiting friends and family back in the states, the wife stated one thing somewhat troubling is how much they noticed the moral character of people has changed here at home since their last visit. The reason this family noticed changes in the lifestyles and spiritual conditions of people, is because they had been living alienated from a worldly and materialistic lifestyle in the states. This separation from the world enabled them to be more sensitive to changes in people's moral character.

It would be hard to imagine what it would be like to live in a location being unable to watch television during the past twenty years, and all of a sudden being able to watch the world news or current evening programming. I'm sure it would be quite shocking for anyone put in this situation. It has always been stated the best way to cook a frog is not to just throw it in hot water, because it would jump out due to the drastic change in its environment. It is said if a person places a frog in warm water and slowly turns up the heat, the frog will not realize it is being cooked. This is very similar to the way Satan has been slowly deceiving the world for years. During the past twenty to thirty years, the entire world is being steadily desensitized through the media, regular TV programming, and the internet. The perfect way to shape a society changing opinions and beliefs relating to spiritual and moral issues, is through a gradual erosion of a societies moral compass.

The Bible warns the church in many places to not be snared by the cares of this world and the pursuit of material possessions. The Bible informs the brethren over thirty five times to be alert and to be watching and waiting, as if the return of the Lord could come at any moment. We as believers are told to live constantly reminding ourselves this world is not our home, and we are just pilgrims passing through this life. We are also reminded in several scriptures these bodies we have are corruptible and will one day wear out like an old tent. The older I become, I am becoming aware of this fact more and more every day.

We are called to be children of the day, people who are commanded to be aware of what is occurring around us in the world we are currently residing. We are commanded in the Bible to not be ignorant of the signs, times, and season we are living realizing where we are in God's prophetic timetable. I understand the Bible gives us many signs to be looking for as we draw closer to the end of this age. It is my belief a major prophetic sign most are overlooking today is the current spiritual condition of the church.

It was approximately four years ago in 2013 I completed an in-depth study on the books of Jude and Revelation. I can remember one of the main themes to the book of Jude involves warning the brethren on the subject of apostasy. As we approach the end of this current age, the church age, we will see a drastic increase in heresy, and the preaching of false doctrines in the churches. Jude states a characteristic of apostasy or the teaching of false doctrine will almost always include the denial of Christ's deity, and the complete rejection of Jesus as the, "Son of God." Colossians chapter 3 gives us further insight concerning the way we should conduct our lives while here on this earth.

> If ye then be risen with Christ, seek those things which are above, where Christ sitteth on the right hand of God.

Set your affections on things above, not on things on the earth.

For ye are dead, and your life is hid with Christ in God.

When Christ, who is our life, shall appear, then shall ye also appear with him in glory.

Mortify therefore your members which are upon the earth; fornication, uncleanness, inordinate affection, evil concupiscence, and covetousness, which is idolatry:

For which things' sake the wrath of God cometh on the children of disobedience:

In the which ye also walked some time, when ye lived in them.

But now ye also put off all these; anger, wrath, malice, blasphemy, filthy communication out of your mouth.

Lie not to one another, seeing that ye have put off the old man with his deeds;

And have put on the new man, which is renewed in knowledge after the image of him that created him:

Where there is neither Greek nor Jew, circumcision nor uncircumcision, Barbarian, Scythian, bond nor free: but Christ is all, and in all.

Put on therefore, as the elect of God, holy and beloved, bowels of mercies, kindness, humbleness of mind, meekness, longsuffering;

Forbearing one another, and forgiving one another, if any man have a quarrel against any: even as Christ forgave you, so also ye do.

And above all these things put on charity, which is the bond of perfectness. (Colossians 3:1–14)

One interesting concept I am discovering as I continue to study the Bible, is the spiritual problems individuals, families, and entire societies struggle with really have changed very little through the years. Although technology has changed over the centuries, people today still struggle with the same moral and ethical issues as people living hundreds of years in the past. The differences seem not to be the types of sins people struggle with, but in the degree of tolerance a society has for specific behaviors. Most people do not understand this truth, but one of the most dangerous sins God's people can commit, is to stand and do nothing while watching others commit horrible sins against God. I once heard a pastor state, "If you put salt on a wound, it stings beyond description." The Bible tells us we are called to be, "Salt and Light," in a world filled with darkness. Sometimes telling someone the truth can be quite painful, although a person must remember counsel on a spiritual issue must always be given with a spirit of love and humility.

We see here in Colossians Paul is writing a letter to this body of believers addressing the heresy evidently going on inside the church. I don't want to deal with all the issues the Colossians were struggling with, but it seems obvious the church was struggling with issues relating to the supremacy of Jesus Christ. Remember, we have already discussed the fact false doctrine and heresy will almost always involve the denial and rejection Christ is the, "Son of God." What do we see occurring in many churches? We see the outright denial of Christ being the literal, "Son of God," being equal to God. We also see many churches denying Christ being the only way, the only truth, and the only life through which a person can be saved.

It is also quite obvious due to the discussion Paul has with the Colossians, the church was having problems with following rules and traditions and not concentrating on a personal walk and relationship with God. The church was having problems with the interference of human wisdom and keeping church traditions. It is interesting the Bible warns us a sign of the end time church will be having an outward form of godliness, but they will ultimately deny the authority of the Bible, and the majesty of God. Churches such as these will gradually fall away from sound doctrine until they reach the point following sound doctrine will be rejected.

This is the reason Paul is setting the record straight here in Colossians, and directly deals with the issue of the supremacy of Christ. I have definitely noticed a problem with this doctrinal truth in many churches today. This issue goes back to the discussion of building a house. If we lack the foundational knowledge of who Christ is, church becomes nothing more than a social gathering, and a place for rules, laws, and traditions. Let's look what Paul has to say to the Colossian church as well as to all churches today regarding the identity of Christ.

> Who is the image of the invisible God, the firstborn of every creature:
> For by him were all things created, that are in heaven, and that are in earth, visible and invisible, whether they be thrones, or dominions, or principalities, or powers: all things were created by him, and for him:
> And he is before all things, and by him all things consist.
> And he is the head of the body, the church: who is the beginning, the firstborn of the dead; that in all things he might have the preeminence.
> For it pleased the Father that in him should all fullness dwell;
> And, having made peace through the blood of his cross, by him to reconcile all things unto himself; by him, I say, whether they be things in earth, or things in heaven. (Colossians 1:15–20)

I have heard many people state Jesus was a great man, and He was a great teacher. I know this response sounds really nice and is an attempt to be politically correct, but in reality it is completely false. Jesus is either literally the, "Son of God," He was a liar, or He was a lunatic. Colossians informs us Jesus is the very image of the Father, and He was the firstborn over all creation. Now we have more understanding as to why Jesus wept as He approached Jerusalem since He knew He would be rejected by His own people. Now we more completely understand why Jesus addressed the Jewish people in parables.

A lot of people have a real problem with this biblical truth, but according to the Bible Jesus created all things. He created all things on the earth and in heaven. Jesus was involved in the creation of the entire spiritual realm. Jesus and Satan were not created as equal beings. Millions of people today are bowing down to many gods including the, "God of this world," known as Satan. The entire spiritual realm was created by Christ for His purpose. As powerful as Satan is, he is a created being, and his days are numbered. Satan will in the future be thrown into the, "Lake of Fire," along with the antichrist and the false prophet. The book of Ezekiel gives us an interesting description of this person the Bible calls Satan.

> Son of man, take up a lamentation upon the king of Tyrus, and say unto him, Thus saith the Lord God; Thou sealest up the sum, full of wisdom, and perfect in beauty.
>
> Thou hast been in Eden the garden of God; every precious stone was thy covering, the sardius, topaz, and the diamond, the beryl, the onyx, and the jasper, the sapphire, the emerald, and the carbuncle, and gold: the workmanship of the tabrets and of the pipes was prepared in thee in the day that thou was created.
>
> Thou art the anointed cherub that covereth; and I have set thee so: thou wast upon the holy mountain of God; thou hast walked up and down in the midst of the stones of fire.
>
> Thou wast perfect in thy ways from the day that thou was created, till iniquity was found in thee. (Ezekiel 28:12–15)

Ezekiel informs us Satan was once the picture of ultimate wisdom and beauty. Ezekiel describes Satan as a mighty Cherub who was recorded in the book of Genesis as being present in the Garden of Eden. This is the description of the spiritual being that caused Adam and Eve to disobey God, and sin against Him. Satan is evidently such a beautifully created being, the only words Ezekiel can use to describe his appearance is through examples of various kinds of precious stones and gold. It has been said Satan may have been at one time God's second in command. Many believe Satan's appearance may have somewhat resembled a glimmering musical instrument due to the description Ezekiel gives of him. We need to understand these created heavenly beings are literally multidimensional in nature, and the only way they can be described in words is through the symbolic use of precious stones. After all, how can a normal person describe such a magnificently created being as this mighty cherub? Satan is described in the Bible as an, "Angel of Light." There are many scripture references in the Bible where mortal people come in contact with angels, and in most all cases people physically and emotionally cannot deal with the encounter. We need to understand as beautiful and powerful as Satan is, he is a created being. Ezekiel informs us Satan's problem began when he became filled with pride. Because of pride, Satan lost his place of authority on the holy mountain of God.

The Bible records Christ as being responsible for all of creation, and it is He who holds everything together. Christ is the first person to defeat death, and rise from the dead. The same power that resurrected Christ gives all those trusting in Him the hope and promise to one day also defeat death. This explains the verse in Corinthians recited during funerals describing how death for those who trust in Christ now has no victory and no sting. Death has been defeated through the person of Christ Jesus. So yes, I would say it is extremely important which god a person bows down to. All religions are not the same, and all gods are not created equal.

Paul also informs us Christ is the head of the church. The pastor is not the head of the church. Christ alone is the head and the bridegroom of the Church. It is Christ who has been given all authority by the Father. It is Christ who holds the keys to death, hell, and the grave. I'm afraid we're not hearing this message preached and proclaimed in most churches today. This type of message is considered to be over the top, and is not considered politically correct in most churches. This type of message makes people feel uncomfortable. The day a sermon in a church makes a person feel comfortable all the time, is the day you need to find another church. I can assure you the truth of God's word is not what the world wants to hear today. Scripture warns us in the last days men will refuse sound doctrine, and employ teachers who will only tell them what their ears desire to hear.

Paul calls the members of the Colossian church to remain faithful to the gospel of Christ and true doctrine. Paul reminds this church since they have been made alive in Christ their priorities should not be focused on earthly things, but on things above. Paul goes on to remind the church the pursuit of material possessions, lust of the flesh, greed, and other earthly desires in the end are all meaningless.

Paul goes on listing examples of earthly desires people can become obsessed with. We understand no place in the Bible will you find it is a sin to work hard, work smart, and to be a good steward with your time and money. No place in the Bible does it say it is a sin to be wealthy. The Bible does not tell us money is the root of all evil, it informs us the love of money is the root of all evil. Actually, this verse in 1 Timothy goes on to tell us having a consuming desire for money and seeking after riches can lead a person from the faith, causing them to endure many unnecessary hardships. The obsession with wealth and material possessions is what Paul in the book of Corinthians describes as corruptible works such as wood, hay, and stubble. When fire is put to works such as these, they are completely burnt up having no eternal value.

The Bible informs us of a rich young ruler who asked Jesus the question dealing with how to inherit eternal life. Jesus knew the man's heart, and understood this man believed eternal life or salvation could be earned and bought with a price. Jesus taught the man eternal life was a gift, and righteousness was something that could not be earned. We notice Jesus did not deny the fact the man was evidently a morally decent person. Jesus knew the man had an obsession with wealth, so the young ruler was instructed to sell everything he had and give it to the poor. Only then would he become eligible to receive riches in heaven. Yes, Jesus knew the heart of this young wealthy man just like He knows the hearts of all people. Money is not in itself evil, we just need to remember where it comes from, and people should understand what the purpose and responsibilities of being wealthy include. When a person understands God owns and has provided us with everything we have, we are spiritually on the right track. We read the Bible records this young rich ruler walked away with his head hung low because he had great wealth.

This is the reason those in the church are commanded to set their hearts on things above. It is for this reason Paul warns Christians to avoid all types of immoralities such as greed, lust of the eye, lust of the flesh, and all forms of evil. It will be people such as these whose lives are characterized by these types of sins, God will in the future pour out His wrath. Paul is not expecting the average Christian to live their life here on earth without struggling to some degree with sin. Paul is informing those in the church their lives should not be characterized or ruled by these sins. If a person has a true relationship with Christ there will be conviction in one's life concerning sin, and a desire to repent and turn from these behaviors.

Sadly, this is not what we are seeing in many churches today. Today, we many times are witnessing the belief if a person is in fact a Christian, there is a license to live a sinful life due to the grace God offers all believers. According to Paul this is a false teaching, and this type of lifestyle should not be taught in the church. Romans chapter 6 also confirms this truth to us.

> What shall we say then? Shall we continue in sin, that grace may abound?
>
> God forbid. How shall we, that are dead to sin, live any longer therein?
>
> Know ye not, that so many of us were baptized into Jesus Christ were baptized into his death?
>
> Therefore we are buried with him by baptism into death: that like as Christ was raised up from the dead by the glory of the Father, even so we also should walk in newness of life.

For if we have been planted together in the likeness of his death, we shall be also in the likeness of his resurrection:

Knowing this, that our old man is crucified with him, that the body of sin might be destroyed, that henceforth we should not serve sin. (Romans 6:1–6)

Paul states to get rid of any sin in our lives having anything to do with our fleshly nature. These evil paths in life Paul is warning people not to take are easy to be deceived into taking. A daily if not minute by minute renewal of the mind is needed to walk the straight and narrow path the Bible commands us to live. The truth is, it is impossible to be victorious in overcoming our sinful nature through our own efforts. It is only by the power of the Holy Spirit residing in all who receive Him, through regular prayer, and reading God's word these evil desires can be put to death.

Are we going to stumble and make mistakes in our daily lives? Are we going to slip up and say things we end up regretting? The answer is most likely a big, "YES." It is for this reason we have been given grace by a loving God. Instead of being characterized by immorality, rage, and filthy language, the Christian life should be characterized with a heart of patience, kindness, and humility. Paul also warns those in the church should have a forgiving heart and not hold grudges against people. We are called to forgive others, because Christ has forgiven us. Christians should be people who have love for one another.

What types of words should the speech of those belonging to God include? A Christian should speak words that build each other up, and give glory to a holy God. We as Christians should be eager to proclaim the gospel message to all willing to listen. Through a spirit of humility, we should always teach and speak truth giving counsel, warning, and expressing disapproval to those in the church straying from sound doctrine. Our lives should be characterized by gratitude and a forgiving heart, because while we were yet sinners, Christ died for us.

Again, my overall purpose for this book is to give people the information they need to discern the times we are living in. The Bible warns us people in the past failed to interpret the signs and the season they were living in. The Bible warns us it will again be just as it was in the days of Noah and Lot. Jesus also warned us of this prophetic truth in Matthew.

> Enter ye in at the strait gate: for wide is the gate, and broad is the way, that leadeth to destruction, and many there be which go in thereat:
> Because strait is the gate, and narrow is the way, which leadeth unto life, and few there be that find it. (Matthew 7:13–14)

People need to come to grasp with what Jesus is warning us in these two verses above. Of all the hundreds of millions of people that have lived on the earth and are currently living, the majority of these people have and will be deceived into taking the wrong path. Taking the broad road which is the way of the world ends up leading a person to spiritual destruction. Jesus goes to explain few people will choose the narrow road which leads a person to everlasting life.

I believe it would be shocking for most people if they really knew the percentage of those in churches today who really believe Jesus is the way, the only truth, and the only person by which eternal life is obtained. You will find many churches today teach there are many roads to heaven. You will find many churches teaching today good works or church membership will qualify a person to enter heaven. How many churches today teach Jesus Christ is literally the Son of the, "Most High God?" How many churches today teach Satan is literally a, "Mighty Cherub," and he is the leader of millions of spiritual beings residing in the spiritual realm? How many churches today teach and believe there is a literal place the Bible refers to as hell? The thought of being thrown into the abyss sure scared the living daylights out of the demons coming into contact with Jesus. The demons were so frightened of the abyss, they begged Christ to allow them to enter into a herd of pigs. The possession of the pigs by these demons drove them to such a state of madness, they all ran over a cliff and died. Should we be surprised we are seeing an increase in demonic behaviors outwardly manifesting themselves in people these days?

I have become quite surprised while teaching even in a conservative church, the number of different ideas people have concerning what they understand as being spiritual truth. The sad fact is, Jesus is informing us most people will make the wrong spiritual decision during their life, resulting in them being eternally separated from a loving God. The Bible records millions of people will declare to God during the, "Great White Throne Judgment," the many wonderful deeds and miracles they have done in His name. The Bible says God will then tell these people He never knew them, and command them to depart from His presence. There is a big difference between having a head knowledge of God and being one of His sheep.

A major sign we are coming to the end of the age will be most churches falling away refusing to teach sound doctrine, although they will have the appearance of being Godly. These churches will deny the deity of Christ, they will deny the power of the Holy Spirit, and they will deny sound doctrine. We need to understand Satan, "The god of this world," does not have a problem with people going to church and even doing good works. Satan does have a problem with people preaching and teaching the word of God, and proclaiming the message of Jesus being the only way to heaven. The teaching of sound doctrine in the churches as we move closer to the end of the age will become less tolerant in many churches and will eventually be banned.

To gain more insight concerning the end time church we need to take a closer look at chapters 2 and 3 of Revelation. Jesus gives us some very crucial information relating to the history, the current condition, and the future of the church. The sad thing is, I have lived most of my life having a limited understanding of the information given to us in Revelation. The truth is, the study of Revelation is shunned in most churches today. I will be discussing in greater detail the contents and events occurring in Revelation in the next chapter. For now, we will be dealing mainly with the topics specifically related to the spiritual condition of the church.

Before we go on, I would like to discuss some basic concepts of the book of Revelation. This again goes back to the concept of building a house. When we get the foundation right, everything else fits into place and makes more sense. The first point we need to understand is the book of Revelation makes quite clear John the apostle is its author. The, "Book of Revelation," was penned by John during a time when he was exiled on the island of Patmos, being persecuted for his work as a Christian missionary. The words of Revelation were made known to John by an angel sent by Christ. It was God the Father who gave this revelation or unveiling to His Son. The purpose of Revelation given to us in verse 1 is to show His servants what must soon take place. The servants of Christ are being informed the entire book of Revelation is a direct warning from Jesus of what will take place in the future. To be quite honest, this idea was quite shocking to me when I realized this several years ago. Here we have an entire book from Jesus Christ directed to the church saints which is seldom read or studied in most churches today. Revelation 1:1 reads as follows:

> The Revelation of Jesus Christ, which God gave unto him, to shew unto his servants things which must shortly come to pass; and he sent and signified it by his angel unto his servant John. (Revelation 1:1)

Another interesting concept to the book of Revelation is it's the only book in the entire Bible promising a blessing to all who read it, understands it, and takes it to heart. In other words, God expects His servants to read and to understand this book. Considerable knowledge and wisdom can be gained by reading and studying the Bible. The Bible is warning the church servants they should do much more than read the book of Revelation. They should be spiritually listening and holding on to the spiritual truths relayed in this book. As we have discussed earlier, knowledge about God or even a belief in God does not make a person righteous in God's eyes. It is a personal faith or reliance in God placing a person in right standing with Him.

These blessings are promised to all who read, hear, and hold onto the truths written in this book.

> Blessed is he that readeth, and they that hear the words of this prophecy, and keep those things which are written therein: for the time is at hand. (Revelation 1:3)

Another spiritual truth we need to understand when studying Revelation is the book is divided into three main sections. When a person reads the book with this understanding much of the confusion most people once had with Revelation is resolved. The Bible gives us this outline in Revelation chapter 1:19. John is here being instructed personally by Jesus Christ to write down the things he had formerly seen, the things which are happening in the present tense, and those things taking place in the future.

We discover in the first chapter of Revelation John is recording the things he had seen. John is attempting to describe a literal glimpse of Jesus Christ while he was, "In the Spirit." John was commanded during this time to write down what he saw, and send it to the seven churches listed in chapters 2 and 3. John then in chapter 1 gives us an incredible description of Christ. It was this description of Jesus John was commanded to write down in chapter 1. This fulfilled the first section of Revelation 1:19 where the things John had seen are written down.

> I John, who also am your brother, and companion in tribulation, and in the kingdom and patience of Jesus Christ, was in the isle that is called Patmos, for the word of God, and the testimony of Jesus Christ.
>
> I was I the Spirit on the Lord's day, and heard behind me a great voice, as of a trumpet,
>
> Saying, I am the Alpha and Omega, the first and the last: and, What thou seest, write in a book, and send it to the seven churches which are in

Asia; unto Ephesus, and unto Smyrna, and unto Pergamos, and unto Thyatira, and unto Sardis, and unto Philadelphia, and unto Laodicea.

And I turned to see the voice that spake with me. And being turned, I saw seven golden candlesticks;

And in the midst of the seven candlesticks one like unto the Son of man, clothed with a garment down to the foot, and girt about the paps with a golden girdle.

His head and his hairs were white like wool, as white as snow; and his eyes were as a flame of fire;

And his feet like unto fine brass, as if they burned in a furnace; and his voice as the sound of many waters.

And he had in his right hand seven stars: and out of his mouth went a sharp twoedged sword: and his countenance was as the sun shineth in his strength.

And when I saw him, I fell at his feet as dead. And he laid his right hand upon me, saying unto me, Fear not; I am the first and the last:

I am he that liveth, and was dead; and behold, I am alive for evermore, Amen; and have the keys of hell and of death.

Write the things which thou hast seen, and the things which are, and the things which shall be hereafter;

The mystery of the seven stars which thou sawest in my right hand, and the seven golden candlesticks. The seven stars are the angels of the seven churches: and the seven candlesticks which thou sawest are the seven churches. (Revelation 1:9–20)

The previous verses gives insight concerning the vision Jesus commanded John to write down. These verses describe the events

John had seen. One of the amazing things I have discovered about the Bible is it does interpret itself. It will usually take some digging, but the Bible will always be the best source in answering questions arising from studying the scriptures. An example of this is given in this same scriptural text where the Bible informs us the seven stars and seven golden lampstands are seven angels over the churches, and the seven lampstands are the seven churches.

Notice the detailed description of Jesus Christ given to us by John. The robe and the golden sash around His chest reveal Jesus as our great, "High Priest." The Bible tells us Christ came of the order of Melchizedek in the sense He was both a, "Priest," and a, "King." The hair of Jesus being pictured white as snow refers to His wisdom and dignity. The eyes of blazing fire refer to His penetrating insight. The feet of bronze refer to His majesty and qualifications as judge over all creation. The double edge sword coming out of His mouth refers to Christ being the, "Living Word," who is given authority to judge all who dwell upon the earth.

For those who attempt to deny this is a literal picture of Christ, Jesus informs John He is the, "First, the Last, and the Living One." Jesus then informs He is the person who was dead and is now alive for ever and ever, and He holds the keys to death and Hades.

John was also commanded by Christ to write down the things happening in the present tense. This primarily would include the time in which John was living, and also during the time the seven churches of Asia existed, continuing through the duration of the church age. The characteristics of these seven churches are discussed in chapters 2 and 3 of Revelation. It is these individual letters from Jesus to the seven churches we will be taking a closer look at. In Revelation chapter 4, we see John discussing events taking place after the church age or age of grace has come to a close. We will be dealing with this final section of Revelation in the following chapter, which basically begins with chapter 4 continuing through the end of the book.

In review, the book of Revelation can be divided into three distinct categories. The first two categories are intended for and directed to the church saints living on earth during the church age. The last category or phase of Revelation reveals a detailed description to a future time of tribulation continuing for a period of seven years, climaxing during the second coming of Christ to earth. After the second coming of Christ there will be a literal millennial or one-thousand-year reign of Christ on earth. During this time there will be peace on the earth. This will be the time when the lion will lay down with the lamb, and the swords will be beat into plowshares.

The third and final section of Revelation records the, "Great White Throne Judgment," where those who are spiritually dead will be judged according to their deeds. During this future time Satan, the antichrist, and the false prophet will be cast into the, "Lake of Fire." Everything will be made new including a new heaven and a new earth during this time. Also during this time, the holy city, "New Jerusalem," will descend from heaven hovering above the earth. This city coming down from heaven will be adorned as a bride in all her beauty, and will literally be the heavenly tabernacle of God dwelling among men.

It is interesting the Bible in several places describes this city as a, "Great Mountain." As stated earlier, I have always wondered if this city descending out of heaven will be in the shape of a pyramid and not a cube as many believe. Revelation gives us an elaborate description of this city including the throne of God, and the river of life. We will be discussing the details of this city called, "New Jerusalem," in more detail as we deal with the third section in Revelation John is instructed to write down. In review, the three categories of Revelation include the following:

- The things which thou hast seen. This section is recorded primarily in Revelation chapter 1.
- The things which are. This section includes Revelation chapters 2 and 3, and deals with a detailed study of seven literal churches existing during the church age.
- The things which shall be hereafter. This final section would include the events in Revelation chapters 4 to 22.

It is this second section of Revelation dealing with, "The Things Which Are," we will now be spending some time on. This section deals with seven specific churches. I believe it is a prophetic picture of the time of the church age in which we are now living. It is somewhat amusing the number of articles I have read, and the videos I have watched where people state we are living in the time of the seven-year tribulation. The seven-year tribulation which the Bible refers to as the time of, "Jacob's Trouble," or, "Daniel's 70th Week," is one of the most factually documented events in the entire Bible. We are not currently living in the time of, "Jacob's Trouble." The Jewish temple is not yet rebuilt and currently in operation, and the prophesied two witnesses have not yet shown up on the scene. The 144,000 having, "God's," name written on their foreheads evangelizing the world has not yet taken place. These 144,000 cannot begin their ministry on earth until the, "Restrainer," is removed which is the Holy Spirit indwelling all true believers. These 144,000 who are sealed by God will bring in a great harvest of souls during the tribulation period. Most importantly, the antichrist who signs this seven-year covenant with Israel has not shown his identity. The antichrist will sign what the Bible refers as the, "Covenant of Death," with the nation of Israel.

At the beginning of the chapter we looked at verses listed in chapter 3 of Colossians. One issue I've stressed over and over again in this book, is words and patterns are very important in the Bible. I know there is disagreement in the church today concerning the time the church saints will be snatched away. It is sad there are even churches today denying this event will take place. When the Bible informs us the dead in Christ will rise first, then those who are alive will be caught up together with them to meet Christ in the air, this is exactly what the Christian needs to believe. There is another verse given in Colossians all people need to read very closely which is given below.

> When Christ, who is our life, shall appear,
> then shall ye also appear with him in glory.
> (Colossians 3:4)

All people need to learn to put aside their opinions and pride concentrating on what the Bible is telling us. I have come to under-

stand what I believe, or what I think about the Bible is not important. What's important is what the Bible says. In the verse above the
Bible tells us when Christ appears and comes in great glory, we who
are, "in Christ," will appear with Him during His second coming to
earth. How can the righteous appear with Christ during His second
coming if He had not previously come for His bride. I will go out
on a limb and make a statement concerning the number of days the
Bible tells us this future time of tribulation will last. I believe the
Bible is in all cases dead on accurate concerning times and dates. I
have touched on this subject earlier when I discussed Joshua's long
day. Didn't Solomon tell us what has been done, will be done again?

The Bible tells us in several places the seven-year tribulation
will be based on a 360-day calendar year. It is interesting both the
Bible and the calendars of several ancient civilizations gives evidence
of a 360-day calendar year. I hold to the belief it is possible the earth
will go through some sort of future cosmic or seismic event causing
the earth's rotation to again be slowed down. This could cause a calendar year to be 360 days in length during the tribulation period.
It may be at such a time as this those, "In Christ," would suddenly
be removed from the earth, and the world would be plunged into
darkness. Because of this, the sudden disappearance of millions of
people leaving the earth may not be immediately noticed. For those
who find this reasoning impossible to believe, below is a statement
from Barbara Marciniak who is a New Age author and Channeler
in her book titled, "Bringers of the Dawn." Notice Barbara through
the channeling of a spirit, is being instructed the sudden removal of
millions of people from the earth will occur during a time of earth
changes.

THE PEOPLE WHO LEAVE THE
PLANET DURING THE TIME OF EARTH
CHANGES DO NOT FIT IN HERE ANY
LONGER, AND THEY ARE STOPPING THE
HARMONY OF EARTH. WHEN THE TIME
COMES THAT PERHAPS 20 MILLION
PEOPLE LEAVE THE PLANET AT ONE TIME

THERE WILL BE A TREMENDOUS SHIFT IN THE CONSCIOUSNESS FOR THOSE WHO ARE REMAINING. Pg. 92 Barbara Marciniak, Bringers of the Dawn: Teachings from the Pleiadians, Bear and Co., 1992

The Bible tells us the signing of a seven-year covenant will be the event that will start the clock ticking down to a period of untold trouble and tribulation lasting for seven years. This covenant the antichrist will make with Israel and possibly other nations is referred to in Isaiah chapter 28 as a, "Covenant With Death." The Bible tells us the first half of this seven-year event will last 42 months or 1,260 days, and the last half of this event will last 42 months or 1,260 days. The Bible informs us midway into this seven-year period of time, the antichrist will desecrate an established Jewish temple making the sacrifices required by the Old Testament Law cease during this time. This event is referred to as the, "Abomination of Desolation."

As we continue on looking at seven specific churches personally selected by Jesus in chapters 2 and 3, it will become more and more obvious we are not currently living during the time of, "Daniel's 70th Week." This future time will include some of the most devastating cataclysmic events ever occurring on earth being far worse than the days of Noah. During this future time of tribulation, approximately eighty percent of earth's population will perish from God's judgment being poured out upon the entire earth. Listen very carefully to the words of Isaiah in chapter 13 concerning this future coming time of wrath. This time of wrath is being stored up for all people refusing the truth, and the gift of salvation God freely offers to all people.

> I have commanded my sanctified ones, I have also called my mighty ones for mine anger, even them that rejoice in my highness.
> The noise of a multitude in the mountains, like as of a great people; a tumultuous noise of the kingdoms of nations gathered together: the Lord of hosts mustereth the host of the battle.

They come from a far country, from the end of heaven, even the Lord, and the weapons of his indignation, to destroy the whole land.

Howl ye; for the day of the Lord is at hand; it shall come as a destruction from the Almighty.

Therefore shall all hands be faint, and every man's heart shall melt:

And they shall be afraid: pangs and sorrows shall take hold of them; they shall be in pain as a woman that travaileth: they shall be amazed one at another; their faces shall be as flames.

Behold, the day of the Lord cometh, cruel both with wrath and fierce anger, to lay the land desolate: and he shall destroy the sinners thereof out of it.

For the stars of heaven and the constellations thereof shall not give their light: the sun shall be darkened in his going forth, and the moon shall not cause her light to shine.

And I will punish the world for their evil, and the wicked for their iniquity; and I will cause the arrogancy of the proud to cease, and will lay low the haughtiness of the terrible.

I will make a man more precious than fine gold; even a man than the golden wedge of Ophir.

Therefore I will shake the heavens, and the earth shall remove out of her place, in the wrath of the Lord of hosts, and in the day of his fierce anger. (Isaiah 13:3–13)

The, "Day of the Lord," is coming, and it will be a day unlike anyone could imagine. Who is this coming day of God's wrath being prepared for? It is for the unrighteous, the arrogant, the wicked, and the proud. It is a day prepared for all who rebel against God and have rejected the sacrifice of His Son, His only Son, Jesus Christ.

Notice Isaiah states there will be war, famine, pestilence, and disease. During this time, God will literally shake the heavens, and the earth will be removed from its place being tossed to and fro as a drunkard. There will be great earthquakes and tsunamis occurring on this earth such as never seen before. There will be such cataclysmic events occurring in the heavens, the Bible declares men's hearts will fail in fear looking at those things coming upon the earth.

This period of time will also include literal manifestations of the spiritual realm on earth. Satan and his hoard of evil angels and demonic spirits will literally manifest themselves on earth, being allowed to rule and reign on the earth during this time of coming wrath. It will be a time worse than the days of Noah and Sodom. Yes, what has happened in the past will repeat itself again. The condition of people's hearts will also be the same as it was during the days of Noah and Sodom. People will be so consumed with their own evil desires living unholy lives, most people will miss the opportunity of grace freely offered to anyone who believes. When the Bible states there is no condemnation and no appointed wrath for those, "In Christ," this is exactly what the Bible means.

One reason I feel compelled to write this book is somebody needs to tell people the truth. You will not hear this message of warning and study these topics in most churches today. I understand telling people the truth is not a popular message and it's not the message most people want to hear, but it is the message people need to hear. God loves all people, and this is the reason He has given us His word. The Bible is clear, God has made a way of escape for all who believe in Him. It is God's will none should perish, but all will inherit eternal life.

In Revelation chapters 2 and 3 we see Jesus commanding John to write down very specific information concerning seven literal churches existing in Asia. The churches John is commanded to write were: Ephesus, Smyrna, Pergamos, Thyatira, Sardis, Philadelphia, and Laodicea.

As we take a deeper look into these seven specific churches. The first thing we need to clearly understand is these were literal churches existing in Asia during the beginning of the church age. An interesting question a person needs to consider is why would Jesus pick these seven specific churches out of the many existing during this time? Another question relates to why Jesus picked these seven churches in this specific order? I have always believed and understood God was personally involved in the writing of every letter, every word, every verse, and every book of the Bible. There is a verse in 2 Peter relating to this biblical truth.

> For the prophecy came not in old time by the
> will of man: but holy men of God spake as they
> were moved by the Holy Ghost (2 Peter 1:21).

We know the Bible was written by over 30 authors over a period of hundreds of years who as stated above were being actively persuaded and moved by God. We know many of these authors were not living during the same period of time. The first thing a person notices while examining the sixty-six books of the Bible is the continuity and agreement with thousands of names, places, and dates. Any rational thinking person would conclude human beings alone could not be responsible for writing the Bible.

We also need to keep in mind the hundreds of prophecies in the Bible written many times hundreds of years in advance of their fulfillment that have come to pass with unbelievable accuracy. Many critics will argue the date of authorship of Daniel stating it would be humanly impossible these prophecies could be recorded with such pinpoint accuracy. Yes, these critics are right, it would be humanly impossible for man alone to create and write such a book as the Bible.

> And the Word was made flesh, and dwelt
> among us, (and we beheld his glory, the glory as
> of the only begotten of the Father,) full of grace
> and truth. John 1:14

Yes, the Bible truly is the, "Living Word." The Bible is not a book of fairy tales and half-truths. The Bible is a book to be taken literally. The Bible is a historical recording of literal events that have happened in the past. The Bible is also a book of prophecy warning all people who will listen of prophetic events yet to take place in the future.

I would like to spend a little time dealing with these seven churches given as examples to the saints personally by Jesus. Why would Jesus choose these seven churches of the hundreds to choose from? It is interesting the number seven in the Bible refers to completion. Tremendous amounts of spiritual and prophetic information is revealed to us by studying each individual church. I also have come to believe these seven churches handpicked by Jesus, collectively may be revealing clues concerning the entire church age from beginning to end.

An important truth to keep in mind is the first three chapters of Revelation are more than likely the most important chapters for the church today. Chapters 2 and 3 in Revelation are personal letters from Jesus Christ to be used as spiritual evaluations for individuals as well as the entire church. The question needing to be asked is why aren't these letters being studied in most churches today? I must admit, I spent most of my fifty-six years growing up in church having very little understanding as to the meaning of these two chapters. Some key points I would ask all people to consider as we take a closer look at these churches would be the following:

- The title and description of each church relates to each individual church's spiritual condition.
- The unique way Jesus Christ addresses Himself to each church relates to the spiritual condition of each church.
- The specific order in which each church is discussed may be a prophetic picture of the progression of spiritual problems arising in the churches throughout the church age.
- The seven letters collectively as well as individually provide spiritual insight benefitting the entire church body.
- The spiritual condition given by Christ of each church compared to the perceived spiritual condition of each church is remarkably different.

- The seven churches collectively may be giving us a spiritual picture of the entire church age from Pentecost until the catching away of the bride of Christ.

As we study these letters to the churches, we need to keep in mind these verses are dealing with the current period of time in which we now living. Revelation chapters 2 and 3 discuss issues which have occurred, and will occur during the period of time known as the church age. Let's now take a brief look at each of these seven churches. The spiritual insight the Bible reveals to us concerning these seven churches was an eye-opening experience for me as I began to understand them. The first letter deals with the church of Ephesus.

> Unto the angel of the church of Ephesus write; These things saith he that holdeth the seven stars in his right hands, who walketh in the midst of the seven golden candlesticks;
>
> I know thy works, and thy labour, and thy patience, and how thou canst not bear them which are evil: and thou hast tried them which say they are apostles, and are not, and hast found them liars:
>
> And hast borne, and hast patience, and for my name's sake hast laboured, and hast not fainted.
>
> Nevertheless I have somewhat against thee, because thou hast left thy first love.
>
> Remember therefore from whence thou are fallen, and repent, and do the first works; or else I will come unto thee quickly, and will remove the candlestick out of his place, except thou repent.
>
> But this thou hast, that thou hatest the deeds of the Nicolaitanes, which I also hate.
>
> He that hath an ear, let him hear what the Spirit saith unto the churches; To him that overcometh will I give to eat of the tree of life,

which is in the midst of the paradise of God.
(Revelation 2:1–7)

The city of Ephesus was one of the largest cities existing during that time. The city was architecturally one of the most beautiful cities in the area. Ephesus was an extremely wealthy city having a major harbor. The primary deity worshipped in the city and surrounding area was the goddess, "Diana." The temple of Diana located in this city was known as one of the great wonders of the world. Both male and female prostitution was included as a part of the worship experience in this temple. As one studies history, they will find there is almost always a direct link between sexual immorality and the occult.

The church of Ephesus received a personal letter from Jesus Christ. The letter is written to the angel or messenger of the Ephesian church. Chapter 1 of Revelation reveals the seven stars are the seven angels to the churches, and the seven golden lampstands are the seven churches. I personally hold to the belief the angels to the seven churches is referencing a literal angel who is watching over each individual church. We find many examples in scripture where angels or spirits watch over individuals or even nations and governments. It is interesting the book of Daniel refers to angels as, "Watchers." The book of Enoch makes reference to these watchers as being both good and evil angels. The name, "Watcher," is probably referring to their characteristics of guarding or keeping watch. We also need to understand the word, "Angel," given here can also mean, "Messenger." It is for this reason some believe the word angel used here in chapters 2 and 3 is making reference to the pastor of each specific church.

Jesus makes it very clear He is very aware of the works being conducted at Ephesus. Jesus commends this church for their hard work and perseverance. Jesus also states He is aware this church does not tolerate those who claim to be righteous, but are found to be false teachers proclaiming a false doctrine. This church is commended for running the race and not growing weary.

It is amazing today we constantly hear many people and even churches making pleas for tolerance. It is interesting here we see Jesus complimenting the church at Ephesus because they have no tolerance for false teaching or false doctrine of any kind. Today tolerance is sold in the churches as a way to be kind and understanding, and a way to increase church enrollment. Jesus commends Ephesus for having no tolerance with wicked people creeping into the churches. The apostle Paul in Acts previously warned the Ephesian elders savage wolves would later creep into the church teaching false doctrine.

> Take heed therefore unto yourselves, and to all the flock, over the which the Holy Ghost hath made you overseers, to feed the church of God, which he hath purchased with his own blood.
>
> For I know this, that after my departing shall grievous wolves enter in among you, not sparing the flock.
>
> Also of your own selves shall men arise, speaking perverse things, to draw away disciples after them.
>
> Therefore watch, and remember, that by the space of three years I ceased not to warn every one night and day with tears.
>
> And now, brethren, I commend you to God, and to the word of his grace, which is able to build you up, and to give you an inheritance among all them which are sanctified. (Acts 20:28–32)

Paul speaks two very powerful words to the church in the above verse. If there were ever two tasks the church should be doing today, it would be, "Watching," and, "Remembering." Paul proclaims the message the church was purchased by the shed blood of Christ. I am increasingly concerned what we are seeing today in many churches is the assembling together, fellowship, singing, and maybe even praying, but the shed blood of Christ being required for the forgiveness of sins is not being proclaimed. Discussing Christ shedding His blood on a cruel cross for the sins of the world is not a popular subject being discussed in many churches today.

It is interesting the church at Ephesus is commended by Christ for their strong stance on defending church doctrine. Paul had earlier warned the Ephesians a day was coming when false teachers with their false doctrines would one day attempt to destroy their church. Evidently the church at Ephesus had heeded Paul's previous warning. I have always liked the way Jude deals with the subject of apostasy. Jude was compelled by the Holy Spirit, strongly commanding and urging the brethren to contend for the faith. God's word as well as the church was definitely under attack during the time of Ephesus, and this spiritual attack will continue to progress through the end of the church age. Jude was urging the church brethren to take a stand for the truth of God's word and the gospel message. Paul here in the verses above was previously warning the church elders to continually be watching for coming apostasy and false teaching entering the church. Paul is holding these elders accountable, and reminding these spiritual leaders they are the overseers of the flock.

What happens when salt loses its saltiness? The Bible states the only thing bad salt is good for is to be poured out in the streets and be trampled on by men. When a church is no longer salt and light, that church becomes no more than a building full of people who have the appearance of godliness. These people will deny the word of God, the power of the Holy Spirit, and deny Jesus Christ as the, "Son of God."

It would seem Christ has given the church at Ephesus a passing grade. At the end of the letter to Ephesus, we find Jesus has one major concern with this church. Jesus informs this church they have lost their first love. What was Jesus trying to tell these people? This church spent a tremendous amount of energy following correct biblical doctrine, and preventing heresy within the church which are in themselves good practices. I believe Jesus was trying to inform this church He was more concerned about a heart relationship with Him instead of a head relationship. Jesus wanted their love and devotion and wanted His followers to seek Him with their hearts.

It's interesting the Bible states of all the spiritual gifts identified in the Bible, the most important gift is love. No other spiritual gift matters if it is not done with a spirit of compassion and love. The

Bible informs us over and over if we are indeed in Christ, we should love and have compassion for one another. The Bible tells us whoever loves his brother lives in the light, but whoever hates his brother lives in darkness. Even when correcting a brother or sister in Christ concerning sin in their life, if a correction cannot be accomplished with humility and love, it should be left alone.

Jesus urges this church at Ephesus to repent and renew their love for Him. Notice the warning Jesus gives to this church if they fail to repent and turn their hearts back to God. Jesus tells this church He will remove their lampstand from its place. Jesus did not tell these brothers and sisters they would lose their salvation. Jesus tells this church the lack of repentance would cause this church to be judged, resulting in a loss of their spiritual power and effectiveness as a church.

A general concept concerning these seven letters to the churches is we need to understand these are letters to physical churches having a name, and a physical address. An individual must have this basic understanding concerning these letters. We will discover as we work through these seven letters, we will see different reactions and responses from Christ concerning various groups of individuals attending each of these churches. We need to understand just because a person attends or is a member of any particular church; nowhere in the Bible does it say an individual is considered righteous in the eyes of God. It is only through a personal relationship and belief in Christ, one is counted righteous before God. Remember, Jesus stated to Nicodemus you must be born of spirit to inherit eternal life.

It would appear most of the members in the Ephesian church knew God in a personal way. Jesus calls this church to remember their first love. A husband cannot tell his wife they need to remember the love they once had for one another, if they were never married in the first place. A very startling reality we will discover as we work through these letters, is we will discover all people attending church are not part of His bride. According to the Bible, these people are not defined as an, "Overcomer." This is a shocking truth needing to be taught and explained in most churches today. It's not about membership or the following of strict doctrine. It's about a loving personal relationship with God. It's the same idea as with the marriage relationship. If a husband and wife will just worry about loving each other with their entire being, everything else will work itself out.

Jesus makes one last complimentary statement to the church at Ephesus. Jesus finds favor with this church because of their stance against a group known as the, "Nicolaitans." It is believed this was a group of heretics who followed the teachings of a person named Nicolas. It is believed this group perverted the concept of grace by using it as a license to sin. In other words, anyone who was saved by grace through faith in Christ had a license to sin. These people believed they were free to live a sexually immoral life because of God's grace if they chose to do so. According to the Bible, this is a false teaching. The Bible commands in several places true Christians should live a life characterized by holy living. Yes, the Christian may sin and stumble in their Christian walk, but overall their lives should be characterized by a desire to live a holy life.

Jesus makes one last plea to all having an ear to hear. Notice this plea goes out to all churches. Whenever the Bible is informing all people that have ears to listen, that is exactly what people need to do. Statements in the Bible such as these are almost always to prepare the reader for something important about to be stated. Jesus states it is the, "Overcomers," in this church which will be given the right to eat of the, "Tree of Life," which is in the garden of God. Some Bible versions will substitute the word, "Victorious," instead of the word, "Overcomer," in these verses.

So the big question is what group of people is Jesus talking to here in Revelation? Who are these people the Bible is referring to as being, "Overcomers?" As always, the answer to the question can be found in the Bible. There are several verses in the Bible we could use to answer this question, but I will use a couple verses in 1 John due to the undeniable clarity these verses give us.

Whosover believeth that Jesus is the Christ is born of God: and every one that loveth him that begat loveth him also that is begotten of him.

By this we know that we love the children of God, when we love God, and keep his commandments.

For this is the love of God, that we keep his commandments: and his commandments are not grievous.

For whatsoever is born of God overcometh the world: and this is the victory that overcometh the world, even our faith.

Who is he that overcometh the world, but he that believeth that Jesus is the Son of God?

This is he that came by water and blood, even Jesus Christ; not by water only, but by water and blood. And it is the Spirit that beareth witness, because the Spirit is truth. (1 John 5:1–6)

So who is an, "Overcomer." It is any person who is born of God believing Jesus is the "Son of God." As we bring this study on Ephesus to an end, let's take just a moment to come to a few conclusions. The church of Ephesus was the first church in the list of seven letters reported on by Jesus Christ. These letters to the churches were given to the church saints and all churches for the purpose of personal examination and correction where needed. As we continue this study with the seven churches we will discover certain groups of people in these churches will be specifically defined as "Overcomers," in all seven letters. There is a tremendous amount of confusion today concerning the identity of this group of people, but the Bible has already very clearly answered this question for us. The, "Overcomer," is anyone born of God and believes Jesus is the, "Son of God." The answer could not be any clearer.

Jesus describes this church as a group of believers who have lost their first love. Jesus had many good things to say about this church, but rebuked them concerning their lack of love for Him. We see by the way this church was addressed by Christ, this church as a collective body of believers appeared to have the capacity to repent and to correct their ways. According to *Hitchcock's* Bible Names Dictionary, the biblical meaning for the name, "Ephesus," is, "Desirable." Jesus saw this church overall as a desirable church. As we continue briefly taking a look at the other six churches, we will notice some startling conclusions and patterns these seven churches will teach us. There is much wisdom to be gained when we realize every name, and every word of the Bible has meaning.

The second letter given to John to write down and give to the churches was written to the church of Smyrna. Smyrna was a very large city in Turkey which may have had a population close to one hundred thousand citizens. Smyrna was an extremely wealthy and beautiful city having a large harbor. Smyrna had several temples including the temple of, "Zeus," who was the father of the gods. This city was a faithful ally to Rome and probably enforced worship to Caesar, the emperor of Rome.

We will again see the name Smyrna will have a direct relationship to the content in the letter given by Jesus Christ. The meaning of the name Smyrna is, "Myrrh." Myrrh is a resin obtained from certain trees used for perfumes, medicines, and incense. Myrrh was and is still used by the Jewish people as an anointing oil and fragrance used during religious ceremonies. The body of Jesus was embalmed with myrrh. The Magi from the East brought gold, frankincense, and myrrh as gifts when they came to worship Jesus as a young child. Since Smyrna means, "Myrrh," we can conclude the church of Smyrna speaks of a church characterized by suffering and death. Let's go ahead and take a look at what Jesus had to say concerning this church.

> And unto the angel of the church in Smyrna write; These things saith the first and the last, which was dead, and is alive.
> I know thy works, and tribulation, and poverty, (but thou art rich) and I know the blas-

phemy of them which say they are Jews, and are not, but are the synagogue of Satan.

Fear none of those things which thou shalt suffer: behold, the devil shall cast some of you into prison, that ye may be tried; and ye shall have tribulation ten days: be thou faithful unto death, and I will give thee a crown of life.

He that hath an ear, let him hear what the Spirit saith unto the churches; He that over-cometh shall not be hurt of the second death. (Revelation 2:8–11)

One interesting thing to note from the verses above is we notice the church of Smyrna is not rebuked in any way from Jesus. Jesus makes no negative comments about this church. We will later on discover there will be only one other church besides Smyrna where Jesus has nothing negative to say.

I find it is very interesting the way Jesus addresses this church. Jesus knew this church would go through horrible persecution and suffering. Jesus addresses this church in this way because He person-ally understood the idea of suffering and was the ultimate example of suffering. Jesus informed this church He was, "The first and the last, who was dead, and now is alive." We discover this letter from Jesus to Smyrna is for the most part, a letter of encouragement.

The word, "Tribulation," spoken by Jesus here brings confusion to many who misunderstand the meaning of the word. Jesus is not telling this church they are going through, "The Great Tribulation," or the, "Day of the Lord," which takes place after the church age has come to completion. Jesus is merely helping us to understand the circumstances these saints were living in and will go through, would include tremendous persecution, tribulation, and even death. The Bible warns the Christian in many places we should be prepared to go through tribulation during our time on earth. Jesus stated the world hated and persecuted Him, and the world would also hate all who believe in Him.

It is a historical fact during this time in history, the Romans under the dictatorship of the Caesar's tortured and killed thousands if not millions of Christians during this time. Jesus again confirms with this church He is aware of their deeds and the afflictions they were going through. We need to keep in mind Jesus knew the suffering this church went through, and He is aware of the suffering Christians are going through today. The Bible tells us there will in the future be a heavy price to pay for all who have shed innocent blood and have tortured and killed those living for Christ. The wrath of God is being prepared for such people.

As I have stated earlier, one thing we will realize is the misconceptions these seven churches will have concerning their spiritual condition. This church saw themselves as being poor due to the poverty and persecution they were experiencing, but Jesus informed this church they were spiritually rich. The comment from Jesus concerning this church being rich is interesting, because we will later discover there is another church who saw themselves as being rich in need of nothing. Jesus stated to this church they were spiritually poor and pitiful.

Jesus also deals with a doctrinal problem existing during this time with some of the Jewish religious leaders. The specifics of some of these problems were probably discussed in Acts chapter 15. These doctrinal issues arose from the religious leaders demanding proper worship should include all Gentiles being circumcised, and these members should also be forced to follow the laws of Moses. Of course, Peter addresses this issue by stating the Gentiles received the Holy Spirit so they must also due to the condition of their hearts be accepted into the body of Christ. These religious leaders were claiming new converts had to first become a follower of Jewish law before they could become a Christian. We see Jesus calling this absolute heresy and referring to these religious leaders as belonging to the synagogue of Satan.

Since I have made reference to Acts chapter 15, there are a few verses we must take a look at. These verses are one of the many forming a pattern as to when the church age will come to completion and

Daniel's 70th Week will commence. This coming period of time is also referred to as, "The Seven-Year Tribulation Period."

> And after they had held their peace, James answered, saying, Men and brethren, hearken unto me:
> Simeon hath declared how God at the first did visit the Gentiles, to take out of them a people for his name.
> And to this agree the words of the prophets; as it is written,
> After this I will return, and will build again the tabernacle of David, which is fallen down; and I will build again the ruins thereof, and I will set it up:
> That the residue of men might seek after the Lord, and all the Gentiles, upon whom my name is called, saith the Lord, who doeth all these things. (Acts 15:13–17)

There are some interesting words from Amos chapter 9 being quoted above in the book of Acts. God has not forgotten about the nation and children of Israel. According to the Bible the tabernacle of David will be rebuilt again, and temple worship will be restored after the church age has come to an end. Then Christ will return physically to this earth reaffirming His covenant with the people of Israel. Christ will again return physically to earth when the people of Israel confess their sins, and call upon Him to rescue them.

Jesus goes on to encourage this church by letting them know He will walk with them through their suffering. There is no promise to this church from Jesus they will escape this suffering. It is a historical fact the church has went through and continues to go through persecution, suffering, and death since the beginning of the church age. Jesus calls this church to be faithful even unto death. Jesus then promises all believers in this church they will one day receive a crown of life.

The letter to Smyrna ends with Christ making a similar comment to that of the church of Ephesus. The letter to Smyrna is also intended for all churches, for all who have an ear and are willing to listen. Jesus again makes a similar promise to the overcomers in this church because of their trust and belief in Christ. The promise made by Jesus is all who, "Overcome," will escape the, "Second Death." A concept all people must understand is although this church went through horrible persecution where most of these saints ended up losing their lives, this was not a result of God's wrath. God's wrath has never or never will be poured out upon those He loves. Remember the promise God made to Abraham concerning the righteous. Abraham stopped at the number 10, but God showed us He will go the extra mile for just one righteous person.

Jesus spoke to the church at Smyrna as if He knew this church was going to die a physical death for the cause of Christ. The first death which is a physical death deals with the separation of the soul from the body. The second death refers to a eternal separation from God which is the eternal separation of the soul from the presence of God. All human beings have a soul, but all human beings do not have the spirit of God living inside them. We need to never forget the words of Jesus to Nicodemus. Jesus stated one must be born of spirit to have eternal life. The born-again believer, those who are born of spirit, will not experience the second death due to their sin debt being paid for on the cross. So the church of Smyrna which name means, "Myrrh," which is symbolic of suffering, is known as the suffering church.

The third letter to the churches is written to the church at Pergamum. *Hitchcock's Bible Names Dictionary* defines the name, "Pergamum," as meaning, "Height or Elevation." The church at Pergamum is historically known as the church which is located at, "Satan's Seat." The church at Pergamum spiritually speaking is known as the church of compromise and tolerance. This church became so doctrinally compromised they were severely rebuked by Jesus for allowing false teachers and false doctrines to creep into the church. During this time, the church began to shift from being persecuted to becoming mixed with the world. It was a time where the comingling of Christianity and paganism was beginning to take place.

The city of Pergamum was located approximately seventy miles north of Smyrna. The city was very rich and prosperous. Pergamum became a major center for pagan worship and occultism. It has been said Zeus was born in this city. Notable structures in the area were the Great Altar of Pergamum, the Hellenistic Theater, the Temple of Dionysus, and the Sanctuary of Athena. The Library of Pergamum was said to hold over two hundred thousand volumes. The city was known for its gymnasiums and hospitals.

This era became known as the, "Great Therapeutic Age." The god, "Asclepius," the god of healing was worshipped in this city. This pagan god is known for his serpent entwined staff which has become symbolic even to this day for pagan and occult healing. Let's now take a look at what Jesus had to say concerning this church.

> And to the angel of the church in Pergamos write; These things saith he which hath the sharp sword with two edges;
>
> I know thy works, and where thou dwellest, even where Satan's seat is: and thou holdest fast my name, and hast not denied my faith, even in those days wherein Antipas was my faithful martyr, who was slain among you, where Satan dwelleth.
>
> But I have a few things against thee, because thou hast there them that hold the doctrine of Balaam, who taught Balac to cast a stumblingblock before the children of Israel, to eat things sacrificed unto idols, and to commit fornication.
>
> So hast thou also them that hold the doctrine of the Nicolaitanes, which thing I hate.
>
> Repent; or else I will come unto thee quickly, and will fight against them with the sword of my mouth.

He that hath an ear, let him hear what the
Spirit saith unto the churches; To him that overcometh will I give to eat of the hidden manna,
and will give him a white stone, and in the stone
a new name written, which no man knoweth saving he that receiveth it. (Revelation 2:12–17)

The Bible states, "To the angel of the church of Pergamum
write." As stated earlier, I hold to the belief each one of these churches
had a literal angel guarding over them. A major difference one notices
in this letter would be the different types of words and symbolism
Jesus uses when addressing this church. Jesus describes Himself to
this church as, "One who has a sharp double edged sword." The Bible
describes Jesus in more than one place as the, "Living Word," and
the, "Word Made Flesh." As stated earlier, the way Jesus describes
Himself will be a direct representation of the spiritual conditions of
these churches. It is interesting the description the book of Hebrews
gives us concerning the word of God.

For the word of God is quick, and powerful, and sharper than any twoedged sword,
piercing even to the dividing asunder of soul and
spirit, and of the joints and marrow, and is a dis-
cerner of the thought and interests of the heart.
(Hebrews 4:12)

These were the words of Jesus the literal, "Living Word." The
word of God brings discernment to the very heart and soul of a man.
We will discover this church had several doctrinal problems, and the
word of God brings discernment concerning doctrinal issues. Jesus
announces to this church He is aware of the environment of paganism they lived in. Jesus acknowledged this church was located in
the city where Satan more than likely literally at one time resided.
This subject has been somewhat addressed in an earlier chapter, but
most churches and even Christians fail to realize many of the gods
worshipped in Old Testament times were spiritual beings known as

fallen angels or demons. The Bible refers to Satan as, "The god of this world." We know according to the Bible Satan is not a god, but a created being referred to in Ezekiel chapter 28 as a, "Guardian Cherub." Satan more than likely was at one time second in command in heaven. It would be one little problem called pride, causing Satan to lose his place of authority and be cast out of heaven taking with him one third of the angelic realm. For those having a problem believing Satan literally resided in this city, need to realize the Bible informs us Satan will literally walk on the earth again during the tribulation period.

It is interesting Jesus literally refers to Pergamum as the city where Satan has his throne. Could this be possible? Yes, I believe so, and it is interesting Jesus mentions this twice in the same verse. It is interesting Apollo was one of the names of a Greek god. It is also interesting Apollo is one of the names given to the angel of the bottomless pit who ascends out of hell entering into the, "Son of perdition." The book of Revelation defines the antichrist as the person who once was, now is not, and ascends out of the bottomless pit. I have for many years believed Greek mythology may very well be a distortion of what historically may have literally taken place in the spiritual realm.

Jesus does compliment at least some members in this church for not denying their faith in spite of the occultism they constantly dealt with. Jesus does criticize the church of Pergamum concerning several issues. One of the criticisms deals with holding to the teaching of a person named, "Balaam." We find information relating to this interesting character in the book of Numbers chapter 22. Balaam was a man who was hired by the enemies of Israel to find ways to compromise and seduce the men of Israel to sin. It is interesting the link we most always find in the Bible with sexual immorality and idol worship. Balaam used the doctrine of compromise to tempt the children of Israel to commit spiritual disobedience. God throughout the entire Bible has always taken a tough stance on sexual immorality. Marriage is a holy covenant created by God between a man and a woman. Marriage is an earthly picture of a heavenly love God has for

His bride, the church. It is for this reason sexual immorality in the church is strictly prohibited by God.

The church of Pergamum was also criticized for embracing the teachings of a group referred to as the, "Nicolaitans," who attended this church. I'm not exactly sure with all the doctrinal issues this heretical group exhibited, except the teachings of this group had something to do with tolerating other pagan religious beliefs. It is possible during this time many churches put into practice the concept of the priesthood ruling over the flock. Instead of the example of Christ where He came to serve and lay down His life for the church, many of these false doctrines taught the priesthood was to be served by the people. The Bible clearly teaches Jesus is, "The Head," of the church, not a priest or any governing body. We see this doctrine and practice trickling into many churches today.

Jesus gives these false teachers in this church a very stern warning. Jesus tells this church to repent and turn back to Him, or He will soon return and fight against them with the sword of His mouth. The Bible gives a similar description of Christ when He physically returns to earth during His second coming. In Revelation 19 Christ is seen returning to earth riding on a White Horse. Jesus is more than likely informing the unrighteous in this church if they are unwilling to repent and give their life to Him, they would face God's wrath during His second coming.

> And I saw heaven opened, and behold a white horse; and he that sat upon him was called Faithful and True, and in righteousness he doth judge and make war.
>
> His eyes were as a flame of fire, and on his head were many crowns; and he had a name written, that no man knew, but he himself.
>
> And he was clothed with a vesture dipped in blood: and his name is called The Word of God.
>
> And the armies which were in heaven followed him upon white horses, clothed in fine linen, white and clean.

> And out of his mouth goeth a sharp sword,
> that with it he should smite the nations: and he
> shall rule them with a rod of iron: and he trea-
> deth the winepress of the fierceness and wrath of
> Almight God. (Revelation 19:11–15)

One of the biggest problems I experience is deciding when to stop discussing the evidence the Bible gives on various topics. We could spend five or six chapters on these five verses alone. When Jesus one day returns a second time literally planting His feet on earth, He will not be returning for His bride. Verse 11 tells us Jesus is returning the second time for the purposes of judging and to make war. Notice the description John gives of Christ having eyes as flames of fire, on His head are many crowns, and His robe is dipped in blood. People, we are not talking about a time of marriage during this event. We are talking about a time of judgment and war. Notice during this event, the armies from heaven are following Him along with those clothed in fine white linen. Looks to me like Jesus is not coming back to earth to get His bride, His bride is already with Him. Jesus warned specific groups of individuals in this church to repent, turn from their evil ways, or they would one day face His wrath.

Notice we again see a call from Jesus to the churches to hear and listen to what the Spirit is saying. We also here again see a similar promise made to the, "Overcomer." We see Jesus promising these overcomers will receive the hidden manna which is the heavenly spiritual nourishment available only to the believer. Jesus during the Lord's Supper informed His disciples He was the, "Bread of Life." Jesus came to the woman of Samaria stating He was the, "Water of Life." Jesus here is stating He is the, "Hidden Manna," sustaining all believers who partake of the life offered by Him. This comment from Jesus also could be relating to the false doctrines occurring in the church during this time, referring to food sacrificed to idols and the teachings of Balaam.

Jesus ends the letter informing the reader, "The Overcomer," will be given a white stone with a new name written on it known only to the believer who receives the stone. This could have several possible answers. In a court of law in those days it is said a white stone is a symbol for innocence, and a black stone was a symbol of guilt. The white stone may also be a symbolic gesture of the righteousness required for admission into the yet future, "Messianic Banquet." I tend to believe the white stone could be spiritually contrasting the pagan worship of a black stone in the temple of Artemis located in Ephesus. The black stone was possibly a meteorite that fell to earth and was worshipped by the pagan religions during that time.

So this concludes a brief study of the church at Pergamum. The church criticized by Christ because of their compromise with the world, and their comingling with false doctrine and false teachers. Remember, these letters are intended for all churches as well as all individuals to be used as a means of personal inspection and correction where needed. These letters are intended for all who have an ear and are willing to listen. We all are being warned by the Creator of the universe concerning things that will soon take place. We are being warned because God loves all people, and His will is that none should perish, but all would have everlasting life.

The fourth church mentioned in Revelation is the church of Thyatira. The meaning of the name Thyatira is, "Daughter." This city was widely known as a merchant and trading city especially known for its purple cloth trade. This city was widely known for its wool, linen, and leather products. The city also had many dyers, leather workers, tanners, potters, and metal workers. The Bible records in Acts 16, an encounter by Paul with a lady named Lydia who was a seller of purple cloth.

According to the book of Revelation, there was a woman living in the city named Jezebel who called herself a prophetess. This woman was teaching and seducing Christians attending the church of Thyatira to commit sins of sexual immorality and eating food sacrificed to idols. We will see this church exhibits the characteristics of spiritual fornication, and the co-mingling of church and idol worship. Let's now take a look at what Jesus has to say concerning the church of Thyatira.

And unto the angel of the church in Thyatira
write; These things saith the Son of God, who

hath his eyes like unto a flame of fire, and his feet are like fine brass;

I know thy works, and charity, and service, and faith, and thy patience, and thy works; and the last to be more than the first.

Notwithstanding I have a few things against thee, because thou suffereth that woman Jezebel, which calleth herself a prophetess, to teach and to seduce my servants to commit fornication, and to eat things sacrificed unto idols.

And I gave her space to repent of her fornication; and she repented not.

Behold, I will cast her into a bed, and them that commit adultery with her into great tribulation, except they repent of their deeds.

And I will kill her children with death; and all the churches shall know that I am he which searcheth the reins and hearts: and I will give unto every one of you according to your works.

But unto you I say, and unto the rest in Thyatira, as many as have not this doctrine, and which have not known the depths of Satan, as they speak; I will put upon you none other burden.

But that which ye have already hold fast till I come.

And he that overcometh, and keepeth my works unto the end, to him will I give power over the nations:

And he shall rule them with a rod of iron; as the vessels of a potter shall they be broken to shivers: even as I received of my Father.

And I will give him the morning star.

He that hath an ear, let him hear what the Spirit saith unto the churches. (Revelation 2:18–29)

Of the seven letters to the churches, we notice the letter to Thyatira is the longest letter of the seven. Again, we see the angel of the church is mentioned as the one receiving the information from Christ. We notice Jesus Christ being described to this church as having eyes like unto flames of fire and having feet like brass. Jesus is portraying Himself to this church as one who is all-seeing, having all power, authority, and judge of all creation.

Jesus first gives this church the good news, and again confirms He is aware of the deeds of this church. Jesus commends this church for their works of love, service, faith, and patience. It is important to note this church evidently is doing some very good works, because Jesus makes some very positive comments about this church.

Jesus then comments on some areas of correction this church needs to consider. We find the chief criticism coming from Christ deals with the toleration of sin in the church. We currently have a major problem with this same issue today in our churches. Just like the world, the church today has become more concerned about being politically correct than doing what is spiritually and biblically right. The chief complaint I hear among people today is the proclamation no person has the right or authority to judge another person. Although there is some truth to this in certain instances, when it comes to the church body, the Bible tells us a life of holiness is expected. All people in the church who hold leadership positions such as pastors, deacons, and teachers are called to a life characterized by holy living. Below is one of the many verses dealing with the issue of immorality amongst the church brethren.

> But fornication, and all uncleanness, or covetousness, let it not be once named among you, as becometh saints. (Ephesians 5:3)

Most understand the concept all Christians are in fact sinners saved by grace. Yes, all Christians stumble, make mistakes, and struggle with sin. We need to understand there is a difference in struggling with sin, and ignoring ongoing issues of various types of sin and sexual immorality taking place openly in the church. Especially if the immorality relates to a church member in an administrative position. We also need to remember anytime a corrective action plan is carried out on a church member; the action is always carried out through a spirit of love and humility. The Bible gives very specific directions as to the way a church member is to be addressed and counseled on ethical and moral issues. Let's take a look at what Paul has to say in 1 Corinthians concerning a sexually immoral issue taking place in the church.

> It is reported commonly that there is fornication among you, and such fornication as is not so much as named among the Gentiles, that one should have his father's wife.
>
> And ye are puffed up, and have not rather mourned, that he hath done this deed might be taken away from among you.
>
> For I verily, as absent in body, but present in spirit, have judged already, as though I were present, concerning him that hath so done this deed,
>
> In the name of our Lord Jesus Christ, when ye are gathered together, and my spirit, with the power of the Lord Jesus Christ.
>
> To deliver such an one unto Satan for the destruction of the flesh, that the spirit may be saved in the day of the Lord Jesus.
>
> Your glorying is not good. Know ye not that a little leaven leaveneth the whole lump?
>
> Purge out therefore the old leaven, that ye may be a new lump, as ye are unleavened. For even Christ our Passover is sacrificed for us. (1 Corinthians 5:1–7)

I believe the above seven verses clarify the issue of sexual immorality in the church. The key concept going on in the church above is not so much the issue of sexual sin in the church which is wrong. It was the fact this church ignored the issue and was even proud about it. Notice the disciplining of this man was not for the purpose of public embarrassment, but for the purpose of bringing repentance and salvation from possible eternal damnation of his soul.

So we now see why Jesus brings strong accusations against the church at Thyatira. This church is tolerating a woman named Jezebel who was guilty of misleading the church into committing sexually immoral acts and eating food sacrificed to idols. This woman refers to herself as a, "Prophetess," who is evidently holding an administrative position in the church.

Notice we see Jesus mentioning He has given the woman a period of time to repent. This is a very interesting comment Jesus makes. There could be a tremendous study conducted or even a book written on this subject alone. Many times the Bible records places where God gives individuals, cities, or even nations a period of time to repent. Even during the days of Noah, God gave the people on earth the period of 120 years to repent and turn from their evil ways. Jesus goes on to say this woman Jezebel was unwilling to repent. It is sad but this is a major sign the Bible is giving us concerning God's prophetic timetable. The Bible declares during the last days people will refuse to repent and turn from their evil ways.

Jesus states there will be serious consequences for this woman named Jezebel, and all people who participate with her if there is no repentance. I have realized over the last few years maybe the church has taken the issue of sin not quite serious enough. I know I've made the comment, "In God's Eyes, Sin is Sin." The older I get, I'm not so sure that statement is true. Yes, all sin brings separation from God, but we see several instances where God sure gets very angry with certain types of sins, especially those dealing with sexual immorality. Jesus informs this church if there is no repentance, tremendous suffering and even death will come upon those who participate in this type of sin. This sin will even result in the death of the children of these individuals. Discipline and judgment is always brought by God to bring correction to a spiritual issue. We need to understand even spiritual adultery which involves going after strange gods will many times lead also to sexual immorality. All types of sin are a symptom of one's disobedience toward God, but they are not considered the same in the eyes of God. There are several examples in the Bible where God personally intervenes in a situation and says enough is enough. To understand the point I am trying to get across, let's take a look at four verses in the book of Proverbs.

> These six things doth the Lord hate: yea, seven are an abomination unto him:
> A proud look, a lying tongue, and hands that shed innocent blood,
> An heart that deviseth wicked imaginations, feet that be swift in running to mischief,
> A false witness that speaketh lies, and he that soweth discord among brethren. (Proverbs 6:16–19)

It is also interesting the Bible instructs Christians to examine themselves before they participate in the Lord's Supper. The drinking of the wine and the eating of bread is a symbolic picture of Jesus giving His blood and body for His church, "The bride." The Bible states many Christians sleep because they have taken the Lord's Supper in an unworthy manner. The word, "Sleep," refers here to the fact these Christians are now physically dead because of sin in their lives. A Christian will again one day rise from the dead at the resurrection, so a physical death to the, "Overcomer," is described symbolically as one who sleeps. A true believer will not suffer the second death which the Bible refers to as an eternal death.

We notice in the letter to Thyatira Jesus again addresses two groups of people in this church in different ways. One concept people seem to not understand today is all people attending or having a membership in a church will not be counted by God as being righteous. The righteous people in the church are identified and addressed as, "Overcomers." Jesus identifies this group of people as those who do not hold to this woman's teachings and have not participated in the deep secrets of Satan. The mixing of pagan and occult worship with the Bible is always seen by God as Satan Worship. This group of people is instructed by Jesus to hold fast until He comes. Jesus warns us in the scriptures, no one can serve two masters.

The overcomers in this church are promised to rule and reign with Christ. Jesus Christ will fulfill this prophecy during the time of His millennial reign here on earth. These overcomers will be given the, "Morning Star," which is another title for Christ. He is also called, The Lamb of God, The Son of Righteousness, The Alpha and Omega, The Bread of Life, The King of Kings, and the Lion of the Tribe of Judah. A similar description of Christ ruling the world with a rod of iron is given in Psalm chapter 2.

Why do the heathen rage, and the people imagine a vain thing?

The kings of the earth set themselves, and the rulers take counsel together, against the Lord, and against his anointed, saying,

Let us break their bands asunder, and cast away their cords from us.

He that sitteth in the heavens shall laugh: the Lord shall have them in derision.

Then shall he speak unto them in his wrath, and vex them in his sore displeasure.

Yet have I set my king upon my holy hill of Zion.

I will declare the decree: the Lord hath said unto me, Thou are my Son; this day have I begotten thee.

Ask of me, and I shall give thee the heathen for thine inheritance, and the uttermost parts of the earth for thy possession.

Thou shalt break them with a rod of iron; thou shalt dash them in pieces like a potter's vessel.

Be wise now therefore, O ye kings: be instructed, ye judges of the earth.

Serve the Lord with fear, and rejoice with trembling. (Psalms 2:1–11)

The angel Gabriel instructed Mary her Son Jesus Christ would one day literally sit on David's throne. Jesus will literally reign for one thousand years from Jerusalem during His future millennial reign on earth. I know there are several who believe this is not a literal event, but the Bible confirms this in several places. Just as the book of Psalms also confirms, Jesus will one day reign from Jerusalem on David's throne.

The Bible also states in Psalms God laughs at the plans of Satan and the nations of the world. Satan, and the kings of the earth will literally believe they are capable of defeating Jesus during His second coming. God in heaven will laugh at the plans of these spiritual and earthly rulers to overthrow and destroy His plan. Jesus will one day literally reign on the earth and will save Israel His chosen people from total annihilation.

Jesus closes the letter by again warning all churches of the need to be spiritually listening and taking these words for the churches very seriously. These letters are intended for all members of all churches on an individual basis, as well as for the collective body. I see a tremendous amount of false teaching and false doctrine being taught in the church today concerning these truths. In this fourth letter to Thyatira we see a change in the way Jesus addresses this church. Jesus appeared to speak to the churches of Ephesus, Smyrna, and Pergamum in a collective sense. The words in these letters from Jesus appear to give the idea the first three churches have the capacity to repent and be counted as righteous. In this fourth letter to Thyatira, Jesus calls out a specific group of believers in this church to stand firm in their faith until He comes again.

We will now move on to the fifth church discussed in Revelation named Sardis. *Hitchcock's Bible Names Dictionary* defines the meaning of Sardis as, "Prince of Joy." My personal name for this church is, "The Church of the Living Dead." The Bible defines the church at Sardis as having a name, but they are spiritually dead. A church is much more than a name on a door. A church, at least in years past was known as the, "House of God," and was made up of a body of believers. We will find as we continue to approach the end of the age, the historical characteristics of churches will continue to evolve into places of social and spiritual enlightenment tolerating all forms of beliefs and doctrines.

We need to keep in mind all seven churches were literal churches dealing with real life issues. We also need to continue to remind ourselves all seven letters were given to the churches by Jesus, and were meant as a spiritual guide for all churches during that time as well as today. We also see these letters were intended for people as an individual tool for measuring spiritual maturity. These letters are intended for anyone willing to listen.

Sardis was also a very wealthy city. Sardis is described as one of the most important cities of the Persian Empire. This city was known for its military strength. It's interesting the people of this city were characterized as soft and fainthearted, and it was more than likely this attitude which led to its later destruction. Historically, Sardis was said to be founded by the sons of Hercules. It is interesting in Greek mythology, Hercules was known as a demi-god whose father was said to be a god, and his mother was a mortal woman. I personally believe Hercules was one of the, "Men of Renown, the Heroes of Old," referred to in Genesis chapter 6. I believe the father of Hercules was more than likely a fallen angel, and his mother was a mortal woman which is strangely similar to the circumstances described to us in Genesis. Hercules would be a hybrid being the Bible would describe as a, "Nephilim."

Sardis was known as a major manufacturing and dyeing center. The streams of Pactolus which literally flowed through the city carried literal gold dust sands from nearby Mt. Tmolus. Sardis, due to its mineral wealth is famed to be the place where coins of currency were invented. The Greek Temple of Artemis as well as a complex named the, "Sardis Synagogue," existed in Sardis. The synagogue consisted of a very large gymnasium and bath complex.

Let's now take a look at Revelation chapter 3 to see what Jesus had to say concerning this church. Keep in mind all seven of these letters are dealing with the time the Bible refers to as, "What is Now," or during the time when these churches literally existed. I hold to the belief we are currently living and fulfilling this period of time which is known as the, "Church Age." We have been in this period of time for approximately two thousand years. This would be the period of time referred to taking place between the sixty-ninth and seventieth week recorded in the ninth chapter of Daniel.

> And unto the angel of the church of Sardis write; These things saith he that hath the seven Spirits of God, and the seven stars; I know thy works, that thou hast a name that thou livest, and art dead.
>
> Be watchful, and strengthen the things which remain, that are ready to die: for I have not found thy works perfect before God.
>
> Remember therefore how thou hast received and heard, and hold fast, and repent. If therefore thou shalt not watch, I will come on thee as a thief, and thou shalt not know what hour I will come upon thee.
>
> Thou hast a few names even in Sardis which have not defiled their garments; and they shall walk with me in white: for they are worthy.
>
> He that overcometh, the same shall be clothed in white raiment; and I will not blot out his name out of the book of life, but I will confess his name before my Father, and before his angels.
>
> He that hath an ear, let him hear what the Spirit saith unto the churches. (Revelation 3:1–5)

Just like the previous letters, we again see John being instructed to write down the words of this letter, and send it to the angel over the church at Sardis. We see here Christ again identifying Himself as the one holding the seven stars or angels of the churches in His hand. In dealing with this church, we see Christ also identifying Himself as one having the seven, "Spirits of God." We will find the definition of the, "Seven Spirits," of God in the book of Isaiah. We will discover these additional characteristics given to us of God will directly relate to issues and concerns addressed in this specific church. The defini-

tion the Bible gives us concerning the, "Seven Spirits," of God quali-
fies God as having the authority to commend, correct, or rebuke this
church concerning their spiritual condition as a church body. We will
see Jesus has some very stern warnings for this church, and it is very
critical all churches understand where this church stands in the eyes
of God. The, "Seven Spirits," of God includes the following:

> And there shall come forth a rod out of the
> stem of Jesse, and a Branch shall grow out of his
> roots:
> And the spirit of the Lord shall rest upon
> him, the spirit of wisdom and understanding, the
> spirit of counsel and might, the spirit of knowl-
> edge and of the fear of the Lord.
> And shall make him of quick understand-
> ing in the fear of the Lord: and he shall judge
> after the sight of his eyes, neither reprove after
> the hearing of his ears:
> But with righteousness shall he judge the
> poor, and reprove with equity for the meek of the
> earth: and he shall smite the earth: with the rod
> of his mouth, and with the breath of his lips shall
> he slay the wicked. (Isaiah 11:1–4)

Jesus Christ is the head of the church, and He alone is qualified
to judge the spiritual condition of any man or any church. Jesus
holds the keys to death, hell, and the grave, and what He says goes.
When Jesus tells a church they are dead it is very sobering, and it is a
very serious spiritual issue. When Jesus tells a person, "Depart From
Me, I Never Knew You," these words are final, and they have eternal
consequences.

Jesus warns this church to get it spiritually right while they still
have little life remaining. Here again in this church, we see evidence
of a small group of believers inside this church trying to be obedient,
since Jesus tells them to stand firm in their faith. As you've heard me
state many times. I believe two of the most important words in the

Bible are, "Remember," and, "Watch." The church at Sardis was told to remember the gospel they received and to safeguard what little faith remained. It is quite interesting the answer you will get when you ask most people attending church to give a definition of the gospel. One of the best definitions of the gospel message can be found in the book of 1 Corinthians.

> Moreover, brethren, I declare unto you the gospel which I preached unto you, which also ye have received, and wherein ye stand;
>
> By which also ye are saved, if ye keep in memory what I preached unto you, unless ye have believed in vain.
>
> For I delivered unto you first of all that which I also received, how that Christ died for our sins according to the scriptures;
>
> And that he was buried, and that he rose again the third day according to the scriptures:
>
> And that he was seen of Cephas, then of the twelve:
>
> After that, he was seen of above five hundred brethren at once; of whom the greater part remain unto this present, but some are fallen asleep.
>
> After that, he was seen of James; then of all the apostles.
>
> And last of all he was seen of me also, as of one born out of due time. (1 Corinthians 15:1–8)

These few verses in Corinthians give the complete definition of what is considered the, "Gospel Message." The gospel message is the fact Christ died for our sins, was buried, and He rose again on the third day. Any other message given contrary to these verses is false teaching and should be considered a false doctrine. This was the message the church of Sardis was asked to remember. Jesus then follows by giving this church a very serious warning. If the church of Sardis fails to follow the gospel message mentioned above, this church will be in danger of Jesus coming and surprising them like a thief. To further clarify what Jesus is saying to this church, all we need to do is a little digging. Take a look to what Jesus tells us in Revelation chapter 16.

> "Behold, I am coming like a thief! Blessed is the one who stays awake, keeping his garments on, that he may not go about naked and be seen exposed!" (Revelation 16:15).

The Bible is the best commentary for the Bible. Notice the clarity we now have dealing with the comments Jesus states to the church at Sardis. Why would Jesus come as a thief to this church? Because many members in this church were not watching for Christ's return, and they had no relationship with Him. Most of the time, when the Bible uses the term, "Nakedness," it is referring to an unrighteous person. A person who is wearing a garment or dressed in white raiment is one who is clothed in the righteousness of Christ. This is the same idea as discussed in a previous chapter where a man was bound, and thrown out of a wedding banquet for not wearing the proper garments. This was not just referring to a story teaching a moral lesson, this is a description of a future literal event involving all unrighteous people.

Jesus goes on in the following verse using this same spiritual context, stating there are a few members in this church who have not defiled their garments. Notice Jesus uses the word, "Few." Jesus states these people will walk with Him in white. The reason is because these few members are righteous in God's eyes. I need to reemphasize Jesus uses the words, "Few Names," when referring to this church. Jesus is more than likely informing us most of the members in this church have no spiritual relationship with God. How many people in churches today are looking and watching for the appearing of Christ? What percentage of people attending church today will be caught by surprise when He returns for His bride? I believe the numbers will be quite staggering.

Jesus closes out this letter to Sardis stating it is the, "Overcomer," who will be clothed in white. The names of these who overcome and are clothed in white will not be blotted out of the, "Book of Life," and will be confessed before the Father and the angels. It is believed all people born are written in the, "Book of Life," and all who reject Christ and His sacrifice on the cross, their names will be taken out of the, "Book of Life." It is quite possible these people who are blotted out of the, "Book of Life," may be recorded in the, "Book of the Dead." There are several verses in the Bible that confirm this belief. A couple examples of these verses include the following:

> And whosoever was not found written in the book of life was cast into the lake of fire. (Revelation 20:15)

> And Moses returned unto the Lord, and said, Oh, this people have sinned a great sin, and have made them gods of gold.
> Yet now, if thou wilt forgive their sin; and if not, blot me, I pray thee, out of thy book which thou hast written.
> And the Lord said unto Moses, whosoever hath sinned against me, him will I blot out of my book. (Exodus 32:31–33)

Whose name will be blotted out of the, "Book of Life?" It is those people who have been counted as unrighteous, having sinned against a holy God. Whose name will Jesus confess before His Father? All who confess Christ to others and are a living testimony to God. We see in Matthew Jesus confirming this spiritual truth. It is interesting during the past four or five years I have been noticing the world is attempting to relay the idea a person's faith should be lived in secret. The world would like to convince the church their faith should only be practiced behind closed doors and not be openly professed in the world. This is nothing but a lie and is pure deception from the god of this world. The Bible clearly states in Matthew chapter 5 the church is intended to be the light of the world. Jesus commanded the church to let their light shine for all the world to see.

> Whosover therefore shall confess me before men, him will I confess also before my Father which is in heaven.
> But whosoever shall deny me before men, him will I also deny before my Father which is in heaven. (Matthew 10:32–33)

Again we see this letter to Sardis is intended for all who have an ear and are willing to listen. This concludes a brief study on the church of Sardis. A church having a name on a door but was spiritually dead. This letter from Jesus is intended as a warning to all churches who will take heed to its message. We as believers need to be constantly watching and looking for the future return of Jesus Christ for His chosen bride, the church. Are you certain your name is written in the, "Book of Life?"

We will now move on to the sixth letter written by Jesus for the churches. This letter is written to the church of Philadelphia. The name Philadelphia means, "City of Brotherly Love." This city was supposedly given this name by King Eumenes II because of his love for a brother named, "Attalus II," who was thought to be his successor. The name literally means, "One who loves his brother."

The city of Philadelphia was a prosperous city producing all types of leather products and a red-colored silk. This city historically was known as, "Little Athens," due to its numerous temples. Due to the city being located near the fertile plain of the Gediz River, it was known for its production of dried fruits such as raisins. The city of Philadelphia was also famous for its wine production.

Just as with the other six churches, it is essential a person pays particular attention to the meaning of Philadelphia. This name literally means, "Brotherly Love." Another interesting thing we need to realize is we will find this church is only one of two churches Jesus had no serious criticisms. The other church which Jesus had nothing negative to say was Smyrna. We will discover Jesus makes two interesting promises to the church at Philadelphia not made to any other church. We will now take a look at what Jesus has to say concerning this church.

> And to the angel of the church of Philadelphia write; These things saith he that is holy, he that is true, he that hath the key of David, he that openeth, and no man shutteth; and shutteth, and no man openeth;
>
> I know thy works: behold, I have set before thee an open door, and no man can shut it: for thou hast a little strength, and hast kept my word, and hast not denied my name.
>
> Behold, I will make them of the synagogue of Satan, which say they are Jews, and are not, but do lie; behold, I will make them to come and worship before thy feet, and to know that I have loved thee.
>
> Because thou hast kept the word of my patience, I also will keep thee from the hour of temptation, which shall come upon all the world, to try them that dwell upon the earth.
>
> Behold I come quickly: hold fast which thou hast, that no man take thy crown.
>
> Him that overcometh will I make a pillar in the temple of my God, and he shall go no more out: and I will write upon him the name of my God, and the name of the city of my God, which is the new Jerusalem, which cometh down out of heaven from my God: and I will write upon him a new name.
>
> He that hath an ear, let him hear what the Spirit saith unto the churches. (Revelation 3:7–13)

As I have said before, sometimes it's hard to know where to begin and where to end. An entire book could easily be written dealing with the seven churches alone. This letter to the church of Philadelphia alone gives acres of information to the churches. There is so much misunderstanding in the church today concerning where the church fits into the prophetic timetable, and God's ultimate plan. We see again John is instructed to write down the words given by Jesus, and send it to the angel of Philadelphia. The letter to the church of Philadelphia gives the reader a very unique description of Jesus Christ which is as follows.

- Jesus is holy.
- Jesus is true.
- Jesus holds the key of David.
- Jesus opens that which no man can shut.
- Jesus shuts that which no man can open.

I know we are living in times where people seem to get easily defended. We are living in times where political correctness has worked its way into many churches. Jesus stated in many places in the Bible giving confirmation, "He is the way, the truth, and the life." The fact of the matter is, statements such as these recorded in the Bible offends many people. Quite honestly, I see a time coming possibly in the near future where the Bible will be banned due to its lack of tolerance on spiritual truths such as this. This still doesn't change the fact people need to be told the truth. One truth I have discovered is as we steadily approach the end of the age, is we will see an increase in deception, false teaching, and a falling away from sound doctrine in the church. The sad thing is the truths in the Bible doesn't bring everyone in the world together. Sadly, we discover the word of God brings a spirit of separation between righteous and unrighteous people. Carefully listen to the words of Jesus below.

> Think not that I am come to send peace on earth: I came not to send peace, but a sword.
> For I am come to set a man at variance against his father, and the daughter against her

> mother, and the daughter-in-law against her
> mother-in-law.
>
> And a man's foes shall be they of his own
> household.
>
> He that loveth father and mother more than
> me is not worthy of me: and he that loveth son
> or daughter more than me is not worthy of me.
> (Matthew 10:34–37)

The truth is the, "Good News," of the gospel is not good news to all people. The truth is many more people will reject Christ than will accept Him. Jesus defines Himself in this letter as holy, true, and one having ultimate authority. Jesus states He holds the keys to death, hell, and the grave. The term, "Key of David," is a term defining Jesus as one having ultimate authority.

The reason there is a tremendous lack of understanding with the book of Revelation is because most are not willing to do their homework. The answers to many questions in the book of Revelation will be found in other scripture references, specifically in the Old Testament. It is sad many in the churches today do not read and study the Old Testament because of the belief it has no relevance for them today. We find the definition to the, "Key of David," is given to us in the book of Isaiah.

> And it shall come to pass in that day, that I
> will call my servant Eliakim the son of Hilkiah:
>
> And I will clothe him with thy robe, and
> strengthen him with thy girdle, and I will com-
> mit thy government into his hand: and he shall
> be a father to the inhabitants of Jerusalem, and to
> the house of Judah.
>
> And the key of the house of David will I lay
> upon his shoulder; so he shall open, and none
> shall shut; and he shall shut, and none shall open.
> (Isaiah 22:20–22)

When a person conducts a Bible name search for, "Eliakim," we find the meaning of the name is, "Resurrection of God." You know after a while people should come to the realization there is no possibility the Bible is the result of human work alone. The Bible is God breathed, and literally every word and every name is inspired by God. I believe the words above in Isaiah are also a foreshadowing of Jesus Christ, the one who holds the, "Key of David," and has been given all authority.

Jesus goes on to inform this church He is very aware of their works. Jesus goes on to commend this church stating although they have little strength left, they have kept God's word, and they have not denied His name. Because this church has been faithful in these two areas, Jesus makes an interesting promise to them. Jesus states He has placed before this church an open door that no man will be able to shut. When I hear someone mention the word, "Door," it reminds me of several other instances in scripture where this word is used.

One instance in the Bible where the word, "Door," is mentioned was during the time of Noah and the Ark. The Bible records the Ark had one door. There was just one way to enter into this Ark of safety. In Genesis chapter 7 the Bible records after Noah, his entire family, and all animals according to their kind were in the Ark, the Bible states God shut the door. I believe God shut the door of the Ark, and no man was then able to enter or exit the Ark. Yes, Noah was safe in the hands of God and no man could pluck him out.

The second instance where scripture makes reference to a door is found during the time of Israel's captivity in Egypt. In Exodus chapter 12 during the time of Passover, the children of Israel were commanded to take the blood of an unblemished lamb, and smear it on the sides and top of the doorframes of each house. The blood of the lamb which signified Jesus Christ who was the perfect unblemished Lamb, would protect the children of Israel from the coming wrath of God. It's sad most in the churches today do not understand the purpose of patterns such as these taking place in scripture. It will be the blood of the Lamb that will again protect those, "In Christ," who are described as, "Overcomers," from God's wrath one day coming upon all unrighteous people.

The third instance in scripture where the word, "Door," is used in the Bible is found in John chapter 10. In Matthew chapter 7 we also find similar verses where Jesus refers to Himself as being, "The Door." Jesus here promises this door will be opened to all whom ask, seek, and knock. It is no coincidence the church of Philadelphia is promised an open door to eternal righteousness, since they have remained faithful to the word of God and have not denied His name. Notice the words spoken by Jesus below in John chapter 10:

> Verily, verily, I say unto you, He that entereth not by the door into the sheepfold, but climbeth up some other way, the same is a thief and a robber.
>
> But he that entereth in by the door is the shepherd of the sheep.
>
> To him the porter openeth; and the sheep hear his voice: and he calleth his own sheep by name, and leadeth them out.
>
> And when he putteth forth his own sheep, he goeth before them, and the sheep follow him: for they know his voice.
>
> And a stranger will they not follow, but will flee from him: for they know not the voice of strangers.
>
> This parable spake Jesus unto them: but they understood not what things they were which he spake unto them.
>
> Then said Jesus unto them again, Verily, verily, I say unto you, I am the door of the sheep.
> (John 10:1–7)

So according to Jesus the Son of the, "Most High God," there is only one door or one entrance into heaven. There is only one door into heaven, and Jesus is the only person being found worthy in all of creation to open and close that door. Jesus states anyone proclaiming eternal life can be achieved by some other means is a liar, a thief, and a robber.

The fourth reference to a door being opened is given in Revelation chapter 4. I believe the description here of an open door in heaven being described by John is a reference to the same door promised to the church of Philadelphia. We will discuss this door being opened for John in further detail later on in the book. I would like to emphasize John records during this time hearing a voice sounding like a trumpet telling him to, "Come Up Hither."

Next, we again see Jesus as with other churches making a symbolic gesture to a specific group of Jews in this church belonging to the synagogue of Satan. We find a lot of the problems the early church experienced came from the Jewish community. Many of the Jewish people were still trying to live under the rules of the Mosaic Law. As we have previously studied, since Israel as a nation had rejected Jesus as Messiah, the benefits and promises to Israel had been temporarily set aside and now fell upon the church.

There is a false doctrine today being taught in many churches referred to as, "Replacement Theology." The basis to this belief is God has given up on Israel, and the Old Testament promises God made to Israel now fall upon the church. The problem with this is the covenant promises God made to Abraham have not been done away with. Although it is true Israel because of their unbelief has been temporarily set aside. God will again during the future, "Seventieth Week of Daniel," restore His relationship with the nation of Israel. God still has a special place in His heart for Israel, because God promises in the Bible any nation who persecutes them will be cursed and strictly disciplined by God.

During the coming, "Tribulation," the entire world including the church will desire to destroy the nation of Israel. We need to remember the world during this time will consist of a comingling of religions and governments forming a world economic system. The steady increase in hatred towards Israel goes all the way back to, "The Garden of Eden." Why will a worldwide hatred toward this nation continue to increase? It was because a virgin by the name of Mary bore a Son named Jesus. Satan is referred to as the, "God of this

World," and he has a special hatred for Israel because she birthed the Savior of the world. This is the reason the armies of the world will one day surround Israel during a future time known as, "Jacob's Trouble," and will attempt to annihilate God's chosen people. This will be the major reason Christ will return to earth again. God will then fight for and rescue His chosen people Israel.

Not only does Jesus promise the church at Philadelphia an open door or a way of escape to heaven. Jesus also promises this church they will be delivered or kept from the hour of trial coming upon the entire world. Notice Jesus refers to this trial as a worldwide trial coming upon all who dwell on the earth. Why would certain members in this church be kept from this time of trial? It is because the members of this church have kept the faith, have not denied His name, and are considered, "Overcomers." The key words one must research concerns the spiritual meaning of, "Those who dwell on the earth." According to the Bible, these people are not considered, "Overcomers."

There is a tremendous amount of confusion in the churches today concerning what groups of people will go through this future time of trouble known as, "The Tribulation." We will be dealing with this period of time more specifically in the next chapter. I can tell you one thing for sure. The person the Bible refers to as, "The Overcomer," will not be present during this event. I have went to great lengths in this book giving biblical evidence of what the spiritual benefits are to those people considered righteous in God's eyes.

The biggest problem I see today is people seem to confuse the concepts of persecution and God's wrath. God's people are informed several times in the Bible they may suffer persecution and even death. The church of Smyrna was told by Jesus to hold fast to their faith even to the point of death. The Bible records two distinct periods of time where God pours out His wrath on the entire world. One of these events, "The Flood of Noah," has already taken place. There will be one more future time where God will again pour out His wrath upon the entire earth. The Bible gives this future period of time several names. A few names for this future event include the following:

- The Day of the Lord
- Daniel's seventieth week
- The Tribulation
- A Day of Wrath
- A Day of Trouble and Distress
- A Day of Destruction of Desolation
- A Day of Darkness and Gloom
- A Day of Clouds and Thick Darkness
- A Day of God's Burning Anger
- A Day of Vengeance

Jesus promises the church of Philadelphia they will be kept from or spared from this time of temptation coming upon the entire earth. It is interesting the word, "Temptation," is used here. This future time will not only be a time of God's wrath, it will be a time of great deception. Listen to what Jesus and Paul both have to say concerning this coming time of wrath and deception.

> Then if any man shall say unto you, Lo, here is Christ, or there; believe it not.
> For there shall arise false Christs, and false prophets, and shall shew great signs and wonders; insomuch that, if it were possible, they shall deceive the very elect.
> Behold, I have told you before.
> (Matthew 24:23–25)

> Even him, whose coming is after the working of Satan with all power and signs and lying wonders,
> And with all deceivableness of unrighteousness in them that perish; because they received not the love of the truth, that they might be saved.

And for this cause God shall send them strong delusion, that they should believe a lie:

That they all might be damned who believed not the truth, but had pleasure in unrighteousness.

But we are bound to give thanks always to God for you, brethren beloved of the Lord, because God hath from the beginning chosen you to salvation through sanctification of the Spirit and belief of the truth (2 Thessalonians 2:9–13).

I am continually shocked with the amount of confusion I see in the church today. Over and over again, the Bible makes it clear, "The Overcomer," those who are, "In Christ," or the, "Bride of Christ," will be kept from this coming time of deception and wrath. The Bible states in several places those, "In Christ," have not been appointed to wrath but unto salvation. What groups of people will be forced to endure this time of tribulation and great deception? Paul in the book of Thessalonians gives us a very clear description listed below:

- Those who are spiritually perishing
- Those who receive not the love of the truth
- Those who have pleasure in unrighteousness
- Those who dwell on the earth

I would like to spend a little more time dealing with the meaning of, "Those Dwelling on the Earth." There are so many patterns in the scriptures giving us clues concerning the differences in the way God deals with the righteous and the unrighteous. Paul in Thessalonians refers to the, "Righteous," as being the, "Sons of Light," or the, "Sons of the Day." Paul then refers to the, "Unrighteous," as being, "Children of Darkness," or the, "Children of the Night."

We see nowhere in scripture where those who are righteous perish from the wrath of God. The Bible does inform us those people who God loves He disciplines, but there is a difference between God disciplining an individual and God pouring His wrath out on someone. Not one righteous person perished in the flood, and not one righteous person perished in the destruction of Sodom and the cities of the plain. As a matter of fact, God promised Abraham if He could find ten righteous people in the city of Sodom, the city would be spared. How many righteous people ended up being led out of this city? According to the Bible, there were four until Lot's wife looked back and was killed. The words in the Bible have spiritual meaning and consequences.

The Bible describes people who are righteous and unrighteous in different ways. To nail down this truth, let's take a look at a few verses in Revelation concerning a group of people referred to as, "Those who dwell on the earth." There is an old gospel hymn whose words inform us, "This world is not our home; we are just a passing through." The righteous are not referred to in the Bible as "Earth Dwellers." The Bible tells us our citizenship is in heaven.

> And they cried with a loud voice, saying, How long, O Lord, holy and true, dost thou not judge and avenge our blood on them that dwell on the earth? (Revelation 6:10)

> And I beheld, and heard an angel flying through the midst of heaven, saying with a loud voice, Woe, woe, woe, to the inhabiters of the earth by reason of the other voices of the trumpet of the three angels, which are yet to sound! (Revelation 8:13)

> And they that dwell upon the earth shall rejoice over them, and make merry, and shall send gifts one to another; because these two prophets tormented them that dwelt on the earth. (Revelation 11:10)

> And all that dwell upon the earth shall worship him, whose names are not written in the

book of life of the Lamb slain from the foundation of the world. (Revelation 13:8)

And he exerciseth all the power of the
first beast before him, and causeth the earth
and them which dwell therin to worship the
first beast, whose deadly wound was healed.
(Revelation 13:12)

And deceiveth them that dwell on the earth
by the means of those miracles which he had
power to do in the sight of the beast; saying to
them that dwell on the earth, that they should
make an image to the beast, which had the wound
by a sword, and did live. (Revelation 13:14)

The beast that thou sawest was, and is not;
and shall ascend out of the bottomless pit, and
go into perdition: and they that dwell on the
earth shall wonder, whose names were not written in the book of life from the foundation of the
world, when they behold the beast that was, and
is not, and yet is. (Revelation 17:8)

I believe the verses above do a good job nailing down the identities of those dwelling on the earth during this time. Several other
places in scripture also make reference to this group of people being
those whose names are not found written in the, "Lamb's Book of
Life."

Jesus then informs the church of Philadelphia He is coming
quickly and to keep their faith ensuring no person takes their crown.
We have discussed this subject in detail in a previous chapter. There
should be no confusion concerning this statement. Jesus did not tell
this church they were in danger of losing their salvation. This is not
what the Bible is telling us. Jesus is informing this church to continue
in their faith and continue to produce good fruit. Jesus warned this

body of believers to not allow any false doctrine or false teaching to cause them to lose their eternal rewards. The possibility exists for the Christian to lose his or her rewards, but they cannot lose their salvation. Every Christian will be rewarded based on the fruit or works they produce while living on this earth.

Those people in this church referred to as, "Overcomers," are promised to be a pillar in the future temple of God coming down out of heaven. All who overcome will receive a new name and become eternal residents of the city referred to as, "The New Jerusalem," coming down out of heaven. The "Overcomer," will be marked as one of God's children. I sometimes hear people expressing concerns whether or not they will one day be required to take the mark of the Beast. I ask these people if they have made a profession of faith asking Christ to become their Lord and Savior. If that person says yes, I then tell them they have already received a mark. This mark according to the Bible is the deposit of the Holy Spirit guaranteeing our inheritance. The mark of the beast is a counterfeit mark offered by Satan identifying those who are his servants.

Jesus closes out the letter to the church of Philadelphia letting all people know who have ears of the need to listen to what the Spirit says to the churches. Here again, these letters are intended for all individuals and churches today, to be used as guidelines for correction and determining one's level of spiritual maturity.

Let's now take a brief look at the seventh and final letter written by Jesus to the church of Laodicea. This church is historically known as the lukewarm church. *Hitchcock's Bible Names Dictionary* defines Laodicea as meaning, "Just People." I again want to stress it is no coincidence the church of Laodicea is the last church Jesus comments on. I believe the church of Laodicea is a spiritual picture of the church during the end of the age. This church has a form of godliness, but Jesus is not the Head of this church body. Laodicea is a church ruled by the people. The church is called to be salt and light. We will see this church was neither salt nor light.

Laodicea was a very large and prosperous city. The city was probably once named Diospolis the, "City of Zeus." Laodicea became one of the most flourishing commercial cities of Asia Minor due to its location. Laodicea was known for its extensive trade in black wool. This city made great advancements in the arts, science, and literature. Laodicea also was home to a medical school and minted its own coins. Laodicea had many buildings including stadiums, baths, temples, gymnasiums, and theaters. Laodicea was also famous for its aqueduct system which brought water from hot springs several miles away. It is said by the time water arrived to the baths in Laodicea, it was lukewarm.

The letter to the church of Laodicea is probably the most depressing of all the letters. Laodicea is one of the two churches too which Jesus has nothing good to say. Let's now take a closer look what Jesus had to say to the church at Laodicea and more importantly, what Jesus has to say to the church today.

> And unto the angel of the church of the Laodiceans write; These things saith the Amen, the faithful and true witness, the beginning of the creation of God;
>
> I know thy works, that thou art neither cold nor hot: I would thou were cold or hot.
>
> So then because thou art lukewarm, and neither cold nor hot, I will spue thee out of my mouth.
>
> Because thou sayest, I am rich, and increased with goods, and have need of nothing; and knowest not that thou are wretched, and miserable, and poor, and blind, and naked:
>
> I counsel thee to buy of me gold tried in the fire, that thou mayest be rich; and white raiment, that thou mayest be clothed, and that the shame of thy nakedness do not appear; and anoint thine eyes with eyesalve, that thou mayest see.
>
> As many as I love, I rebuke and chasten: be zealous therefore, and repent.
>
> Behold, I stand at the door, and knock: If any man hear my voice, and open the door, I will

come in to him, and will sup with him, and he with me.

To him that overcometh will I grant to sit with me in my throne, even as I also overcame, and am set down with my Father in his throne.

He that hath an ear, let him hear what the Spirit saith unto the churches. (Revelation 3:14–22)

John is instructed to pen this last letter to the church at Laodicea. John records the words given by Jesus to be sent to the angel residing over this church. This letter written by Jesus to the church of Laodicea is also similar to the previous six letters in the sense it is a warning to the spiritual conditions of all churches. Notice here Jesus identifies Himself as the, "Amen, The Faithful and True Witness, and the Beginning of Creation." These names are all identifying characteristics of Jesus Christ. Jesus is trustworthy, and He is faithful. Jesus was with God and was present during creation. Jesus is the, "Living Word," of God. These are words the church today needs to heed, especially dealing with Jesus being the, "Beginning of Creation." Take a look at what Colossians has to say concerning the preeminence of Christ.

Who is the image of the invisible God, the firstborn of every creature:

For by him were all things created, that are in heaven, and that are in earth, visible and invisible, whether they be thrones, or dominions, or principalities, or powers: all things were created by him, and for him:

And he is before all things, and by him all things consist.

And he is the head of the body, the church: who is the beginning, the firstborn from the dead; that in all things he might have the preeminence. (Colossians 1:15–18)

We notice by the way Jesus addresses the church of Laodicea, this church had some major spiritual issues. We see here in this letter Jesus cannot make one positive comment about this church. This church has no good works to discuss. I have read many polls over the years concerning what people believe. I was shocked to discover the percentages of people who regularly attend churches today who do not believe the Bible can be taken literally. Many in the church today believe Satan is not a literal spiritual being but is just a figment of one's imagination. Many in the church today refuse to believe events in the Old Testament such as the Flood actually took place. Many people in the church today doubt heaven and hell are literal places. I believe many churches today can be characterized as being dead or lukewarm. The idea Jesus is one day coming back for His bride is seen as completely ridiculous in many churches today.

Jesus accuses this church of being neither cold nor hot. Jesus refers to the church of Laodicea as being, "Lukewarm," thus making Him want to vomit them out of His mouth. Jesus quite honestly is disgusted with this church. This is a church filled with tolerance and compromise. This is a church characterized by false teaching and false doctrine. This is a picture of a church having no passion for the gospel of Jesus Christ. The church of Laodicea is similar to many of the churches today.

How many churches today teach Jesus is not the only way to heaven? How many pastors do we have today standing in pulpits, who do not believe marriage is a holy covenant from God between a man and woman? We even have pastors standing in pulpits today claiming they do not believe in God. If people choose to believe there is no God they have the right to do so. I would have never dreamed there could be such a thing as a pastor of a church who claims to be an atheist. How could it be possible for a pastor claiming to be an atheist to literally open up the Bible and read from God's word? It is when a church has a form of godliness but denies the existence and the power of God this becomes possible. Take a look at what 2 Timothy has to say concerning this issue. I believe I may have discussed some of these verses in a previous chapter but as a disc jockey once stated, we need to play this one again.

This know also, that in the last days perilous times shall come.

For men shall be lovers of their own selves, covetous, boasters, proud, blasphemers, disobedient to parents, unthankful, unholy,

Without natural affection, trucebreakers, false accusers, incontinent, fierce, despisers of those that are good,

Traitors, heady, highminded, lovers of pleasure more than lovers of God;

Having a form of godliness, but denying the power thereof: from such turn away. (2 Timothy 3:1–5)

Let me make a few things clear. These comments are in no way intended to be hate speech. These are tough comments that are not politically correct. The Bible makes it very clear. Any person having a leadership role in a church is called by God to be a person of the highest ethical and moral standards. The reason the Bible demands a pastor or elder have character above approach is for the purpose of preventing compromise. It's kind of like telling a recovering alcoholic it would be fine if they were to have one beer or one shot of whiskey every day.

The Bible recommends to the church a man who has gone through a divorce should not be the pastor or elder of a church. The reason is not due to the person being an evil or bad person. The divorce may have not even been his fault. The reason is because God sets the bar high to prevent spiritual compromise, so He recommends a pastor or elder be the man of one wife as well as having a life characterized by moral and ethical integrity. Once a church succumbs to the compromising of God's word, the church starts down a slippery slope of compromise impossible to recover from. Let's take a look at the spiritual qualities the Bible recommends for the positions of pastor and elder. Keep in mind these spiritual truths are not my statements or opinions, these words come directly from God.

This is a true saying, if a man desire the office of a bishop, he desireth a good work.

A bishop then must be blameless, the husband of one wife, vigilant, sober, of good behaviour, given to hospitality, apt to teach;

Not given to wine, no striker, not greedy of filthy lucre; but patient, not a brawler, not covetous;

One that ruleth well his own house, have his children is subjection with all gravity;

(For if a man know not how to rule his own house, how shall he take care of the church of God?)

Not a novice, lest being lifted up with pride he fall into the condemnation of the devil.

Moreover he must have a good report of them which are without; lest he fall into reproach and the snare of the devil.

Likewise must the deacons be grave, not doubletongued, not given to too much wine, not greedy of filthy lucre;

Holding the mystery of the faith in a pure conscience.

And let these also first be proved; then let them use the office of a deacon, being found blameless.

Even so must their wives be grave, not slanderers, sober, faithful in all things.

Let the deacons be the husbands of one wife, ruling their children and their own houses well. (1 Timothy 3:1–12)

So we can see from the above scripture references, the positions of pastor and elder are to be filled with men who are blameless. Men who have the highest moral character and are above reproach. These men are to be the husband of one wife. I can recall an incident years ago when a man in a church I attended informed me the phrase,

"Husband of one wife," was referring to a man having one wife at a time. I didn't argue with the man, but I can assure you this is not what the Bible is informing us. God sets high standards for the positions of pastor and elder to preserve the spiritual integrity of the church. When churches continue to lower the standards required for church leadership, the church at some point becomes no more than a building with a name. The church of Laodicea is a warning sign for all churches today, and should be used as a spiritual guideline evaluating the spiritual condition of the church.

Jesus then gives us some very valuable insight as to the spiritual condition of this church. To state in modern terms, the church at Laodicea was large and would be filled with every modern convenience available to us today. The church pews were padded. The church had several recreation areas, probably a gym and maybe even a theater. The church had several employees on staff, had a very large budget, and their bank account was full. Because this church was so wealthy and luxurious, the members of this church came to believe there was no more in their spiritual lives they were in need of.

Jesus tells this church although they thought they were rich and in need of nothing, spiritually they were extremely poor. It is interesting the church of Laodicea thought they were rich, and the church at Smyrna thought they were poor. Jesus informed Laodicea they were poor in spirit and informed Smyrna they were spiritually rich. Jesus goes on to reveal the true spiritual picture of Laodicea. Jesus informs this church they were wretched, miserable, poor, blind, and naked. Jesus diagnoses the church of Laodicea as being, "Spiritually Dead." These are tough words for a church to hear.

Jesus accused this church of being spiritually blind. This church was incapable of recognizing their true spiritual condition. Blindness is a word used in the Bible many times to symbolize either spiritual immaturity or spiritual unrighteousness. We need to understand as we come closer to the end of the age, spiritual blindness will become the norm for those dwelling on the earth and even for those in the church. The Bible states in many places when people refuse to repent of their evil ways, God finally has no choice but to give people over to a reprobate mind. The church of Laodicea is a spiritual picture of where a lot of churches are today, and where most are headed. Look at what the word of God tells us in Deuteronomy.

> The Lord shall smite thee with madness, and blindness, and astonishment of heart:
> And thou shalt grope at noonday, as the blind gropeth in darkness, and thou shalt not prosper in thy ways: and thou shalt be only oppressed and spoiled evermore, and no man shall save thee. (Deuteronomy 28:28–29)

This church was spiritually blind. Jesus also describes this church as being naked. Nakedness in the Bible in many cases symbolizes spiritual unrighteousness. The church of Laodicea was considered unrighteous in God's eyes. What is Jesus trying to tell this church? Jesus is informing this church they are not, "His Sheep," they are not part of, "His Bride," and they do not know Him. There will be many churches like the church of Laodicea who will go into the future time of Tribulation, because the members of these churches have no relationship with Jesus. People ask me all the time who will be left behind on this earth to suffer God's wrath. The answer is those who are spiritually blind, naked, and are not identified as, "Overcomers."

Because Jesus loves all people and desires them to accept His offer of salvation by faith, Jesus counsels this church to repent, and turn toward Him. Jesus gives counsel to this church using terminology relating to their spiritual condition of unrighteousness and their materialistic view of life. Since this church believes they are spiritually rich, Jesus symbolically asks this church to buy the gold and white robes offered by Him so they can be spiritually rich and cover their unrighteousness. Jesus also uses symbolism when informing this church to put eye salve in their eyes so they can truly see. The best scripture reference to spiritual nakedness in the Bible is found in the book of Genesis.

> And when the woman saw that the tree was good for food, and that it was pleasant to

the eyes, and a tree to be desired to make one wise, she took of the fruit thereof, and did eat, and gave also unto her husband with her; and he did eat.

And the eyes of them both were opened, and they knew that they were naked; and they sewed fig leaves together, and made themselves aprons.

And they heard the voice of the Lord God walking in the garden in the cool of the day: and Adam and his wife hid themselves from the presence of the Lord God amongst the trees of the garden. (Genesis 3:6–8)

Nakedness from the beginning in the Bible has been a picture of unrighteousness. When Adam and Eve sinned against God their day to day personal relationship with God immediately came to an end. It is only through Christ, a person's spiritual relationship with God can be reestablished. Jesus told Nicodemus a person must be, "Born of Spirit," to be able to enter the kingdom of God. The Bible also informs us in Genesis God provided animal skins to cover the nakedness of Adam and Eve. This was also a spiritual picture reminding us the shedding of blood is always required as a covering and payment for sin.

If a person loves their children, they will correct and discipline them when they are young hopefully preventing them from making serious mistakes later on in life. Jesus reminds this church they are being rebuked and disciplined because He loves them.

Jesus informs the church of Laodicea He is standing at their heart's door, and He is knocking. We see a unique contrast between the churches of Laodicea and Philadelphia. Notice Jesus states to the church of Philadelphia He had set before them an, "Open Door," but Jesus is described standing and knocking continually trying to get in the door to Laodicea. What an interesting picture. Jesus knocks at the door of people's heart, but it is the individual who has to open their heart and let Him in. Salvation is a gift offered by God to all who will receive it.

Jesus promises all overcomers at Laodicea they will be given the authority to reign with Him from His throne in heaven. The reason all people who trust in Christ are considered an, "Overcomer," is because Jesus overcame death. Because Jesus lives and is seated at God's right hand, the righteous will also one day conquer death ruling and reigning with Him.

Jesus closes out the letter to Laodicea with the same comment He makes to the other six churches. These letters are intended for all churches, and for anyone who is willing to listen. From what I can see going on in most churches today, there is definitely a lack of hearing, listening, and remembering. I know these seven letters are tough to read, especially this last letter. We need to remember Jesus states He disciplines and rebukes those people He loves. To all those churches, pastors, teachers, and church members who love God and are contending for the faith, Jesus encourages them to keep the faith, finish the race, and let no man steal your crown.

I would like to close out this chapter listing the characteristics Jesus gives in these seven letters of those who, "Overcome." There should be no doubt in anybody's mind who the Bible is referring to when it makes references to this group of people. It is quite oblivious Jesus is referencing those people who are His sheep, and those who are considered as righteous. Here is the list of characteristics the book of Revelation gives us relating to those people the Bible refers to as, "Overcomers."

- Those who will eat of the tree of life
- Those who will escape the second death
- Those who will eat hidden manna
- Those who will receive a white stone
- Those who will receive a new name
- Those who will be given power over the nations
- Those who will receive the Morning Star
- Those who are clothed in white robes

- Those whose names will not be blotted out of the book of life
- Those whose name will be confessed before the Father and the angels
- Those who will be kept from the hour of temptation coming upon the whole earth
- Those who will be made a pillar in the temple of God
- Those who have written on them the name of God
- Those who have the name of the city of God written upon them
- Those who will sit with Jesus on His throne

A Day of Great Tribulation

I have been somewhat prepared in advance to discuss details relating to the day God's wrath will come upon the entire earth. A few years ago, I completed a verse by verse study on the book of Revelation. Revelation is one of the most amazing studies I have ever completed. It is common to study books in the Bible such as Psalms and spend several weeks going through the book. A verse by verse study on the book of Revelation is rare, because it is a very difficult book to understand. I have come to realize to understand Revelation a general knowledge of the entire Bible especially the Old Testament is required. The book of Revelation uses a tremendous amount of symbolism, and a person will discover answers to most questions in this book will be found in the Old Testament. The name, "Revelation," refers to an uncovering or unveiling of things taking place in the future. The book of Revelation was revealed to Jesus by God the Father and was written by John while exiled on the isle of Patmos.

The purpose of the book is to reveal to God's servants what will take place shortly. Revelation is the only book in the Bible giving a blessing to all who read it. I find most people and even churches tend to avoid reading and studying Revelation due to its complexity and the amount of symbolism contained in the book. Those people willing to do their homework will receive a blessing due to the spiritual insight they will gain. To give a short example with the amount of confusion most people have with this book, a person needs to look no further than the very first chapter of Revelation.

> Behold, he cometh with clouds; and every
> eye shall see him, and they also which pierced
> him: and all kindreds of the earth shall wail
> because of him. Even so, Amen. (Revelation 1:7)

Above we see a description of Jesus coming with the clouds. This verse also states during this event every eye shall see Him, even those people who pierced and crucified Him. The verse continues saying all people who are dwelling on the earth during this time will mourn when they see Him coming. To gain further understanding as to the meaning of this verse a person must do their research. As I have stated before, the best commentary to the Bible will always be the Bible. We find four verses in the book of Zechariah giving us clues to the true meaning of what John is informing the saints in this verse.

> In that day shall the Lord defend the inhab-
> itants of Jerusalem; and he that is feeble among
> them at that day shall be as David; and the house
> of David shall be as God, as the angel of the Lord
> before them.
> And it shall come to pass in that day, that
> I will seek to destroy all the nations that come
> against Jerusalem.
> And I will pour upon the house of David,
> and upon the inhabitants of Jerusalem, the spirit
> of grace and of supplications: and they shall look
> upon him whom they have pierced, and they
> shall mourn for him, as one mourneth for his
> only son, and shall be in bitterness for him, as
> one that is in bitterness for his firstborn.
> In that day shall there be a great mourning
> in Jerusalem, as the mourning of Hadadrimmon
> in the valley of Megiddon. (Zechariah 12:8–11)

In most instances, any time the Bible mentions the words referring to, "That Day," it is usually referencing a future event known

as the, "Day of the Lord." The book of Zechariah is informing us during this coming, "Day of the Lord," Jesus Christ will return again to earth. One major purpose for His return will be to protect the nation of Israel. Jesus will establish His earthly kingdom on earth during this time and will rule and reign from Jerusalem for a thousand years. This will also fulfill the prophecy we have discussed earlier, where the angel, "Gabriel," instructs Mary her Son Jesus would rule from David's throne.

Most nations will not heed this warning given by Zechariah. Any nation who comes against Israel during this time will be destroyed by Christ, and His armies following Him from heaven. Revelation chapter 19 describes this event where Jesus comes from heaven riding a white horse. Verse 11 of Revelation 19 informs us the two fold purpose of His second coming. The purpose for Jesus coming to earth a second time is to, "Judge," and to, "Make War." This event does not involve the catching away of His bride. Verse 15 in Revelation 19 informs us during this time Jesus will smite the nations, and rule them with a rod of iron. It will be a time of fierceness and wrath from Almighty God like the world has never seen before. It will not be a time for wedding ceremonies, but a time of judgment and war.

So yes, this will be a time of great mourning for the world. This will be a sad time for all who dwell on the earth. All people who have rejected Christ and have refused to turn from their evil works, will during this time know their end has come. There will also be weeping and mourning in the land of Israel, because they as a nation will realize during this time they have rejected Jesus as, "Messiah," and, "King," and have sinned greatly against their God. The nation of Israel will mourn because they will realize they are guilty of rejecting and crucifying Jesus their Messiah. When there is true repentance there usually is mourning and weeping for sins committed against a holy God.

There is far too much confusion among believers concerning this period of time. This will be an event where Jesus literally comes to earth a second time. The Bible also describes another event including those people who belong to Him, when those who are, "In Christ," will meet Him in the air. We will discuss this idea in the next chapter when we discuss the blessed hope all people have who have placed their faith and trust in the risen Christ. Before we move on, I would like to share one other scriptural reference further explaining the second coming of Christ and its purpose.

Who is this that cometh from Edom, with dyed garments from Bozrah? this that is glorious in his apparel, travelling in the greatness of his strength? I that speak in righteousness, mighty to save.

Wherefore art thou red in thine apparel, and thy garments like him that treadeth in the winefat?

I have trodden the winepress alone; and of the people there was none with me: for I will tread them in mine anger, and trample them in my fury; and their blood shall be sprinkled upon my garments, and I will stain all my raiment.

For the day of vengeance is in mine heart, and the year of my redeemed is come.

And I looked, and there was none to help; and I wondered that there was one to uphold: therefore mine own arm brought salvation unto me; and my fury, it upheld me.

And I will tread down the people in mine anger, and make them drunk in my fury, and I will bring down their strength to the earth.

I will mention the loving kindness of the Lord, and the praises of the Lord, according to all that the Lord hath bestowed on us, and the great goodness toward the house of Israel, which he hath bestowed on them according to his mercies, and according to the multitude of his loving kindness.

For he said, Surely they are my people, children that will not lie: so he was their Saviour.

> In all their affliction he was afflicted, and the angel of his presence saved them: in his love and in his pity he redeemed them; and he bare them, and carried them all the days of old.
>
> But they rebelled, and vexed his holy Spirit: therefore he was turned to be their enemy, and he fought against them.
>
> Then he remembered the days of old, Moses, and his people, saying, Where is he that brought them up out of the sea with the shepherd of his flock? where is he that put his holy Spirit within him? (Isaiah 63:1–11)

If people can understand just these eleven verses in Isaiah, much of the Bible and most of the book of Revelation will be much easier to comprehend. What we see in these verses is in a sense a love letter where God explains His brokenness for His people Israel. Jesus came to be their Messiah, and the children of Israel rejected Him. There is coming a time in the future when the nation of Israel will repent of their sins when they rejected their Messiah, and they will again cry out to God to rescue them. The last three verses in this same chapter as well as one verse in Hosea records this future time of Israel's repentance.

> O Lord, why hast thou made us to err from thy ways, and hardened our heart from thy fear? Return for thy servants' sake, the tribe of thine inheritance.
>
> The people of thy holiness have possessed it but a little while: our adversaries have trodden down thy sanctuary.
>
> We are thine: thou never barest rule over them; they were not called by thy name. (Isaiah 63:17–19)

> I will go and return to my place, till they acknowledge their offense, and seek my face: in their affliction they will seek me early. (Hosea 5:15)

From the above scripture references, we can see it appears one event is required that must take place before Jesus Christ comes to earth a second time. The nation of Israel will during a future time of distress and tribulation confess and repent of their sins. Until this future time of repentance occurs, God will continue to withdraw Himself from Israel. The above scripture literally states there is a day coming when the nation of Israel will again cry out to God, "Return for Thy people's sake." This is the major reason for the second coming of Christ. It will be a very dark day for Israel because they have rejected their Messiah. It will be a dark day for all people dwelling on the earth because they have rejected God's love and forgiveness and have persecuted God's chosen people. It is amazing how much spiritual insight in Revelation has been gained by doing a little research, and taking a look at ten or fifteen verses in the Old Testament.

For the remainder of the chapter, we will deal with some of the major events taking place in Revelation. Another point I again would remind people when studying Revelation is the book is divided into three main sections. We find this outline in chapter 1. Notice this outline is given to John by Jesus instructing him of what will be the order of the book. John is instructed to write down the following in Revelation 1:19:

- Write the things which thou hast seen.
- Write the things which are.
- Write the things which shall be hereafter.

When a person understands some basic principles to Revelation the book makes much more sense. The things John had seen are recorded in Revelation 1:12–20, where he describes turning around and literally sees Jesus Christ the, "Son of God." John states when he saw Christ, he fell at His feet as though he were dead. John then records Jesus touched him with His right hand and states to him in the verses below.

> Fear not; I am the first and the last: I am he
> that liveth, and was dead; and, behold, I am alive
> for evermore, Amen; and have the keys of hell
> and of death. (Revelation 1: 17–18)

The second section to the book of Revelation deals with John writing down the things, "Which Are," or the things taking place during the church age. This section includes chapters 2 and 3 discussing the spiritual conditions of seven specific churches.

The third section to Revelation deals with things that, "Shall be Hereafter," or things taking place following the church age. This third section or final section of Revelation, is where we will be spending the bulk of our time in this chapter. This period of time includes most of the book of Revelation starting with chapter 4 and continuing through the remainder of the book. This future period of time will commence when the church age comes to a close. This time will then go through the seven-year tribulation period climaxing during the event known as the, "Battle of Armageddon." After the conclusion of Armageddon, the next major event the Bible informs us will take place is the, "One-Thousand-Year Millennial Reign," of Christ, and the, "New Jerusalem," coming down from heaven. Information on the "Great White Throne Judgment," including the fate of all beings both in the natural and supernatural realm, will also be revealed in the final chapters of Revelation. We will during this time see Satan being thrown into the, "Lake of Fire," where the antichrist and false prophet already resides and will see death and hell coming to an end. We will then be given a glimpse into a future period of time the Bible refers to as eternity.

One of the major areas of confusion I see among believers today deals with the issue of what groups of people will have to endure this future time of tribulation known as, "Daniel's 70th Week," or the, "Day of the Lord." I have gone into great detail throughout the book giving people an understanding concerning who this future period of time is intended. The Bible goes out of its way to warn people in numerous places what this coming day of God's wrath will entail. The Bible explains in great detail not one righteous person perished in the flood, no righteous people perished in Sodom, and no person covered by the blood of the lamb in Egypt suffered the wrath of God. No person who is called: Righteous, an Overcomer, the Bride of Christ, or In Christ will suffer God's wrath. The righteous may endure tribulation, persecution, and even death, but as the Bible declares, they will be saved from the wrath to come.

There is one other key scriptural reference giving discernment concerning this coming time of God's wrath. You have probably discovered by now this book has many more scripture references than most books. I make no apologies for this. I learned years ago talk is cheap and words are meaningless if they cannot be backed up with the truth of scripture. When dealing with an individual's eternal spiritual condition, a person needs to go to the only source of truth, the word of God. Let's now take a look at what Daniel chapter 9 has to say concerning this coming day of wrath coming upon all people dwelling on the earth.

> And whiles I was speaking, and praying, and confessing my sin and the sin of my people Israel, and presenting my supplication before the Lord my God for the holy mountain of my God.
> Yea, whiles I was speaking in prayer, even the man Gabriel, whom I had seen in the vision at the beginning, being caused to fly swiftly, touched me about the time of the evening oblation.
> And he informed me, and talked with me, and said, O Daniel, I am now come forth to give thee skill and understanding.
> At the beginning of thy supplications the commandment came forth, and I am come to shew thee; for thou art greatly beloved: therefore understand the matter, and consider the vision.

Seventy weeks are determined upon thy people and upon thy holy city, to finish transgression, and to make an end of sins, and to make reconciliation for iniquity, and to bring in everlasting righteousness, and to seal up the vision and prophecy, and to anoint the most Holy.

Know therefore and understand, that from the going forth of the commandment to restore and build Jerusalem unto the Messiah the Prince shall be seven weeks, and threescore and two weeks: the street shall be built again, and the wall, even in troublous times.

And after threescore and two weeks shall the Messiah be cut off, but not for himself: and the people of the prince that shall come shall destroy the city and the sanctuary; and the end thereof shall be with a flood, and unto the end of the war desolations are determined.

And he shall confirm the covenant with many for one week: and in the midst of the week he shall cause the sacrifice and the oblation to cease, and for the overspreading of abominations he shall make it desolate, even until the consummation, and that determined shall be poured upon the desolate. (Daniel 9:20–27)

Daniel chapter 9 gives us some of the most valuable information in the entire Bible concerning an event known as, "Daniel's 70th Week." Daniel is given insight from an angel named Gabriel concerning the future of Israel. Daniel receives a divine revelation from Gabriel during a time in prayer when he is pleading to God for mercy and forgiveness for his sins, and the sins of Israel. Gabriel gives Daniel information concerning the future of Israel with such precise accuracy causing many skeptics to debate or deny the date Daniel was written. We know the book of Daniel was written somewhere around 600 BC, due to the references of Kings reigning during that time. These kings would include Jehoiakim, Nebuchadnezzar, and Darius. There is absolutely no way it could be possible for man alone to get these prophetic dates perfectly right to the day. The Bible is truly written under the inspiration and direction of God.

The angel Gabriel was sent by God to give Daniel discernment as to Israel's future. Gabriel states to Daniel seventy weeks of years have been determined for the nation Israel. The angel Gabriel states this period of time will start with the command to restore and rebuild Jerusalem. Nehemiah chapter 2 informs us this event took place when, "Artaxerxes," was king. Wikipedia identifies this event occurring during the twenty first-year reign of king, "Artaxerxes," in the year 445 BC.

The angel Gabriel is informing Daniel what events will take place during a 490-year period of time in Israel's future. This 490-year period of time will start with the command to restore and rebuild Jerusalem. Gabriel informs Daniel from the time the command to rebuild Israel is given to the time of Christ will be seven weeks, plus sixty weeks, and then two more weeks, making a total of sixty-nine weeks of years. This would bring the total number of years from the command to rebuild Jerusalem recorded in Nehemiah, to the time Christ is, "Cut Off," or crucified to 483 years.

Gabriel continues by giving Daniel further clarification concerning what will take place during this 483-year time frame. During this period of years the Jerusalem wall and the street will be rebuilt during times of trouble. Gabriel also states this period of time will end with the death of the Messiah when He would be crucified on a cross not for Himself, but for the sins of the world. Most do not realize the magnitude of the event when Israel rejected Jesus as Messiah during His prophetic, "Triumphal," entry into Jerusalem. During this time, the true, "Passover Lamb," rode into Jerusalem as a perfect sacrifice for the sins of the people. During the same time a Jewish priest was offering up the shed blood of an unblemished lamb, the true, "Lamb of God," was shedding His blood on a cross. This is why John the Baptist called Jesus, "The Lamb of God," who takes away the sins of the world. This event changed Israel's future in a very drastic way.

It was for this reason Jesus wept as He approached Jerusalem. Jesus foreknew what the consequences of Israel rejecting Him would be. Jesus truly did come for, "His Own," and they received Him not. There are a couple very significant verses in Luke chapter 19 giving insight concerning the significance of this event.

> And when he was come near, he beheld the city, and wept over it,
> Saying, If thou hadst known, even thou, at least in this thy day, the things which belong unto the peace! But now they are hid from thine eyes.
> For the days shall come upon thee, that thine enemies shall cast a trench about thee, and compass thee round, and keep thee in on every side,
> And shall lay thee even with the ground, and thy children within thee; and they shall not leave in thee one stone upon another; because thou knewest not the time of thy visitation. (Luke 19:41–44)

Notice in the previous verses Jesus foretells of a future event where Rome in 70 AD would completely destroy Jerusalem, and many men, women, and children would be killed and taken captive. The final words from Jesus in verse 44 are essential in understanding God's future plans for Israel. Jesus states all these events including the future destruction of Jerusalem will be because the children of Israel failed to recognize who He was. Israel will continue to experience spiritual blindness and be persecuted severely, because they failed to recognize this man born of a virgin who walked the streets of Jerusalem. The man who gave sight to the blind, raised the dead, was crucified, now is risen, and is currently seated at the right hand of the Father.

Notice how accurately the angel Gabriel describes the future captivity and destruction of Jerusalem which was also described by Jesus. Daniel receives this information from Gabriel hundreds of years before the time Jesus would later ride into Jerusalem on a donkey. The crucifixion of Jesus Christ would end a 483 year period of prophecy for Israel. There will be one last seven-year period of time Israel will have to go through before this prophecy will be completely fulfilled. This coming period of time known as, "Daniel's 70th Week," will complete this prophecy given to Daniel over 2500 years ago. Gabriel informs Daniel this period of time is specifically prepared for Israel and upon the city of Jerusalem. God will use this last seven year period of time to cause Israel to turn their heart back to Him. Jeremiah chapter 30 gives us further definition as to the purpose of this period of time.

> For thus saith the Lord; We have heard a voice of trembling, of fear, and not of peace.
>
> Ask ye now, and see whether a man doth travail with child? Wherefore do I see every man with his hands on his loins, as a woman in travail, and all faces are turned into paleness?
>
> Alas! for that day is great, so that none is like it: it is even the time of Jacob's trouble, but he shall be saved out of it. (Jeremiah 30:5–7)

The Bible specifically calls this coming seven-year period of time, a time of, "Jacob's Trouble." It will be a horrible time of trouble for the nation of Israel and all others dwelling on the earth. This time of trouble is not intended for the overcomer, the bride of Christ, or any other name you want to call those counted as righteous. There is far too much confusion in the churches and among believers relating to this issue. When people understand just a few of these basic spiritual truths, the entire book of Revelation makes much more sense. You will not find the word, "Church," mentioned again in the book of Revelation after chapter 3. You will find the words, "Saints, Bride, and Overcomers," is mentioned, but this deals with an entirely different group of people than those merely attending a church.

A question I am routinely asked relates to the identity of those people in Revelation who receive white robes and are referred to as saints. The answer to this question always refers to what the Bible calls the, "Mystery of the Church," or, "The Bride." We will be discussing this in further detail in the following chapter. The Old Testament saints and the Tribulation saints are different in the sense these two groups are not specifically defined in the Bible as those who are, "In Christ." The Old Testament saints will be counted righteous due to their faith and their belief in God. The Tribulation saints will be counted righteous and receive white robes, because they will refuse to take the mark and worship the Beast who declares himself as God. Here again, people need to understand all saints whether, "Old Testament," those, "In Christ," or the, "Tribulation," saints, will not be treated in the same way. Yes, all people who put their faith in God will receive eternal life, but the Bible does, "NOT," define all saints as being part of the bride of Christ. The Bible defines the bride of Christ as those who are, "In Christ," having one body with many members. Let's take a look at a few more verses giving clarity to this issue.

> And he believed in the Lord; and he counted it to him for righteousness. (Genesis 15:6)

> Verily I say unto you, Among them that are born of women there hath not risen a greater than John the Baptist: notwithstanding he that is least in the kingdom of heaven is greater than he. (Matthew 11:11)

> And one of the elders answered, saying unto me, What are these which are arrayed in white robes? and whence came they?
> And I said unto him, Sir, thou knowest. And he said to me, These are they which came out of great tribulation, and have washed their robes, and made them white in the blood of the Lamb.
> Therefore are they before the throne of God, and serve him day and night in his tem-

ple: and he that sitteth on the throne shall dwell among them. (Revelation 7:13–15)

And many of them that sleep in the dust of the earth shall awake, some to everlasting life, and some to shame (and) everlasting contempt. (Daniel 12:2)

Those who are part of the bride of Christ are referred to in the Bible as those, "In Christ." There are three primary participants in a wedding. There is the, "Groom," who the Bible defines as Jesus. There is the bride of Christ which is those people who are, "In Christ." This body of believers is referred to by Christ as, "Overcomers," in the letters to the seven churches. Finally, there are those people who the Bible refers to as, "Wedding Guests." If the bride is made up of all believers including Old Testament and Tribulation saints, then who are the wedding guests described in Revelation chapter 19?

And a voice came out of the throne, saying, Praise our God, all ye his servants, and ye that fear him, both small and great.

And I heard as it were the voice of a great multitude, and as the voice of many waters, and as the voice of mighty thunderings, saying, Alleluia: for the Lord God omnipotent reigneth.

Let us be glad and rejoice, and give honour to him: for the marriage of the Lamb is come, and his wife hath made herself ready.

And to her was granted that she should be arrayed in fine linen, clean and white: for the fine linen is the righteousness of saints.

And he saith unto me, Write, Blessed are they which are called unto the marriage supper of the Lamb. And he saith unto me, These are the true sayings of God. (Revelation 19:5–9)

There really seems to be no other way to bring people truth, but to show it to them in God's word. Notice the words above in verse 9 of Revelation 19. Does anybody truly believe it would be necessary for a bride to receive an invitation to her own marriage supper. The bride is the entire purpose for the marriage supper. The Bible speaks truth and answers all our questions if we will just do the research. Too many people today sit in a pew or in a class and put their full trust in a person without doing their own homework. Doesn't the Bible tell us to study to show thyself approved so we will be able to rightly divide and discern what is truth? Isn't it always a good idea when making a purchase to read the fine print before signing on the dotted line? Every person will one day individually give an account for the decisions they have made in life. It's actually a much more serious issue than this. I believe every parent will one day give account for the way they have taught and raised their children. We who are parents and grandparents have been given a lot of responsibility when we really think about it.

Getting back to the verses in Daniel chapter 9, I want to stress what the angel Gabriel states will be accomplished during this seven-year period of great distress coming upon the world. Daniel tells us this period of time will be for the purpose of bringing in everlasting righteousness, and an end to sin and wickedness on the earth as well as in the spiritual realm. It will be a time bringing a completion to all things including prophecy. This seven-year period will be a time for cleansing the earth of evil and preparing it for Christ's one-thousand-year millennial reign on earth.

The book of Daniel gives us valuable insight regarding an event starting the countdown of the seven year tribulation. The person the Bible refers to as the antichrist will confirm a covenant with Israel and possibly other nations for a period of seven years. It's amazing how many people do not believe this period of time should be taken literally. There are several passages in the Bible such as here in Daniel and Revelation making reference to this event. The Bible informs us in many places Daniel's seventieth week will last seven years, and the event known as the, "Abomination of Desolation," will take place 42 months or 1,260 days from the beginning of this covenant agreement. Without spending a lot of time on this issue, the Bible clearly refers to this time of tribulation as a literal event. Notice how the book of Isaiah makes reference to this event.

> Because ye have said, We have made a covenant with death, and with hell are we at agreement when the overflowing scourge shall pass through, it shall not come unto us: for we have made lies our refuge, and under falsehood have we hid ourselves. (Isaiah 28:15)

Because the nation of Israel has rejected the true Messiah, they will be deceived into making a covenant with the antichrist which will end up being their demise. God will in His sovereignty use this event as a disciplinary measure to turn the heart of His people back to Him. Remember the words of Solomon stating, "What Has Been Done, Will Be Done Again." God will bring Israel back into an Old Testament type experience in order to bring them to a spiritual state of repentance. Now we see the prophetic message Jesus states in the book of John, makes perfect sense.

> I am come in my Father's name, and ye receive me not: if another shall come in his own name, him ye will receive. (John 5:43)

Yes, Israel will be deceived by this coming man of sin. It will be a short honeymoon for Israel. According to Daniel this coming, "Son of Perdition," will break the covenant made with many nations. The antichrist will defile the holy temple after forty-two months, or at the middle point of this seven year agreement. Another important insight the angel Gabriel gives us is at least by the midpoint of the seven-year tribulation period, Israel will have an established temple, and Old Testament temple practices will again be reestablished. Remember, this period of time will be after the current church age, and the age of grace has come to a close. When Jesus stated today is the day of salvation, this is exactly what He meant. The world will be living in a new age during this time. Jesus informed the disciples of this same event in Matthew chapter 24, giving valuable information concerning what the nation of Israel will have to experience during this time.

> When ye therefore shall see the abomination of desolation, spoken of by Daniel the prophet, stand in the holy place, (whoso readeth, let him understand:)
>
> Then let them which be in Judaea flee in the mountains:
>
> Let him which is on the housetop not come down to take any thing out of his house:
>
> Neither let him which is in the field return back to take his clothes.
>
> And woe unto them that are with child, and to them that give suck in those days!
>
> But pray ye that your flight be not in the winter, neither on the sabbath day:
>
> For then shall be great tribulation, such as was not since the beginning of the world to this time, no, nor ever shall be.
>
> And except those days should be shortened, there should no flesh be saved: but for the elect's sake those days shall be shortened.
>
> Then if any man shall say unto you, Lo, here is the Christ, or there; believe it not.
>
> For there shall arise false Christs, and false prophets, and shall shew great signs and wonders; insomuch that, if it were possible, they shall deceive the very elect.
>
> Behold, I have told you before.
>
> Wherefore if they shall say unto you, Behold, he is in the desert; go not forth: behold, he is in the secret chambers; believe it not.

> For as lightning cometh out of the east, and
> shineth even unto the west; so shall also the com-
> ing of the Son of man be. (Matthew 24:15–27)

We notice in the book of Matthew Jesus gives credibility to the words spoken by Daniel. There are a lot of people who have a problem with the validity of Daniel but as we see here, Jesus doesn't appear to have any concerns about what Daniel records. Notice Jesus informs us this will be a time of, "Great Tribulation." It will be a time like there has never been or will be again. We know the earth has gone through extreme cataclysmic events before such as the flood of Noah, but Jesus states nothing will compare to this time. The church needs to be reminded these events are coming. The question is, are people spiritually awake and are they spiritually prepared for these future events. It is impossible to imagine what this coming time will be like, since events this severe have never happened in our recent past. Can one imagine what it will be like on earth when every mountain and every island is removed from its place? I have always believed being prepared for catastrophes is a smart thing. Some extra supplies and extra food is a good idea. I am telling people there is not a bunker or any amount of food, supplies, or weapons that will enable a person to survive this coming period of God's wrath.

> And the kings of the earth, and the great
> men, and the rich men, and the chief captains,
> and the mighty men, and every bondman, and
> every free man, hid themselves in the dens and in
> the rocks of the mountains;
> And said to the mountains and rocks, Fall
> on us, and hide us from the face of him that sit-
> teth on the throne, and from the wrath of the
> Lamb: (Revelation 6:15–16)

We also notice these events are meant to be a time of spiritual awakening for Israel. Jesus warns when the people of Israel see the antichrist standing in the, "Holy of Holies," of a new functioning Jewish Temple declaring himself as God, they need to run for the hills. This will fulfill the event known as the, "Abomination of Desolation," spoken of by the prophets, because the antichrist will stop temple sacrifices and desecrate the temple.

Gabriel gives Daniel some final words of wisdom concerning this man known as the antichrist. We need to always keep in mind God is in control and there are no surprises for him. The antichrist will be allowed according to scriptures to have absolute power and control over the earth for forty-two months. After this time, he will be destroyed and thrown into the, "Lake of Fire," along with the false prophet. This concept confuses most people even in the church, but during this period of forty-two months the antichrist will be given authority over the saints to overcome them. Notice the Bible does not say he will be given power to overcome, "The Church." The true church or bride, those who have, "Overcome," will not be on earth during these events. What has the scripture taught us? The Tribulation will be a period of time determined for Israel, Jerusalem, and those who dwell on the earth. It will be a time of, "Jacob's Trouble." Daniel chapter 7 gives us further insight to this man known as the antichrist.

> I came near unto one of them that stood by, and asked him the truth of all this. So he told me, and made me know the interpretation of the things.
>
> These great beasts, which are four, are four kings, which shall arise out of the earth.
>
> But the saints of the most High shall take the kingdom, and possess the kingdom for ever, even for ever and ever.
>
> Then I would know the truth of the fourth beast, which was diverse from all the others, exceeding dreadful, whose teeth were of iron, and his nails of brass; which devoured, brake in pieces, and stamped the residue with his feet;

And of the ten horns that were in his head, and of the other which came up, and before whom three fell; even of that horn that had eyes, and a mouth that spake very great things, whose look was more stout than his fellows.

I beheld, and the same horn made war with the saints, and prevailed against them;

Until the Ancient of days came, and judgment was given to the saints of the most High; and the time came that the saints possessed the kingdom.

Thus he said, The fourth beast shall be the fourth kingdom upon earth, which shall be diverse from all kingdoms, and shall devour the whole earth, and shall tread it down, and break it into pieces.

And the ten horns out of this kingdom are ten kings that shall arise: and another shall rise after them; and he shall be diverse from the first, and he shall subdue three kings.

And he shall speak great words against the most High, and shall wear out the saints of the most High, and think to change times and laws: and they shall be given into his hand until a time and times and the dividing of time.

But the judgment shall sit, and they shall take away his dominion, to consume and to destroy it unto the end. (Daniel 7:16–26)

A future kingdom will arise and conquer the entire globe during this time of coming Tribulation. This kingdom will be ruled by one of the most evil and fierce rulers that has ever existed. He is referred to as the antichrist or the Beast. The Bible refers to this person as the man who once was alive, now is not, and will ascend out of the Abyss. This ruler will have no compassion for people, and he will hate anything having to do with God. His ultimate goals will be to destroy Israel and kill all people dwelling on the earth refusing to worship him. Sadly, hundreds of thousands, perhaps millions of saints will be murdered during this time. This man of sin will have a simple philosophy, worship him or die. The age of grace has passed. Those dwelling on earth during this time will be forced to make a spiritual choice. Worship the antichrist, take the mark, and deal with the circumstances, or deny the antichrist, refuse the mark, and die. I have heard many people make the comment there is no way they will ever kneel down and worship anyone. During this time, a choice will be required. Worship the Beast, or die.

This man called the antichrist will not be a normal man. Notice Daniel describes this man as being, "More Stout," or opposing than the other kings. I believe this man will literally be the offspring of Satan referred to by God in the book of Genesis. This man will literally be of the seed of the serpent. John in the book of Revelation informs us this man once existed, now is not, and will ascend out of the abyss. John informs us his name is, "Apollo." It is interesting Apollo was worshipped in the past as a Greek God. Being in some ways similar to Christ, this person once walked the earth but unlike Christ, this man now is dead. Jesus Christ will one day descend from heaven and the person known as the antichrist, he ascends out of the bottomless pit. And for those who believe this Beast is just referring to a world power, the Bible makes clear more than once he has eyes like a man and a mouth that speaks boastfully constantly blaspheming God.

I have for years believed the time of Gentile rule on the earth will end in the way it began. Yes, there really is nothing new under the sun. I firmly believe the antichrist very well could be a resurrected, "Nimrod." I firmly believe his spirit which is currently locked in the abyss, will be somehow released by God to reenter the body of a resurrected Nimrod. I know this sounds hard to believe, but this is what I believe the bible is trying to tell us. And yes, I have been laughed at many times, and I know people thought my beliefs were a little strange. Most people in the church do not want to hear this information. I have to admit, it is a little hard to believe. People need to realize we have reached the point with technology all we really need is the, "DNA," of any human or animal, and we can recreate it. If the body of Nimrod or a Nephilim king could be found, the impossible becomes possible. I have listened to several people stating Nimrod's body may very well have been found years ago in Iraq. Nimrod, a man known by many names, may have also been called, "Gilgamesh." A great source for continued study on the subject of DNA manipulation would be to access the Internet and research the subject, "Transhumanism."

John records in Revelation this information was given to him by Jesus Christ as a warning to His servants of what will take place in the future. The reason the church was given this information was for the purposes of education and warning. It is the church who has been given the responsibilities of being salt and light. It is for this reason Jesus had stern warnings for many of the seven churches in Asia. Jesus informed the last church named Laodicea they were poor, pitiful, blind, and naked. In other words, this church had no relationship with Christ. Jesus stated He knows His sheep, and His sheep know His voice.

It will be churches who are similar to Laodicea who will go through this time of horrible deception, temptation, and wrath. It was the church at Philadelphia who was given an, "Open Door," and promised personally by Christ to be kept from this future time of testing. Jesus warned us over and over again to not be deceived. Jesus also gives us a very strange warning in the previous scripture text in Matthew. Jesus warns if anyone makes reference to Christ one day being found in the desert or in a secret chamber, do not believe them. Could Jesus be making reference to an ancient tomb in the desert that has been or will be discovered? Below is the scripture text in Matthew relating to this subject.

> Behold, I have told you before.
> Wherefore if they shall say unto you, Behold, he is in the desert; go not forth: behold, he is in the secret chambers; believe it not. (Matthew 24: 25–26)

The Bible gives us some very interesting information relating to Nimrod. The Bible informs us for some reason God had to intervene in the affairs of Nimrod and put an end to his plans. It is interesting according to *Hitchcock's Bible Names Dictionary*, the name Nimrod means, "Rebellion." This dictionary also defines the meaning for the name Babel as, "Gate to God," It is possible Nimrod was attempting to open a spiritual doorway to the spirit world and was receiving power and authority from Satan, fallen angels, and demonic forces to achieve this goal. The Bible makes reference to a heavenly ladder in which angels are seen ascending and descending to the earth. There is an old gospel song referencing angels ascending and descending Jacob's ladder, and most people probably have no idea what this ladder is referring too. Take a look at what the Bible has to say in Genesis concerning this man called Nimrod.

> And the Lord came down to see the city and the tower, which the children of men builded.
> And the Lord said, Behold, the people is one, and they have all one language; and this they begin to do: and now nothing will be restrained from them, which they have imagined to do.
> Go to, let us go down, and there confound their language, that they may not understand one another's speech. (Genesis 11:5–7)

I believe Nimrod and the government system he was attempting to create, is a picture of the future antichrist and the future worldwide control he will bring upon the entire earth. This future world system will consist of total governmental, economic, and religious control over the entire world. The antichrist's reign on earth will begin with a seven-year agreement or covenant he will make with many nations, but will primarily be intended for the nation of Israel.

When a person researches the period of time in which Nimrod lived, we come to the realization most all cults and religions of the world can be traced back to the times of Assyria and Babylon. The

Bible gives us another interesting characteristic of Nimrod in Genesis chapter 10.

> He was a mighty hunter before the Lord:
> wherefore it is said, Even as Nimrod the mighty
> hunter before the Lord. (Genesis 10:9)

So Nimrod was known as a mighty hunter. Historical artifacts have been found supposedly of Nimrod, and in a lot of cases this great warrior is seen riding on a horse with a bow in his hand. I believe Revelation chapter 6 is giving us a picture of this mighty hunter.

> And I saw, and behold a white horse: and he
> that sat on him had a bow: and a crown was given
> unto him: and he went forth conquering, and to
> conquer. (Revelation 6:2)

In Revelation chapter 19, we see a very similar description of another person riding on a white horse which is Jesus Christ. Notice the similarities of these two individuals. This is a picture of the level of deception the appearing of the antichrist will have. The antichrist will deceive Israel, and all people dwelling on the earth during this time. This man will be coming, "As Christ," or, "In the place of Christ," and he will deceive the world. This will be a time of great deception. These two verses will be the ultimate fulfillment of the two seeds discussed earlier in the book. Jesus Christ is the, "Seed of the Woman," and the antichrist is the, "Seed of Satan."

> And I saw heaven opened, and behold a
> white horse; and he that sat upon him was called
> Faithful and True, and in righteousness he doth
> judge and make war.
> His eyes were as a flame of fire, and on his
> head were many crowns; and he had a name

written, that no man knew, be he himself. (Revelation 19:11–12)

Although there are similarities between these two riders on white horses, there are major differences. One rider is named, "Faithful and True," and on His head were many crowns. Since Christ has been given ultimate authority over all the earth, He has a name too which He alone knows, and a name which is above every other name.

The antichrist who is also referred to as, "The God of Many Names," is described riding on a white horse being a great conqueror. I believe it is no coincidence Nimrod was also given the title of a mighty hunter. The Bible informs us God confused the language of people during the construction phase of the tower of Babel. When the people were scattered and they settled into new areas, Nimrod more than likely became known throughout the land and was worshipped as a, "god." Some people suggest Nimrod very well could have been a hybrid being Genesis chapter 6 refers to as a, "Nephilim."

There are many legends suggesting Nimrod was a giant, a man of great stature. If this is true, Nimrod would definitely be qualified for the position of antichrist, because he would have the seed of the Serpent. One last interesting comment relating to Nimrod is the Egyptians worship a god by the name of, "Osiris." Osiris is known as the, "God of the underworld," or the, "God of the dead." Osiris is also known as the, "Dying and rising god." The Bible informs us a characteristic of the antichrist is he is known as the man who was alive, now is dead, and will rise out of the bottomless pit. Sounds like a description of a dying and rising god to me. The Egyptians also worshipped the stars and the constellation Orion which is also defined as the, "Mighty Hunter." This may be just another coincidence. The problem is, I don't believe in coincidences any longer. Could it be this man the Bible refers to as Nimrod was also known and worshipped by other names such as: Orion, Osiris, Apollo, Gilgamesh, Marduk, Saturn, and Baal. Let's look at a couple more verses in Revelation making references to this man called the antichrist.

The beast that thou sawest was, and is not; and shall ascend out of the bottomless pit, and go into perdition: and they that dwell on the earth shall wonder, whose names were not written in the book of life from the foundation of the world, when they behold the beast that was, and is not, and yet is.

And the beast that was, and is not, even he is the eighth, and is of the seven, and goeth into perdition. (Revelation 17:8, 11)

This spirit the Bible refers to as, "The Beast," comes out of the bottomless pit, possessing a man the Bible calls the, "Son of Perdition." The antichrist will be a reappearance of one of seven great Gentile kings that once ruled the world. The angel informs John in Revelation this man will be somehow resurrected and the spirit of, "Apollo," will inhabit him, and he will literally walk the earth again as the antichrist. Because this world ruler was one of seven mighty kings ruling the world who will return again, John refers to this man as the, "Eighth King." The Bible tells us the whole world will be astonished when they see this man. Those dwelling on the earth being deceived during this time will not be those who are "In Christ." It will be those people dwelling on the earth whose names are not written in the book of life.

This will be a period of time where an unholy trinity will rule the world. Satan will be allowed to take the role of the, "Most High God," during this time. After all, his goal in life has always been to find a way to overthrow God seating himself on God's throne. So in a sense, mankind is caught in the middle of a spiritual battle between the forces of good and evil. Here's what the book of Isaiah tells us concerning the ultimate goal of Satan.

I will ascend above the heights of the clouds;
I will be like the most High. (Isaiah 14:14)

Satan's ultimate goal in life is to be like God. It seems strange Satan could bring himself to the level he will actually believe he can take God's throne. For some reason, Satan comes to believe through the joining of the nations of the world along with his hoard of evil forces, he will be able to achieve his goals. I believe there have been many events in history where Satan thought he had the upper hand, but God was always one step ahead of him. The crucifixion of Christ would be one of those examples. During this time Satan will be allowed to have his time on the center stage of the world. Satan will truly will live up to his name as the, "God of this world," for a period of forty two months. Satan, as well as the kings of the world will not realize they are being used as pawns by God to carry out His ultimate will.

Another person playing an active role of deception during the tribulation will be a person the Bible refers to as the, "False Prophet." A description of this man is given in Revelation chapter 13. The false prophet will receive his power from Satan who is referred to in the Bible as, "The Dragon." The false prophet will deceive all who dwell on the earth with all types of wondrous signs and miracles. The Bible states this man will be able to bring fire down from heaven. The false prophet will point people to the antichrist, and will play a major role in forcing all on the earth during this time to worship him. I have heard people make the comment nobody will ever tell them when to worship or who to worship. During this time nobody will have the freedom to live as they please. They will take the mark, worship the Beast, or they will be killed. Here's what the Bible has to say about this man called the, "False Prophet."

> And I beheld another beast coming up out of the earth; and he had two horns like a lamb, and he spake as a dragon.
> And he exerciseth all the power of the first beast before him, and causeth the earth and them which dwell therein to worship the first beast, whose deadly wound was healed.

And he doeth great wonders, so that he maketh fire come down from heaven on the earth in the sight of men,

And deceiveth them that dwell on the earth by the means of those miracles which he had power to do in the sight of the beast; saying to them that dwell on the earth, that they should make an image to the beast, which had the wound by a sword, and did live.

And he had power to give life unto the image of the beast, that the image of the beast should both speak, and cause that as many as would not worship the image of the beast should be killed.

And he causeth all, both small and great, rich and poor, free and bond, to receive a mark in their right hand, or in their foreheads:

And that no man might buy or sell, save he that had the mark, or the name of the beast, or the number of his name. (Revelation 13:11–17)

First of all, it would be interesting to go back and count how many times the Bible makes reference to, "Those who dwell on the earth." I believe God is going out of His way to make the point very clear to the reader the identity of these people. Secondly, if anybody tells you they understand every word of the book of Revelation, you probably should start running fast in the other direction. After close to thirty years of reading, studying, and listening to countless theories on bible prophecy, there are still many answers to questions I am still searching for. There is one thing I do know for sure. I do not want to be one of those people dwelling on the earth during this time of, "Great Tribulation."

The false prophet will if I might say be the, "False Elijah," of the group. If people could just grasp the concept that Satan's entire agenda will be comprised of lies and deception. This man will perform great miracles even causing fire to come down from heaven in the sight of many. Through the acts of these miracles, the people living on the earth during this time will be deceived. The false prophet will play the religious role of the, "Holy Spirit," in this evil trinity. Although a true worship of Christ will not be allowed or tolerated during this time, church and religion will play a major role in the level of deception taking place during this time. When one controls the government, controls the economy, and controls the religions of the world, we have a situation where there is complete global control. Revelation tells us this man will present himself as a, "Lamb," but he will speak as a, "Dragon." This will be a time of, "Great Deception," such as the world has never seen before.

The false prophet will force all people on earth no matter their earthly status to receive a mark in their right hand, or in their forehead. This will be a time of total control, and a loss of all freedoms. If you want to participate in the world financial or governmental systems during this time, you will need to take the mark. I have always believed the mark of the, "Beast," will be sold to the masses as giving people more security, preventing identify theft, and saving people more time due to no longer needing to store passwords and security codes. The mark will involve and control all types of economic transactions, as well as provide 24-hour monitoring of every person dwelling on the earth. The world is constantly improving computer and WiFi capability. I believe this technology is all part of the, "Beast System," which is already in place, and will one day control and monitor every person dwelling on the earth. The world is ready to move to a cashless society and live life in a whole new era of digital reality.

The other facet to the mark of the, "Beast," most do not consider, is it literally will be spiritual in nature. I have believed for years and recently I am more convinced, the mark will include not only injecting a microchip under a person's skin, but also the changing of a person's DNA. I am of the belief the mark will be Satan's counterfeit for the Holy Spirit. The Bible informs us in Ephesians, the Holy Spirit is a mark sealing or guaranteeing an eternal inheritance to those who trust and believe in Christ. I believe the mark of the, "Beast," is a counterfeit for the Holy Spirit eternally damning the souls of any person who receives it. I believe one of the supposed benefits Satan will offer those taking the mark will be immortality by altering a person's DNA. The mark will not only possibly involve a microchip implant, it will involve a spiritual decision. It is for this reason the Bible informs all people refusing the mark of the Beast will escape the, "Second Death," and all who take the mark will experience the, "Second Death." It is interesting Revelation chapter 16 tells us ugly and painful sores break out on all people receiving the mark. I have wondered if these sores were a direct judgment from God or merely the body rejecting these evil manipulations of DNA. I believe the answer is they are both. In the same way the indwelling of the Holy Spirit causes a rebirth of a person's spiritual condition with God, the mark of the, "Beast," will also eternally change a person spiritually.

For those who believe this is nonsense, I would suggest researching what science has now been doing for years in the areas of DNA manipulation. As stated earlier, we are now technologically to the point if we have the DNA of a human or any kind of animal, we can literally clone, recreate, or comingle foreign DNA with the human body. Scientists have been warning the public for years we may be on the verge of scientific and medical breakthroughs, we may one day drastically regret.

The major objective of the false prophet will be to force those dwelling on the earth to worship the antichrist. It is interesting the Bible refers to the antichrist as being fatally wounded by a sword, and yet this man lives. I am of the impression this may be one of the reasons the entire world will be astonished when they see this man. I am not stating with complete certainty, but I do not believe the antichrist shows up on the scene, is killed by a sword, and then the world is astonished or shocked he comes back to life again. I tend to believe the world will be astonished and will marvel at this man, because people will realize this man once walked the earth, was possibly killed by a sword, and now he is alive for all to see. It is interesting what the book of Jasher tells us concerning the death of Nimrod.

And Nimrod and two of his men that were
with him came to the place where they were, when

Esau started suddenly from his lurking place, and drew his sword, and hastened and ran to Nimrod and cut off his head. Jasher, Chapter 27:7

We need to remember John states the antichrist once was alive, now is dead, and he will ascend out of the abyss. We see these similar descriptions of this future world leader told over and over in the Bible. Revelation chapter 17 gives us more insight concerning this person.

And I saw one of his heads as it were wounded to death; and his deadly wound was healed: and all the world wondered after the beast.

And they worshipped the dragon which gave power unto the beast: and they worshipped the beast, saying, Who is like unto the beast? who is able to make war with him?

And there was given unto him a mouth speaking great things and blasphemies; and power was given unto him to continue forty and two months.

And he opened his mouth in blasphemy against God, to blaspheme his name, and his tabernacle, and them that dwell in heaven.

And it was given unto him to make war with the saints, and to overcome them: and power was given him over all kindreds, and tongues, and nations.

And all that dwell upon the earth shall worship him, whose names are not written in the book of life of the Lamb slain from the foundation of the world. (Revelation 13:3–8)

It is interesting when the Bible wants us to pick up on a particular truth, it will repeat certain characteristics or facts to us over and over again. This is what we see taking place in the Bible concerning this coming ruler. We see this man has some real spiritual problems, because in several scripture passages the Bible informs us this man is full of pride, he is arrogant, and evidently has a problem controlling his mouth. This man constantly curses and blasphemes God and even curses those people dwelling in heaven. The antichrist hates the saints, and is even for a period of forty-two months allowed to persecute and kill them. The antichrist hates Israel, and his overwhelming desire is to totally annihilate them. We can recall in Genesis where God informs Adam, Eve, and the Serpent there would be enmity or hatred between Satan and the woman. The woman in the garden is a spiritual picture of Israel who would one day birth the Messiah. The antichrist is given total global control of the world for forty-two months. All who dwell on the earth whose names are not written in the, "Book of Life," will be deceived into worshipping this man.

Due to the impossibility of covering all the significant events occurring in Revelation, I would like to touch on a few other important events occurring during this time. In chapters 4 and 5 we are given some very important information where we are shown a scene of God's throne in heaven. Notice the words used by John in the first verse of chapter 4.

> After this I looked, and, behold, a door was opened in heaven: and the first voice I heard was as it were a trumpet talking with me; which said, Come up hither, and I will shew thee things which must be hereafter. (Revelation 4:1)

Here we see John mentioning a door in heaven opening. I believe this is a picture of the same door promised to the church of Philadelphia due to this church keeping the faith. Notice John describes the voice of God sounding like a trumpet. The Bible describes an event taking place in the future where there will first be a shout, followed by the, "Trump of God." We will discuss this further in the next chapter. Notice this voice from God tells John to, "Come up Hither." I believe this verse is a symbolic reference to the gathering together of the bride of Christ. John is then informed by

God he will be shown things which must take place, "Hereafter," or, "After This." Since John had just finished with the letters to the seven churches, I believe these words are making reference to events occurring after the completion of the church age. It is my belief chapter 4 and all chapters following through the end of the book of Revelation, deals with a future time after the church age has been completed.

In chapters 4 and 5 of Revelation we are being shown an almost indescribable scene in heaven referred to as the throne of God. We need to keep in mind when John is attempting to describe what he is being allowed to see, he is describing sights which words are incapable of expressing. John is caught up in the spirit to heaven and is attempting to explain in the best way humanly possible, what he is seeing in the spiritual or multidimensional realm.

We need to understand that God, these Four Beasts or Creatures, the angels, and all demonic spirits operates in the spiritual realm. Mortal beings such as us can only live and operate in the dimensions of length, width, height, and time. The supernatural realm is not confined to these four dimensions. The Bible tells us God is able to see the beginning from the end and the end from the beginning. God is able to operate in several dimensions of time alone. What I am trying to say, is in the spiritual realm the impossible becomes possible. The three verses below gives us a glimpse of how one day we will as Paul states, "Put on immortality."

> Beloved, now are we the sons of God, and it doth not yet appear what we shall be: but we know that, when he shall appear, we shall be like him; for we shall see him as he is. (1 John 3:2)

> But as it is written, Eye hath not seen, nor ear heard, neither have entered into the heart of man, the things which God hath prepared for them that love him (1 Corinthians 2:9).

> For now we see through a glass, darkly; but then face to face: now I know in part; but

then shall I know even as also I am known
(1 Corinthians 13:12).

I must quickly touch on an interesting promise 1 John gives us. When will we be like Him? When Christ appears is what the Bible informs us. I believe this will occur in the moment, in a twinkling of an eye. The one idea I am trying to get across is as we study what takes place in the future, we will never in our present state totally understand it all. Aren't we told the definition of faith is trusting in something we cannot see or prove?

Before we move on one last thing we need to realize concerning the book of Revelation, is from chapter 4 to the end of the book the information is not in chronological order. A person needs to understand John is attempting to describe events happening on earth and in the spiritual realm at the same time. John is like a person narrating a play or parade attempting to describe multiple events or scenes occurring simultaneously. He is attempting to explain multiple events taking place in heaven and on the earth, occurring in the natural and the supernatural realm.

We find the major point to the, "Throne in Heaven," scene taking place in chapter 5. Revelation chapter 5 gives us a picture of the sovereignty and authority given to Jesus Christ the, "Lamb," that was slain. A person should take note in chapters 4 and 5 we see Jesus in a sense taking on a new role. Jesus, "The Lamb of God," has been seated at the right hand of the Father making intercession for the saints during the church age. Now we Jesus and Him alone taking a sealed scroll out of the right hand of God and being found worthy to break its seals. Jesus has been portrayed during the church age as the, "Lamb of God," making intercession for the saints. Now Jesus is being portrayed as the, "Lion of the Tribe of Judah," given authority to judge the world. There are literally thousands of various gods, spirits, and angels being worshipped today by millions of people through many types of religions. Revelation informs us no man in heaven, the entire earth, or under the earth is found worthy to open the scroll but Jesus Christ, "The Lamb of

God." Here's a list of verses in chapter 5 informing us of Christ's authority.

> And I saw in the right hand of him that sat on the throne a book written within and on the backside, sealed with seven seals.
>
> And I saw a strong angel proclaiming with a loud voice, Who is worthy to open the book, and to loose the seals thereof?
>
> And no man in heaven, nor in earth, neither under the earth, was able to open the book, neither to look thereon.
>
> And I wept much, because no man was found worthy to open and to read the book, neither to look thereon.
>
> And one of the elders saith unto me, Weep not: behold, the Lion of the tribe of Judah, the Root of David, hath prevailed to open the book, and to loose the seven seals thereof.
>
> And I beheld, and, lo, in the midst of the throne and of the four beasts, and in the midst of the elders, stood a lamb as it had been slain, having seven horns and seven eyes, which are the seven Spirits of God sent forth into all the earth.
>
> And he came and took the book out of the right hand of him that sat upon the throne.
>
> And when he had taken the book, the four beasts and four and twenty elders fell down before the Lamb, having every one of them harps, and golden vials full of odours, which are the prayers of saints.
>
> And they sung a new song, saying, Thou art worthy to take the book, and to open the seals thereof: for thou was slain, and hast redeemed us to God by thy blood out of every kindred, and tongue, and people, and nation;

> And hast made us unto our God kings
> and priests: and we shall reign on the earth.
> (Revelation 5:1–10)

We see Jesus, "The Lamb of God," is now being portrayed as the, "Lion of the Tribe of Judah." The, "Lion of the Tribe of Judah," is an Old Testament definition of Jesus Christ. Jesus is the only man in all creation spiritually qualified to break the seals of the scroll and read its contents. Jesus Christ came as a, "Lamb," when He was born in the city of Bethlehem. He will come as a, "Lion," to earth the second time. The breaking of these seven seals will start a chain reaction of events which will occur on the earth, in the heavens, and in the spiritual realm unlike never seen before. I also must comment on the identity of this group of people seen around God's throne. They are redeemed by the blood of the Lamb, out of every kindred, tongue, people, and nation having been made, "Kings," and, "Priests." You know the Bible informs us in several places, "The Bride," will one day rule and reign with Christ.

Beginning in Revelation 6 and continuing through chapter 16, we see the majority of this information refers to judgments occurring to those dwelling on the earth during this time. Many of these judgments referred to as seal, trumpet, and vial (bowl) judgments will happen in progression, but one needs to understand some of these judgments will possibly cause a chain reaction of events to occur. For example, if an asteroid was to strike the earth we know it likely would have a domino effect causing cataclysmic events such as earthquakes and tsunamis. These events would possibly trigger other major health, environmental, and economic judgments to occur on the earth. Notice here again we see repetitive patterns of sevens dealing with these judgments.

I would like to give a very brief overview describing the basic details of these judgments, and give a short response concerning the impact they will have on those dwelling on the earth. We need to realize it is Jesus and Him only who is qualified to break the seals to this scroll, and start this procession of judgment events to come upon the earth. Another interesting point a person will need to recognize is the way these judgments will be similar in nature to the judgments which occurred in Egypt during Israel's captivity. Again, we should be reminded of the words of Solomon where he stated, "What Has Been Done, Will Be Done Again."

Seal #1: A white horse appears symbolizing power and righteousness. This rider wears a crown and carries a bow symbolizing authority to rule, and power to overcome and conquer. His name is not, "Faithful and True." This man more than likely is the antichrist coming as a false Christ. Daniel states he destroys wonderfully, meaning the world will at first marvel over his wisdom, and he will be worshipped and admired by those dwelling on the earth. The antichrist will destroy through peace and governmental regulation. By the middle of, "Daniel's 70th Week," or the 1,260 day timeline, he will be given worldwide control.

Seal #2: A red horse symbolizing war appears on the world scene who takes peace from the world, and many people will be killed by the sword.

Seal #3: A black horse appears symbolizing a time of extreme famine and hunger on the earth.

Seal #4: A pale horse appears symbolizing death and hell. During this time, 25 percent of earth's population is killed by the sword, by hunger, and death. It is very probable during the time of these seal judgments there will be a worldwide war, and this war may very well involve an extensive nuclear exchange between the nations of the world.

Seal #5: The souls slain during the tribulation for their word and testimony to God, cry out to Him to avenge and judge those on earth who have killed them. They are given white robes and told to wait until this time of wrath has run its full course, since there still exists people on earth who will be killed for their testimony to God.

Seal #6: There is a great earthquake during this time. The sun and moon literally are blotted out. Asteroids, meteorites, also referred to in the Bible as fiery hail, are hurled to the earth during this time. Great cataclysmic events literally take place in the heavens. Mountains and islands are literally moved from their place. This event likely fulfills Isaiah's prophecy where the earth wobbles to and fro as a drunkard, and when John describes the heavens appearing to roll up like a scroll. People dwelling on the earth during this time hide in caves or bunkers fearing greatly, because of the events taking place on the earth during this time of wrath. There will be electrical discharges from heavenly objects passing close to earth during this time. These discharges will be so severe they will literally melt mountains. In ancient times these electrical discharges were known as, "Lightning Bolts," of the gods.

Seal #7: The seventh seal is opened causing silence in heaven for half an hour. The silence more than likely refers to an intermission or break in the action before a second wave of wrath will be hurled upon the earth. The seventh seal is comprised of seven trumpet judgments.

Trumpet #1: The first angel sounds, and fiery hail probably referring to meteorites or asteroids pound the earth burning up one third of the earth's trees and grasses. One third of the earth may refer to a specific part of the earth facing this onslaught from heaven.

Trumpet #2: The Bible states something like a great mountain burning with fire, more than likely referring to a large asteroid impacts the ocean causing one third to become red like blood. This event will cause one third of ocean life to perish and one third of all ships sailing the oceans to be destroyed.

Trumpet #3: More than likely another huge asteroid falls from the heavens burning like a lamp on one third of all rivers and streams. This event makes these waters bitter and toxic. The name of this falling star is called, "Wormwood," which refers to bitterness. Many people on the earth die because of this event.

Trumpet #4: The celestial events previously mentioned possibly cause one third of the earth to have no sunlight, no moonlight, and no starlight. The only other possible interpretation would be one third of the sunlight, moonlight, and starlight would be blotted out due to the amount of smoke and dust in the atmosphere from these celestial impacts on earth.

Trumpet #5: An angel is given power to open a spiritual doorway to the bottomless pit allowing hordes of demonic creatures upon the earth. These demonic creatures are giving power not to kill, but to torture those dwelling on the earth for five months. These are not literal locusts, because they are instructed not to hurt the grass or any green thing. The number of these beings is 200 million. We will discuss this subject later on in more detail.

Trumpet #6: Four fallen angels are loosed who are evidently bound in the vicinity of the river Euphrates. These angels will kill one-third of the population on earth during this time. They are loosed on the earth for a little over a year. During this time of wrath, the armies of God will not only come down from heaven, they will be allowed to come up out of the earth.

Trumpet #7: The seventh trumpet will be the end of the second woe upon earth, and the preparation of the last woe being seven vials or bowls of wrath. During this event there is lightning, thunder, an earthquake, and great hail. The final seven bowls of wrath will be seven final plagues being poured out upon the earth.

Bowl #1: Those who have received the mark of the Beast and worship his image develop very grievous sores on their bodies.

Bowl #2: The oceans become toxic and become red like blood killing all life in them. This is probably not referring to literal blood, but the oceans will become toxic to all life and may literally look like blood. It is said the ancient Egyptians have documented during the time of the Exodus, a poisonous red dust fell from the sky during this time.

Bowl #3: During this event all rivers and streams become as blood. Many of these events are a prophetic repeat of the Egyptian plagues. The purpose of these events is due to the innocent blood of the prophets, saints, and God's chosen people being needlessly spilt throughout history.

Bowl #4: The fourth bowl involves an event with the sun which is more than likely a solar flare so severe it scorches men with great heat.

Bowl #5: The fifth bowl describes limited darkness in the kingdom where the antichrist resides, causing men to be in great anguish. A volcanic eruption or some similar event may explain this occurrence. Through all this time of wrath men will still refuse to repent of their evil deeds and continue to blaspheme God.

Bowl #6: Bowl number six causes the river Euphrates to dry up. This will prepare a way for the future invasion from the kings of the East. Three unclean spirits described as frogs are released on the earth. This is for the sole purpose of deceiving the kings and rulers of the earth to gather together for the battle of Armageddon. There will be great hailstones falling on men weighing anywhere from fifty to one hundred pounds during this time. These stones are more than likely asteroids impacting the earth.

Bowl #7: A voice out of heaven informs all, "It is finished." Lightning, thunder, and voices follow, and there is an earthquake so great there has never been one like it since men dwelt on the earth. The city of Jerusalem during this time is divided into three parts because of this earthquake. The cities of the world are destroyed, and every island and mountain ceases to exist. Jesus warned during this time the seas would, "Roar." There will be earth cataclysms and tsunamis during this time beyond a person's wildest imagination.

This concludes a brief description of judgment events affecting those people dwelling on the earth. These events are recorded in chapters 6 through 16 of Revelation. I would like to discuss in further detail a couple other events occurring during this time in Revelation. One thing people do not realize, is during this seven-year period of God's judgment there will be a tremendous harvest of souls into God's kingdom. Although many of these people who reject Satan's world system will pay the ultimate sacrifice by losing their life, these people will receive white robes, and they will receive eternal life.

Since the true church will already have been snatched away no longer dwelling on the earth during this time, the question arises to what group of people will be responsible for this great harvest of souls. This great worldwide evangelistic event will be accomplished by 144,000 Jewish people who will be sealed and protected by God, and they will bring in a great harvest of souls. This group will consist of twelve thousand people from each of the twelve tribes of Israel. It will be during this time, the following verses in the book of Matthew will be fulfilled.

Then shall they deliver you up to be afflicted, and shall kill you: and ye shall be hated of all nations for my name's sake.

And then shall many be offended, and shall betray one another, and shall hate one another.

And many false prophets shall arise, and shall deceive many.

And because iniquity shall abound, the love of many shall wax cold.

But he that shall endure unto the end, the same shall be saved.

And the gospel of the kingdom shall be preached in all the world for a witness unto all nations; and then shall the end come.

When ye therefore shall see the abomination of desolation, spoken of by Daniel the prophet, stand in the holy place, (whoso readeth, let him understand). (Matthew 24:9–15)

It will be during the time of the, "Seven-Year Tribulation," the gospel of the kingdom will be preached unto all nations. The bride of Christ, the restraining force of salt and light, will be taken out of the way first. After this, the torch will be passed to a special called out group of Jewish people who will evangelize the world during this time. There are many theories and beliefs concerning who this group of 144,000 will consist of. The good thing is, the Bible informs us in great detail as to the identity of this group. We find the answer to who these 144,000 are in Revelation chapter 7.

And after these things I saw four angels standing on the four corners of the earth, holding the four winds of the earth, that the wind should not blow on the earth, nor on the sea, nor on any tree.

And I saw another angel ascending from the east, having the seal of the living God: and he cried with a loud voice to the four angels, to whom it was given to hurt the earth and the sea,

Saying, Hurt not the earth, neither the sea, nor the trees, till we have sealed the servants of our God in their foreheads.

And I heard the number of them which were sealed: and there were sealed an hundred and forty and four thousand of all the tribes of the children of Israel.

Of the tribe of Juda were sealed twelve thousand. Of the tribe of Reuben were sealed twelve thousand. Of the tribe of Gad were sealed twelve thousand.

Of the tribe of Aser were sealed twelve thousand. Of the tribe of Nephthalim were sealed twelve thousand. Of the tribe of Manasses were sealed twelve thousand.

Of the tribe of Simeon were sealed twelve thousand. Of the tribe of Levi were sealed twelve thousand. Of the tribe of Issachar were sealed twelve thousand.

Of the tribe of Zabulon were sealed twelve thousand. Of the tribe of Joseph were sealed twelve thousand. Of the tribe of Benjamin were sealed twelve thousand.

After this I beheld, and, lo, a great multitude, which no man could number, of all nations, and kindreds, and people, and tongues, stood before the throne, and before the Lamb, clothed with white robes, and palms in their hands. (Revelation 7:1–9)

A great harvest of souls is coming. A great multitude of people that no man can count from all nations will stand before the throne of God being given white robes. All those who refuse to worship Satan during this time and cry out to God will be spared from the second death. These people going through this fearful and dreadful time receiving white robes will have likely been killed by the antichrist, but these people will receive eternal life. In Revelation chapter 14 we are given the identity of those arrayed in white robes. It is those people who have come out of, "Great Tribulation," and have washed their robes in the blood of the Lamb. Notice the Bible mentions the pain and suffering these people have endured on the earth. These people will no longer hunger, thirst, and the sun will no longer scorch them.

During this future time of wrath God will go out of His way to show mercy to Israel, His chosen people. The people of Israel have a good understanding of many of the Old Testament prophecies. During this time known as, "Jacob's Trouble," the nation of Israel will begin to pick up on the prophetic patterns of events happening around them. Israel will recognize the, "Abomination of Desolation," when it occurs at the exact midpoint of, "Daniel's 70th Week," as a prophetic sign to flee Jerusalem. Another sign occurring during this seven-year period of time, will be the appearance of the, "Two Witnesses." We will touch on a couple things concerning these two individuals without going into great detail concerning their identities, or what will be their purpose while on the earth for 42 months. I will state the Jewish people have a tradition they keep to this day where they prepare a table for the prophet Elijah and expect him to appear during the feast of Passover. There is an interesting promise in the book of Malachi which promises Elijah the prophet will be sent to Israel before an event of, "Great Tribulation," will someday take place. Keep in mind, even Jesus spoke of a coming time of, "Great Tribulation," taking place during the last forty-two months of Daniels seventieth week.

> Behold, I will send you Elijah the prophet
> before the coming of the great and dreadful day
> of the Lord. (Malachi 4:5)

According to the book of Malachi, Elijah could definitely be one of the two witnesses. Another thing interesting about this idea is one of the miracles performed by these two witnesses will be shutting heaven so it does not rain. Other possibilities for these witnesses are Moses, Enoch, and John. It is interesting in the book of Jude we see the archangel Michael disputing with Satan over the body of Moses. This does make one wonder what deceptive plan could Satan possibly of had in mind with the body of Moses? Could Satan have somehow known there may be a future plan for Moses, or would Satan have plans to use his body for some other deceptive event with Israel? Let's look at a few verses in Revelation describing this unbelievable event.

And I will give power unto my two witnesses, and they shall prophesy a thousand two hundred and threescore days, clothed in sackcloth.

These are the two olive trees, and the two candlesticks standing before the God of the earth.

And if any man will hurt them, fire proceedeth out of their mouth, and devoureth their enemies: and if any man will hurt them, he must in this manner be killed.

These have power to shut heaven, that it rain not in the days of their prophecy: and have power over waters to turn them to blood, and to smite the earth with all plagues, as often as they will.

And when they shall have finished their testimony, the beast that ascendeth out of the bottomless pit shall make war against them, and shall overcome them, and kill them.

And their dead bodies shall lie in the street of the great city, which spiritually is called Sodom and Egypt, where also our Lord was crucified

And they of the people and kindreds and tongues and nations shall see their dead bodies three days and a half, and shall not suffer their dead bodies to be put in graves.

> And they that dwell upon the earth shall
> rejoice over them, and make merry, and shall send
> gifts one to another; because these two prophets
> tormented them that dwelt on the earth.
>
> And after three days and an half the spirit of
> life from God entered into them, and they stood
> upon their feet; and great fear fell upon them
> which saw them.
>
> And they heard a great voice from heaven
> saying unto them, Come up hither. And they
> ascended up to heaven in a cloud; and their ene-
> mies beheld them. (Revelation 11:3–12)

This has to be one of the most amazing and unbelievable stories in the Bible. This event will literally take place in the future. It's as if we are going back to the times of the Old Testament. During this time, Israel will have a functioning temple reinstating the customs and sacrifices required in Old Testament law. In Revelation chapter 11 an angel gives John a measuring rod, and he is told to measure the temple and altar of God where the people worship. If an angel instructed John to measure the temple and the altar of God, these structures must have literally existed during this time. A person cannot measure an object that does not exist.

Notice these two witnesses will be given power and authority to prophesy for 1,260 days or three and one half years. Revelation chapter 11 describes these two witnesses as being the two olive trees and two candlesticks standing before the God of earth. The Old Testament book of Zechariah describes these two olive trees as the two anointed ones standing by the Lord of the whole earth. Who are these two witnesses discussed here in Revelation? We don't know for sure, but I do believe these two anointed ones standing by the Lord will have many similarities to Moses and Aaron when they withstood Pharaoh. We also need to understand these two witnesses will be a literal living testimony of God's power to Israel during this time. Israel more than likely will recognize and recall the words of the prophet Zechariah when they see these two witnesses performing great miracles. Here's what Zechariah chapter 4 has to say concerning these two olive branches.

> Then answered I, and said unto him, What are those two olive trees upon the right side of the candlestick and upon the left side thereof?
> And I answered again, and said unto him, What be these two olive branches which through the two golden pipes empty the golden oil out of themselves?
> And he answered me and said, Knowest thou not what these be? And I said, No, my lord.
> Then said he, These are the two anointed ones, that stand by the Lord of the whole earth. (Zechariah 4:11–14)

These two witnesses are specifically called prophets, and notice they are clothed in sackcloth. We see pictures in the Bible when people would clothe themselves in sackcloth, and it was usually a picture of mourning and repentance over sin in a person's life. We see many of the patterns in Revelation making one think they are reading from the Old Testament. We notice this from the name of Jesus where He is now referred to the, "Lion of the Tribe of Judah," to the rebuilding of a temple and the reestablishment of temple sacrifices. We see the two witnesses appearing clothed in sackcloth, and we notice an overall Old Testament theme during this time. This period of time will resemble the times of Old Testament Law, not the age of grace or the church age. We will also notice as this seven-year period of tribulation continues to draw closer, the plot to the story will center more and more around Israel, and the city of Jerusalem.

These witnesses will be able to shut up heaven, bring fire down from heaven, turn water into blood, and send plagues upon the land. I can definitely see why many people identify the two witnesses as Moses and Elijah due to the similarities in the miracles being performed.

I believe these two witnesses will show up at the beginning of, "Daniel's 70th Week," being killed at the 3.5-year mark after prophesying for a period of 1,260 days. The antichrist will be given authority to overcome them and kill them. For the last half of this seven-year event or 1,260 days, the antichrist will be given total control of the world. The bodies of these two witnesses will lie in the street for three and one half days for the entire world to witness. According to the Bible, there will be partying and celebration in the streets when these two witnesses die, because of the plagues and disasters they have sent on all people dwelling on the earth.

There is a big push today even in the churches to play down events such as these. I hold to the belief these two witnesses will be a literal reappearance of two great prophets of the Bible. It is interesting there were two people named Enoch and Elijah who never experienced a physical death. These two people were caught up to God, and existed no more. Could Enoch and Elijah be the two witnesses? Yes it's possible, but I'm not planning to be present on earth during this event to see whether I'm right or wrong. After three and one half days, life will come back into the bodies of these two witnesses. More than likely every cable TV show will be broadcasting this event for the world to see. These two witnesses will then stand to their feet and ascend into heaven, as the entire population dwelling on the earth more than likely witness this event. The Bible states great fear will fall upon all who witness this event. All dwelling on the earth during this time will literally witness the resurrecting power of God. One thing I know for sure is Moses, Aaron, and Pharaoh were prophetic pictures of the coming two witnesses and the antichrist. What has been done, will be done again.

There are a couple more main events I would like to touch on before we close out this chapter dealing with this coming day of wrath. The first event we will discuss is what I will refer to as the, "Coming Demonic Invasion." What people do not realize is there will be a literal manifestation of the spiritual realm taking place on the earth during this time. Similar events happened during the days of Jared and Noah, and throughout much of the Old Testament. The Bible states, "Woe to the earth, because Satan that old serpent has come down to earth having great fury, because he knows his time is short." These are not just poetic words. These words are referring to coming literal events. Similar events such as these have happened before, and they will happen again.

One of the most shocking events yet to take place involves an invasion on earth by spiritual beings the Bible refers to as locusts. This event is discussed in Revelation chapter 9. If you were to have asked me fifteen years ago what this event referred to, I would have given you a much different answer than what I am giving in this book. With years of thought, research, prayer, and a greater realization of what the Bible is actually telling us, I am now telling you this will be one of the most fearful events ever occurring on earth.

Years ago, I would have told you what John was describing here in the best way he could was probably advanced military technology. I would have stated John is attempting to explain what may be apache helicopters or other advanced weaponry. When you literally walk up to one of these helicopters or see pictures of one, a person can see they do somewhat resemble a locust or a scorpion. We even have the roar of the engine, the eerie sound of the rotors, and we see fire coming from its mouth and its tail. This Biblical description sounds and looks like helicopters to me, or so I thought.

As I continued to grow in Christ and acquired more knowledge and understanding of scripture especially in the areas of biblical prophecy, I began to question some of my past beliefs about the Bible. This increase in an understanding of the Bible is a major reason for the book. Through the years I began to realize there is much more to the story than we are being told. I began to see there is much more to reality than what we see with our eyes. This is interesting, because this is exactly what the Bible refers to as the biblical definition of faith.

> "Now faith is the substance of things hoped for, the evidence of things not seen" (Hebrews 11:1).

Reality as we know it does not necessarily involve things we see, touch, hear, and smell. Reality also includes the things a person cannot see. This is what the Bible is trying to teach us. What is in store for the, "Overcomer," is far more amazing than what a person experiences while living here on earth. I have heard people make the comment many times stating they will not believe something until they can see it with their own eyes. Most people don't realize the visible light a human can see includes less than 5 percent of the total electromagnetic spectrum. There are many more kinds of light a person cannot see than what they are able to see. To state it factually, humans are only able to see or experience a fraction of what is defined as reality. So the statement is true, there truly is more to reality than what meets the eye. This is very interesting, because this is exactly what the Bible tells us.

> Then Elisha prayed, "O Lord, open his eyes so he can see." The Lord opened the servant's eyes and he saw that the hill was full of horses and chariots of fire all around Elisha. (2 Kings 6:17)

> But the natural man receiveth not the things of the Spirit of God: for they are foolishness unto him: neither can he know (them), because they are spiritually discerned. (1 Corinthians 2:14)

Over time I began to study the Bible with more and more of an open mind not letting religion and traditions, but the words of the Bible influence my belief system. I began to enjoy reading and studying the Bible and developed a growing desire to gain understanding in what the Bible was really trying to tell me. Yes, I began to take the Bible in a more literal way letting the Bible begin to interpret itself.

Over the next several years, I discovered many questions I once had about the Bible along with some scriptural texts were beginning to make more sense. I have learned we could study the Bible for ten lifetimes and still not understand everything the Bible has to tell us.

I began to realize over time Bible prophecy was really not so impossible to believe when a person has a basic understanding of what has historically taken place. When an entire society comes to the point they doubt God is creator of everything, they doubt the credibility of the Old Testament, and even doubt the existence of God, people will also naturally doubt the truth of Bible prophecy. After all, if a person has no belief God even exists or created everything, why should we expect a person to believe God will one day come again? Satan, "The god of this world," has been extremely successful in deceiving the world including a significant number of the churches concerning these beliefs.

Ephesians chapter 6 reminds us of the fact we wrestle not against flesh and blood, but against spiritual wickedness in high places. There is a spiritual realm, and it is just as real as the physical realm we currently live in. This is why there has been such a push to try to explain away and even cover up information related to history and the stories of the Bible. There is an old saying that states, "If you tell people the same lie over and over again, after a period of time people will begin to accept the lie as truth." Satan, "The god of this world," has convinced most people into believing a lie. There is a great deception coming on the horizon. Who is this deception for? It is for those who are perishing and for those people who refuse the truth.

When we keep this perspective in mind as we study the entire Bible, now many Bible verses and stories begin to take on new meaning. This brings new understanding as to the real purpose for the flood of Noah, the destruction of Sodom, the Exodus, and all other scriptures including prophecy.

So now after years of Bible study and research, I can tell people with absolute certainty when John sees locusts coming out of a bottomless pit, this event will happen, and it should be taken literally. Helicopters do not come out of a bottomless pit. The Bible tells us hell is a literal place prepared for Satan, his fallen angels, and his demonic forces. Hell is also a place with real gates and real bars reserved for those who reject God. The Bible is here referring to a literal event occurring in the spiritual realm. John attempts to describe these demonic creatures in the best way he possibly can. The prophet

Joel also describes these creatures in the best way he can by comparing these creatures to a literal locust army, blotting out the sun, stripping away vegetation, and leaving the land desolate. It is interesting Revelation chapter 9 informs us these locusts are commanded to not hurt any form of green vegetation. God in this situation is likely not giving commands to armies of insects, but God does have the authority to command demons in what they are permitted or not permitted to do. Keeping all this in mind, let's now take a fresh look at Revelation chapter 9.

> And the fifth angel sounded, and I saw a star fall from heaven unto earth: and to him was given a key of the bottomless pit.
>
> And he opened the bottomless pit; and there arose a smoke out of the pit, as the smoke of a great furnace; and the sun and the air were darkened by reason of the smoke of the pit.
>
> And there came out of the smoke locusts upon the earth: and unto them was given power, as the scorpions of the earth have power.
>
> And it was commanded them that they should not hurt the grass of the earth, neither any green thing, neither any tree; but only those men which have not the seal of God in their foreheads.
>
> And to them it was given that they should not kill them, but that they should be tormented five months: and their torment was as the torment of a scorpion, when he striketh a man.
>
> And in those days shall men seek death, and shall not find it; and shall desire to die, and death shall flee from them.
>
> And the shapes of the locusts were like unto horses prepared unto battle; and on their heads were as it were crowns like gold, and their faces were as the faces of men.

And they had hair as the hair of women, and their teeth were as the teeth of lions.

And they had breastplates, as it were breastplates of iron; and the sound of their wings was as the sound of chariots of many horses running to battle.

And they had tails like unto scorpions, and there were stings in their tails: and their power was to hurt men five months.

And they had a king over them, which is the angel of the bottomless pit, whose name in the Hebrew tongue is Abaddon, but in the Greek tongue hath his name Apollyon. (Revelation 9:1–11)

John gives the reader information on what has to be one of the most frightening events ever occurring in the entire Bible. This event takes place after the fifth angel sounds his trumpet. John tells us a star falls from heaven to earth having a key and is allowed to open a doorway to the bottomless pit. A star in the Bible is usually a reference to an angel. It is interesting many of the stars and planets in the solar system are named after gods which in most cases is referring to angels.

If a person will do their homework you will find out as stated in Psalms, the heavens were originally created to declare the glory of God. The Bible goes on to say day after day the heavens utter speech, and night after night they display God's wisdom. One example of this fact would deal with the symbolic meaning of the planet Mars. The meaning of the name Mars is, "God of War." This name originally symbolized the archangel Michael who the Bible refers to as the, "Warring Angel." In Greek mythology, the planet Mars is identified as the god, "Ares." If a person will do their research on this subject, one will find the original interpretations and meanings for the stars and planets are one of many things having been corrupted by Satan now taking on occult meanings. I believe in Old Testament times, the people of Israel literally looked up into the sky and told their children stories of the gospel message written in the heavens.

It is not by coincidence the signs of the zodiac include a virgin woman now named Virgo and end with Leo the Lion. The constellation Virgo was originally meant to symbolize the virgin who conceived the Messiah, and Leo the Lion actually symbolized Jesus, "The Lion of the Tribe of Judah." This angel who the Bible refers to as a, "Star," is given a key that will literally open a doorway, a gate, or a portal to the abyss.

We notice the opening of this abyss has an immediate physical effect on the earth, because smoke rises out of this abyss to the extent the sun and atmosphere are darkened. It is possible the opening up of this abyss could literally cause some type of geologic event such as a volcano to erupt on the earth. It's sad most people will not take this event literally, but events happening in the spiritual realm will have a direct effect on the physical realm.

We need to keep in mind all these events are being controlled and allowed by God. Notice again these creatures are commanded to not hurt any green vegetation of any kind. These locusts are commanded only to torture those men who do not have the seal of God written in the foreheads. These locusts are given power and authority on the earth for five months not to kill, but to torment those dwelling on the earth. John describes the torment of these locusts as being similar to that of a scorpion. John also tells us during this time men will want to die, but death will flee from them. I have always believed for many years the mark of the Beast will be much more than a computer chip. The mark will also include a spiritual profession of faith to Satan resulting in the altering of a person's DNA.

During this period of time man may be offered a life of immortality as a supposed benefit of worshipping the Beast. After all, who wouldn't want to live forever? As I've explained in earlier chapters, I believe it has always been much more about genetics than we've imagined. When Adam and Eve sinned in the garden not only did they lose their spiritual relationship with God, they were immediately changed physically from being immortal to mortal. They then recognized their spiritual condition with God had changed. I believe

the Bible informs us in the Old Testament there has been a tamper-
ing with the genetics of mankind in the past, and I believe the Bible
tells us these events will repeat themselves again.

Scientists have actually been working to achieve immortality through genetic manipulation for years. I believe the first event
where this occurred caused God to send a flood destroying all flesh
on earth, and the second event will take place during the coming
time of tribulation. People need to understand angels both good and
bad are immortal beings. Paul tells us in 1 Corinthians all flesh is
not the same. Has a person ever considered what it would be like if
Satan was to allow the mixture of his genetic seed with the genetic
seed of a man? Kind of sounds like a science fiction movie doesn't it?
No, it kind of sounds to me like what occurred during the days of
Noah. It is very interesting Revelation tells us during this time death
will flee from people, and they will break out with terrible sores.
Sounds to me like a genetic experiment gone wrong causing devastating circumstances.

John then continues in verse 7 giving us a description of these
creatures. The overall characteristics of these beings is they resemble
horses wearing all the necessary shields for battle. These creatures
although they have the appearance of horses, they have faces like
men, crowns upon their heads, and the hair on their heads resembles
the hair of a woman. Crowns in the Bible are usually symbols of
authority. These creatures also have wings, and the sounds of their
wings were as the sounds of chariots running to battle. These creatures have faces like men, but they have teeth looking like that of a
lion. These creatures appear to be heavily armored having breastplates of steel. Finally, these creatures have tails closely resembling a
scorpion, and they are able to strike and sting men with their tails.
These creatures have been given the authority to torment those people who do not have the seal of God written in their foreheads. Notice
the distinct differences in the way the Bible distinguishes those who
belong to God and those belonging to Satan. The 144,000 are sealed
and marked by God, and those worshipping Satan during this time
are also sealed with a mark. Those people having the seal of God is

referencing the 144,000 sealed from the twelve tribes of Israel who will evangelize the world during this time of tribulation.

These creatures are not literal insects or advanced military machines. These are demonic creatures ascending out of the abyss being allowed by God to torment those dwelling on the earth for five months. These creatures are wearing crowns, and they complete their mission with order. These locusts do not hurt the earth, but sting only those dwelling on the earth who have not been sealed by God. Not only do they have order and purpose, they have a king over them. Their king is the angel of the bottomless pit. The Bible in Revelation 9, gives us the Hebrew and Greek names of this king who descends out of the bottomless pit inhabiting the, "Son of Perdition."

I have believed for many years there were only two possibilities for this being the Bible refers to as; "The Antichrist." The first possibility would be this man is a fallen angel, and the second possibility is he is a, "Demonic King," rising out of the abyss. This, "Demonic King," would possess a man known as the, "Son of Perdition," who would ultimately be used for God's purpose. The Hebrew name for this angel of the bottomless pit is, "The Destroyer," and the Greek name for this man is, "Apollyon." It is interesting according to Greek mythology Apollo was the son of Zeus, and in Greek mythology Zeus was the ruler of the gods.

The more you study this subject the stranger it gets. Who is this king of the bottomless pit? His name was and is Apollo. He once walked the earth and was worshipped as a god. He now is locked in the abyss, and he will be allowed to one-day reign for forty-two months. His spirit will one day ascend out of the abyss. Genesis chapter 6 makes reference to fallen angels descending on the earth lusting after the daughters of men and bearing children. The Bible calls these children, "Nephilim," referring to them as the heroes of old, the men of renown. What has been done, will be done again. The truth has been right in front of us the entire time.

It was probably close to five years ago, I was surfing on the internet looking at pictures of ancient archaeology and ancient structures located around the world. I have always been fascinated with this subject, because it further suggests mankind was in the past visited by extraterrestrial beings. Yes, these beings were extraterrestrial in nature, but in reality they were extradimensional beings. They are what the Bible would refer to as fallen angels. The Bible tells us angels long ago left their first estate stepping into our reality corrupting all flesh on earth. The Bible, the book of Enoch, the book of Jasher, and other historical writings mention during the days before the Flood all flesh on earth was corrupted resulting in a worldwide flood. Yes, even the animals were corrupted during this time. This was the reason for the flood. This was the reason God had to wipe the slate clean.

One thing I have come to realize over the past four or five years, is we really do wrestle against spiritual wickedness in high places. Maybe it's time we as a church started to believe this. While I was viewing pictures of strange structures and sculptures around the world, I noticed there are sculptures of, "Horse Like," creatures in Iraq known as a, "Lamassu." To be quite honest, I believe my jaw hit the floor when I saw pictures of these ancient deities. When I saw photographs of these figures my mind went straight to Revelation 9. I believe God has confirmed in my spirit over the years these beings very well may be a picture of what literally exists in the spiritual realm. Wikipedia defines these creatures as an Assyrian protective deity.

These beings have bodies of what looks like horses or bulls. They have wings and human heads with long hair. The have a face like a man and crowns on their head. When I viewed pictures of these beings I thought to myself could these hybrid creatures have once walked the earth before the flood of Noah? Could these beings be the result of a past corruption of animal DNA by fallen angels? Could these creatures referred to as, "Lamassu," be similar to what John is attempting to describe to us in Revelation? On the front cover you will find a picture of one of these ancient demonic creatures. Yes, what has been done, will be done again.

Another subject we need to take a look at before we move on will deal with an event most people are familiar with known as, "The Battle of Armageddon." The word, "Armageddon," probably refers to the, "Mountain or Hills of Megiddo." Armageddon is a word which usually refers to any major event or battle taking place or is about to take place. In reality, the word, "Armageddon," more than likely refers more to an event than a place. The word is only found once in the Bible occurring in the book of Revelation.

> And he gathered them together into a place called in the Hebrew tongue Armageddon. (Revelation 16:16)

The yet future battle of Armageddon will bring an ending to Gentile reign on earth. This will be the final battle between the forces of good and evil. The kings of the earth will be gathered together to Israel to meet their doom. The answers to how and who will gather these kings of the world together is also explained in Revelation chapter 16. God will use demonic spirits to entice and draw the nations of the world to Israel. Remember, we wrestle not against flesh and blood, but against wickedness in high places. The Bible clearly warns us as we approach the end of the age demonic activity will increase. More and more regularly I witness on the local news the steady increase in madness, violence, and immorality going on in our world.

People fail to realize this spiritual truth, but demonic oppression and possession usually causes madness to those they possess. We need to usually be not so concerned about who the leaders of nations are, but who are the spirits overseeing the affairs of these leaders and nations. Revelation chapter 16 informs us demonic spirits will draw the nations to Israel for this final battle.

An ever increasing hatred toward the nation of Israel is a prophetic sign of the times. The nations and leaders of the world will be deceived by Satan and his allies into believing they can destroy the nation of Israel. It will be the time when it appears all hope has been lost for the survival of Israel, then Jesus will suddenly appear on the scene to rescue them. There are several places in the Bible giving a description of this event, but we will just look at two Old Testament references listed below in the books of Joel and Daniel.

For, behold, in those days, and in that time, when I shall bring again the captivity of Judah and Jerusalem,

I will also gather all nations, and will bring them down into the valley of Jehoshahat, and will plead with them there for my people and for my heritage Israel, whom they have scattered among the nations, and parted my land.

And they have cast lots for my people; and have given a boy for an harlot, and sold a girl for wine, that they might drink.

Yea, and what have ye to do with me, O Tyre, and Zidon, and all the coasts of Palestine? Will ye render me a recompence? and if ye recompense me, swiftly and speedily will I return your recompence upon your own head;

Because ye have taken my silver and gold, and have carried into your temples my goodly pleasant things:

The children also of Judah and the children of Jerusalem have ye sold unto the Grecians, that ye might remove them far from their border.

Behold, I will raise them out of the place whither ye have sold them, and will return your recompence upon your own head:

And I will sell your sons and your daughters into the hand of the children of Judah, and they shall sell them to the Sabeans, to a people far off: for the Lord hath spoken it.

Proclaim ye this among the Gentiles; Prepare war, wake up the mighty men, let all the men of war draw near; let them come up:

Beat your plowshares into swords and your pruninghooks into spears: let the weak say, I am strong.

Assemble yourselves, and come, all ye heathen, and gather yourselves together round about: thither cause thy mighty ones to come down, O Lord.

Let the heathen be wakened, and come up to the valley of Jehosaphat: for there will I sit to judge all the heathen round about.

Put ye in the sickle, for the harvest is ripe: come, get your down; for the press is full, the fats overflow; for the wickedness is great.

Multitudes, multitudes in the valley of decision: for the day of the Lord is near in the valley of decision.

The sun and the moon shall be darkened, and the stars shall withdraw their shining.

The Lord shall roar out of Zion, and utter his voice from Jerusalem; and the heavens and the earth shall shake: but the Lord will be the hope of his people, and the strength of the children of Israel.

So shall ye know that I am the Lord your God dwelling in Zion, my holy mountain: then shall Jerusalem be holy, and there shall no strangers pass through her any more.

And it shall come to pass in that day, that the mountains shall drop down new wine, and the hills shall flow with milk, and all the rivers of Judah shall flow with waters, and a fountain shall come forth out of the house of the Lord, and shall water the valley of Shittim.

Egypt shall be a desolation, and Edom shall be a desolate wilderness, for the violence against the children of Judah, because they have shed innocent blood in their land.

But Judah shall dwell for ever, and Jerusalem from generation to generation.

> For I will cleanse their blood that I have
> not cleansed: for the Lord dwelleth in Zion.
> (Joel 3:1–21)

The Bible states during a time when all hope appears gone, the Lord will be the hope and the strength of Israel. This is a time of great judgment. You will recall a previous event in Revelation describing the souls in heaven being slain on the earth for their testimony to God. These souls are described crying out to God stating, "How long, oh Sovereign Lord, before the inhabitants of the earth are judged, and our blood is avenged." I can tell you their prayers will be answered during this time. The blood of all innocent and righteous people spilled throughout the ages will be avenged during this time.

There is a prayer most people have memorized and can recite it at will. Most people including those attending churches have little understanding as to its meaning. I am referring to the Lord's Prayer. The kingdom of God is coming to this earth. The will of God will be accomplished not only in heaven but also on the earth. A righteous and holy God must judge and hold people accountable for the sins they have committed. All innocent blood that has been shed and will be shed will be avenged. All sin and evil will one day be judged. The earth will be cleansed during this time of all sin and evil.

Notice in verses nine and eleven Joel makes some very strange references relating to events occurring during this time. We find other references such as this in other books of the Bible such as Isaiah and Revelation. It is my belief during this time known as, "Daniel's 70th Week," there will be a manifestation of the spiritual realm on earth. During this time there literally will be demonic and angelic forces loosed and walking on the earth. It is possible as the Bible describes, mighty men of God will literally be awakened and will come up out of hell while spiritual beings descend from the heavens. I know people are quick to conclude events occurring such as these are impossible and very unlikely. I would suggest reading 2 Kings 19:35 where the Bible states the, "Angel of the Lord," killed 185,000 Assyrian solders in one night.

The thing we need to remember is during this future time, the Lord will literally gather the armies of the world to Israel in the valley of Jehoshaphat for the purpose of judgment. The ironic thing about this is the armies of the world are going to Israel with the intentions of destroying God's chosen people, and they will end up being the ones who are destroyed. Joel even gives us the ultimate purpose of God's judgment upon these nations. It is because the world is guilty of shedding the innocent blood of His people, for scattering them among the nations, and dividing His land.

One more spiritual truth I would again like to stress is according to the Bible the earth will go through more than one harvest. The harvest of grapes Joel describes occurring during this time is also mentioned specifically by Jesus and is mentioned several other places in the scriptures. This harvest is referred to as the, "Harvest of Grapes," or the, "Great Winepress of God's Wrath." This harvest according to the Bible is conducted not by God but by the angels. The Bible gives us a symbolic picture where angels are being commanded to take their sickles, and harvest the grapes of the unrighteous souls dwelling on the earth. It is because the earth is ripe and is ready to be harvested. These grapes or people will be thrown into the great winepress of God's fury where they will be trampled by God outside the city of Jerusalem. Another harvest of souls is also described in Matthew 13 as the parable of the weeds. The servants of the owner to a field notice weeds growing among the wheat, so these servants ask the owner if they can pull the weeds. The owner of the field stated to the servants let both the wheat and the weeds grow until the harvest. The weeds would first be harvested, tied up in bundles, and then burned. This is a prophetic picture of what will take place during the end of Christ's 1000-year millennial reign on earth with those people who are evil and sinful during this time. During the, "Harvest of Grapes," which is conducted by the angels, the Bible gives us a chilling picture of a great amount of blood covering the ground for 1,600 stadia or 971,200 feet. What a gruesome and horrible scene this will be. This distance the blood of the unrighteous will flow would be equal to approximately 185 miles.

We will take a look at a couple more Old Testament texts before we conclude this chapter dealing with this future day of wrath. Let's now take a look at two verses in the second chapter of Daniel. These two verses in Daniel gives us a quick overview relating to the end of Gentile reign on earth. There will be a total of seven great Gentile kingdoms ruling the world from the beginning of time coming to completion during Daniel's seventieth week. The seven Gentile kingdoms of the world described by Daniel includes; Assyria, Egypt, Babylon, Medo-Persia, Greek, Rome, and Revived Rome. John informs us there will be seven great kings associated with these kingdoms, but there will be a final king and kingdom that will arise coming from the original seven kingdoms. This eighth king and kingdom will arise to power gaining world domination during the final forty-two months of, "Daniel's 70th Week." It will be this eighth king who the Bible refers to as the, "antichrist," who will deceive the world, and gather the nations to come against Israel. The two verses in Daniel referring to this event states the following.

> And in the days of these kings shall the God of heaven set up a kingdom, which shall never be destroyed: and the kingdom shall not be left to other people, but it shall break in pieces and consume all these kingdoms, and it shall stand forever.
> Forasmuch as thou sawest that the stone was cut out of the mountain without hands, and that it brake in pieces the iron, the brass, the clay, the silver, and the gold; the great God hath made known to the king what shall come to pass hereafter: and the dream is certain, and the interpretation thereof sure. (Daniel 2:44–45)

Daniel chapter 2:44–45 includes part of an interpretation to a troubling dream experienced by king Nebuchadnezzar, ruler of Babylon. This Bible story informs us all of the king's sorcerers, magicians, and astrologers were unable to interpret this dream. Daniel is the only man found who is able to interpret this dream. The dream King Nebuchadnezzar had involved a large statue having a head of gold, chest and arms of silver, belly and thighs of brass, legs of iron, and its feet as well as its ten toes were mixed with iron and clay. This statue explained above is representative of the five great Gentile kingdoms which have ruled the world beginning with Babylon and King Nebuchadnezzar. The two great kingdoms existing before the time of Babylon would be Assyria and Egypt making a total of seven Gentile kingdoms. Daniel chapter 7 gives us further insight concerning the last kingdom which is made up of iron and clay having ten toes. The ten toes is a reference to ten kings that one day will arise out of this future kingdom. Let's take a brief look at a few verses in the Bible, where Daniel is informed by an angel of what will take place concerning this future kingdom.

Thus he said, The fourth beast shall be the fourth kingdom upon earth, which shall be diverse form all kingdoms, and shall devour the whole earth, and shall tread it down, and break it in pieces.

And the ten horns out of this kingdom are ten kings that shall arise: and another shall rise after them; and he shall be diverse from the first, and he shall subdue three kings.

And he shall speak great words against the most High, and shall wear out the saints of the most High, and think to change times and laws: and they shall be given into his hand until a time and times and the dividing of time.

But the judgment shall sit, and they shall take away his dominion, to consume and to destroy it unto the end.

And the kingdom and dominion, and the greatness of the kingdom under the whole heaven, shall be given to the people of the saints of the most High, whose kingdom is an everlasting kingdom, and all dominions shall serve and obey him. (Daniel 7:23–27)

Daniel is given prophetic insight from an angel concerning these future kingdoms. Notice the king of Babylon saw these kingdoms pictured as a great statue, and these same kingdoms were seen as great beasts to Daniel. Daniel saw these kingdoms from the spiritual perspective of being beasts. Here we see in Daniel the Bible confirming to us similar characteristics of the antichrist to that of John. Daniel confirms he will blaspheme the, "Most High God," and he will be given power to overcome the saints for 3.5 years or forty-two months.

We will now close out this chapter taking a look at one more scripture reference in Revelation chapter 19. We will only address the last five verses in this chapter due to already identifying who this rider on the white horse is. This rider is named, "Faithful and True," and He is wearing many crowns. He is coming, "To Judge," and to, "Make War." I believe it's quite oblivious who this rider is. He is the only person in all of creation found worthy to break the seals to the scroll. He is the only one in heaven, on earth, and under the earth found worthy to take the scroll out of the right hand of the, "Most High God." He is the, "Lion of the tribe of Judah." He is the, "Lamb," that was slain and is alive. He is, "The Christ." Let's take a look at these five verses in Revelation chapter 19.

And I saw an angel standing in the sun; and he cried with a loud voice, saying to all the fowls that fly in the midst of heaven, Come and gather yourselves together unto the supper of the great God;

That ye may eat the flesh of kings, and the flesh of captains, and the flesh of mighty men, and the flesh of horses, and them that sit on them, and the flesh of all men, both free and bond, both small and great.

> And I saw the beast, and the kings of the earth, and their armies, gathered together to make war against him that sat on the horse, and against his army.
>
> And the beast was taken, and with him the false prophet that wrought miracles before him, with which he deceived them that had received the mark of the beast, and them that worshipped his image. These both were cast alive into a lake of fire burning with brimstone.
>
> And the remnant were slain with the sword of him that sat upon the horse, which sword proceeded out of his mouth: and all the fowls were filled with their flesh. (Revelation 19:17–21)

What a sobering picture the Bible gives us here concerning the fate of all who reject God. All the kings and armies of the world will be gathering themselves together attempting to destroy the nation of Israel. Instead of destroying Israel, all nations coming against them will be destroyed. The information provided in the Bible is definitely not politically correct and is not concerned with hurting a person's feelings. The Bible gives us the truth, the whole truth, and nothing but the truth. The Bible informs us an angel will command the birds to gather together, gorging themselves on the flesh of all humans and animals which are slain in this battle.

The Bible gives us a very clear picture concerning what happens to the Beast and the false prophet. The Beast and the false prophet will be captured and thrown alive into a fiery lake of burning sulphur. If there is any kind of a positive message one can take away from this story, it would be this event is yet to take place. If you are alive, breathing, and reading these words I can tell you there is still hope for you, and anyone else that has not yet put their faith and trust in God. Trust Christ while you still have time. I can assure you these events will one day take place. Jesus Christ came as a, "Lamb." Jesus Christ is coming again as a, "Lion." The Bible states it is God' s will no one would have to face this horrible time of, "Great Tribulation." Today is the day of salvation. I can assure you God will have no mercy on those refusing to accept His Son, His only Son, Jesus Christ. There is no reason not to trust Him today.

Hope for the Overcomer

I would like to close out this book on a positive note. This past ten to fifteen years has taken me on an interesting journey. It has been my goal from the beginning to share some questions about the Bible I have struggled with over the years. My studies will hopefully provide a few answers to some questions concerning the Bible others may have. This book has taken us all the way from Genesis to Revelation. In this book I have shared some very interesting conclusions to many of the questions I have struggled with. The answers to these questions has come through many hours of thought, prayer, researching, and quite honestly putting everything aside, letting the Bible be my guide for knowledge and truth. I can tell you with all sincerity there is hope for all who put their faith and trust in the God of the Bible.

I realize some of the material we have covered in this book was at times hard for an individual to deal with and wrap their mind around. When a person understands we serve a God who has always existed, is all seeing, all knowing, and sent His Son so we can have life, this is also a hard concept to wrap one's mind around. The idea God loved and cared for Noah so much He went to such great lengths to save one person's life is hard to comprehend. The idea Jesus, "The Son of God," was born of a virgin and was willing to lay down His life for such a horrible sinner as me is beyond my capacity of reasoning. God in His infinite wisdom through the Bible has shown all people willing to listen beforehand how the movie will one day end. One of the great learning moments of my life was when I realized with all certainty, God's ultimate plan will be accomplished whether a person accepts or rejects it. The stories recorded in the Bible will one day end exactly in the way God planned it. With God, there never were and never will be any surprises. God foreknew the entire contents of the Bible before the words, "In the beginning," was ever written down. God recorded these stories and events informing us of the past and is warning us of what will occur in the future. The reason is because God loves us wishing none should perish but all would trust Him as Lord. In spite of all the horrible things that will come upon this earth, there is a future filled with hope, peace, and joy for all who choose to be an, "Overcomer."

The Bible tells us God will one day put an end to all pain and suffering. The curse which was brought upon mankind through the disobedience of Adam and Eve will one day be done away with. There will one day be no more tears and suffering, and there will be no more hatred, greed, malice, and murder. There will be no more sickness, disease, suffering, and death. Look at the horrible mess man has made of this world. God will one day make things new again. With God there truly is hope. God loved mankind so much He surrounded us with the irrefutable evidence and design of His creation. God gave us His word, and He gave us His Son, His only Son. God has made a way for all those who are willing to put their faith and trust in Him.

We will continue to see a steady increase in spiritual deception as we draw closer to the end of this age. We are living in a time where people are being taught there is no such thing as absolutes. Whether we believe this deception or not, the reality is the laws of science, physics, and even spiritual laws do exist. For instance, a person can deny the existence of gravity, but when a person jumps off a bridge or a high building, there will be consequences to one's actions whether they believe in the law of gravity or not. It is the same principal when dealing with the spiritual and moral laws God has also established. All people will one day stand before God even if they deny the truth of the Bible and the existence of God. All people will one day be held accountable for the deeds they have done during their time here on this earth, and they will reap what they have sown.

When Adam and Eve sinned against God while in the garden, blood had to be shed as payment for their sin. When a person thinks about it, Adam and Eve had everything one could desire yet they blew it. They were not going to die, and they were not experiencing pain or suffering. They had no worries and no bills coming due, but they blew it. Jesus, "The Lamb of God," freely went to the cross and became sin so we born of sin can be counted righteous. For those who have been counted righteous our future is not one of doom and gloom. It is one of hope, peace, and joy, and it will be a glorious day when He appears. For those dwelling on the earth that reject God and His salvation offered to all who ask and seek Him, it will be a time of horror, fear, and weeping. Revelation chapter 21 gives us insight concerning this future period of time, "The Overcomer," will one day experience.

> And I saw a new heaven and a new earth: for the first heaven and the first earth were passed away; and there was no more sea.
>
> And I John saw the holy city, new Jerusalem, coming down from God out of heaven, prepared as a bride adorned for her husband.
>
> And I heard a great voice out of heaven saying, Behold, the tabernacle of God is with men, and he will dwell with them, and they shall be his people, and God himself shall be with them, and be their God.
>
> And God shall wipe away all tears from their eyes; and there shall be no more death, neither sorrow, nor crying, neither shall there by any more pain: for the former things are passed away.
>
> And he that sat upon the throne said, Behold, I make all things new. And he said unto me, Write: for these words are true and faithful.
>
> And he said unto me, It is done. I am the Alpha and Omega, the beginning and the end. I will give unto him that is athirst of the fountain of the water of life freely.

He that overcometh shall inherit all things;
and I will be his God, and he shall be my son.

But the fearful, and unbelieving, and the
abominable, and murderers, and whoremongers,
and sorcerers, and idolaters, and all liars, shall
have their part in the lake which burneth with
fire and brimstone: which is the second death.
(Revelation 21:1–8)

In these verses we are given a glimpse into the future. God is telling us the old things will be done away with, and there will be a new heaven, and a new earth. God will make all things new. The curse of sin and death has long been done away with. Because of this, there will be no more pain, suffering, and sorrow during this time. We need to remember these verses are describing events taking place in the future.

How many times do we hear people state the Bible is outdated and no longer credible to use as a spiritual guide during these modern times? Not only is the Bible credible for us today, the Bible documents events happening over one thousand years into the future. When we consider the future, "Seven-Year Tribulation," coming upon the earth and the, "One Thousand-Year Millennial Reign," of Christ, the Bible informs us of events occurring 1,007 years in the future with these two events alone. Anyone who states the Bible is not written for us today lacks spiritual understanding and is being deceived.

Have you ever heard of someone receiving a letter in the mail informing them they will be receiving a large inheritance? The Bible informs us all people who keep the faith and finish the race will receive a huge inheritance. Do we realize our Heavenly Father owns it all, and the Bible tells us we are joint heirs with Him. You name it, God owns it.

During this time, God will literally dwell with men. God has always desired to dwell with Israel and be their God. Israel was God's chosen people, but they rejected Him. During this time, the tabernacle of God, "The New Jerusalem," will literally descend down from heaven hovering above the earth. It is interesting one of the traditions of the, "Jewish Wedding," was after the engagement with his bride was official, the groom would go back to his father, and build a room on the side of his father's house. I believe this, "Holy City," descending down from heaven is the house Jesus has prepared for His bride. Living water coming from under God's throne will flow out of this city down onto the earth below. God throughout the Bible has always been portrayed as, "Living Water." God was the living water for His chosen people wondering in the wilderness when Moses struck the rock bringing forth living water sustaining the children of Israel. The living water coming from the rock was a prophetic picture of Jesus who provides living water to all who will drink. Jesus told the woman at the well if she would drink from the water He alone provides, she would never thirst again.

This city coming down out of heaven is also referred to as, "The Bride of the Lamb," because this city shines with the glory of God, and its brilliance resembles precious jewels worn by a bride. This literal city is not only the residence of the bride but also symbolizes the beauty of His bride. The books of Proverbs and Isaiah has these words to say concerning a beautiful bride.

> Who can find a virtuous woman? For her price is far above rubies. (Proverbs 31:10)

> I will greatly rejoice in the Lord, my soul shall be joyful in my God; for he hath clothed me with the garments of salvation, he hath covered me with the robe of righteousness, as a bridegroom decketh himself with ornaments, and as a bride adorneth herself with her jewels. (Isaiah 61:10)

This entire city shines as if it were a very precious jewel clear as crystal. This city has twelve gates, three gates on each of its four sides. On each of the twelve gates is listed one of the names of the twelve tribes of Israel. The city has twelve foundations, and on each foundation is a name of one of the twelve apostles. The walls of the city were made of jasper, and the city was made of gold so pure it was transparent. The foundations of this city are decorated with every type of precious stone imaginable.

John was given a measuring rod and instructed by an angel to measure the city, the gates of the city, and the walls. It has always amazed me how many people believe this is not a literal city, but only an allegorical illusion meant for moral and spiritual inspiration. This city is so real and literal it can be measured. You cannot measure something that does not exist. The city is laid out like a square, and its length, width, and height were all the same measuring 12,000 stadia. If one stadia is approximately 220 yards in length, this would make this city be around 1,500 miles in length, width, and height. The Bible informs the walls of this city are approximately 200-feet thick. Most people believe this city is in the shape of a cube, but I happen to believe it is in the shape of an equal sided pyramid. I have stated earlier in this book, the Bible makes several references to, "The Mountain of God." A pyramid looks like a mountain. I have also believed for years the thousands of pyramids on earth are an earthly representation of what exists in the heavens. Notice the words in Revelation chapter 21 describing this city.

> And there came unto me one of the seven angels which had the seven vials full of the seven last plagues, and talked with me, saying, Come hither, I will shew thee the bride, the Lamb's wife.
> And he carried me away in the spirit to a great and high mountain, and shewed me that great city, the holy Jerusalem, descending out of heaven from God. (Revelation 21:9–10)

The angel tells John to come with him, and he would be shown a great and high mountain. This is something we can agree to disagree on, but I happen to believe this city coming down from heaven is shaped like a mountain. All who overcome and are found righteous in God's eyes will have an eternal residence in this city. Along with a promise of inheritance there is also a warning from God here in these verses. God warns mankind over and over again in the same way a loving father or mother will warn their children of coming danger. This warning from God is very clear. The unbelieving, murderers, the sexually immoral, all idolaters, and all others who practice evil will have no residence in this holy city.

The Bible warns all people whose lives are characterized by these types of sins will be thrown into a literal, "Lake of Fire." This is the second death, and it is eternal. To escape this second death one must be clothed in the righteousness of Christ. As the parable states, a person must be clothed in the appropriate garments offered only by the King. Those clothed in righteousness will be allowed entrance and become permanent residents to this great city. Remember the words Jesus had to say concerning this city to all having ears to listen?

> Let not your heart be troubled: ye believe in God, believe also in me.
>
> In my Father's house are many mansions: If it were not so, I would have told you. I go to prepare a place for you.
>
> And if I go and prepare a place for you, I will come again, and receive you unto myself; that where I am, there ye may be also. (John 14:1–3)

It would be an interesting study to research the times the Bible makes statements such as let not your heart be troubled, comfort one another with these words, there is now no condemnation, or we have not been appointed to wrath. Jesus, the Son of the, "Most High God," promises a place is prepared in this great city, "The New Jerusalem," for all overcomers.

If a person was to conduct a study on the Jewish wedding ceremony, a person would be surprised how closely Jesus kept these same traditions with His bride. One of the steps to the Jewish marriage ceremony would occur after the groom would choose his bride and finalize the betrothal process. The son or groom would then prepare a room for his bride in his father's house or on the side of his father's house. This is just exactly what Jesus has accomplished for His bride. If you are an, "Overcomer," you have a place in heaven already prepared for you.

We find a parable in the Bible referring to five wise and five foolish virgins. I have lived most of my Christian life having no real understanding as to the meaning of this parable. In the Jewish wedding ceremony there were bridesmaids who participated in the ceremony. According to the Bible these bridesmaids were all virgins, but five of them were wise, and five were foolish. While the groom is away for an undetermined amount of time preparing a house for the two to live, the bride was to keep herself clothed in white and be watching for the sudden return of her groom. The bridesmaids are to also be watching and ready having their lamps trimmed along with extra oil. The groom traditionally would come as a thief during the night with a shout and a trumpet blast to snatch the bride away. In the parable of the wise and foolish virgins, the foolish virgins who had no oil is symbolic of those who will not be spiritually ready and awake when Christ appears in the clouds, and those who are righteous will be caught up to meet Him in the twinkling of an eye. These foolish bridesmaids who have no oil for their lamps is a prophetic picture of those people not born of spirit. It is while these bridesmaids are trying to find oil for their lamps the Groom suddenly appears, and the door is shut preventing these unrighteous people from participating in the wedding banquet. These foolish virgins arrive late to the banquet pleading for the door to be opened allowing them to enter in. The Bible tells us these foolish virgins were denied access to the wedding banquet. This parable is then closed with a warning from Jesus to keep watch, and be ready for His return.

In the Jewish wedding ceremony, after the son or groom has built a room usually adjoining his father's house, the father would inspect the room. If the room was ready, the father would then tell his son to go get his bride. The groom and his wedding party would then usually during the midnight hour return to the house of his bride with a shout and trumpet blast, quickly stealing his bride away. After a while a person has to come to the realization all these patterns in the Bible cannot be coincidental. I believe the following verses confirm this event described in the parable of the ten virgins will one day take place for all people who are called, "Overcomers."

> But I would not have you to be ignorant, brethren, concerning them which are asleep, that ye sorrow not, even as others which have no hope.
>
> For if we believe that Jesus died and rose again, even so them also which sleep in Jesus will God bring with him.
>
> For this we say unto you by the word of the Lord, that we which are alive and remain unto the coming of the Lord shall not prevent them which are asleep.
>
> For the Lord himself shall descend from heaven with a shout, with the voice of the archangel, and with the trump of God: and the dead in Christ shall rise first:
>
> Then we which are alive and remain shall be caught up together with them in the clouds, to meet the Lord in the air: and so shall we ever be with the Lord.
>
> Wherefore comfort one another with these words. (1 Thessalonians 4:13–18)

Here we see the Bible informing the brethren to comfort one another with these words. Paul here is attempting to calm down the members of this church putting to rest the possibility a false report or letter was being circulated teaching, "The Day of the Lord," had already come. These church members were being taught their loved ones who had previously passed away had missed the resurrection. It is interesting in the following chapter, Paul informs this church, "The Day of the Lord," comes as a thief in the night. In other words, Paul tells this church the resurrection has not taken place and clearly states those people who, "Sleep In Christ," will actually be resurrected first.

Paul warns these brethren in this church not to be deceived into believing those who now sleep have no hope. Notice the word,

"Sleep," is used here. It is because those who are "in Christ" are in a sense sleeping when they die, because their bodies will one day rise to new life. Paul reassures these brethren stating because all church saints believe Jesus Christ conquered death, those who sleep, "In Christ," will live again.

Paul then goes on to give us the specific order in which these events will occur. First, the Lord Himself will descend from heaven pronounced by a shout from an archangel proceeding with a trumpet blast from God. The Bible informs us it will be Christ Himself who descends from heaven. The harvest of these righteous people who are, "In Christ," will not be completed by the angels. Just like in the Jewish wedding tradition, it will be the Groom alone who comes for His bride. Secondly, those who are dead or sleeping, "In Christ," will rise first. The Bible states Jesus will bring back with Him the spirits of those who are asleep, and they will then be reunited with their now immortal bodies in the moment, in the twinkling of an eye. Thirdly, those who are still alive, "In Christ," will be caught up together immediately following those resurrected to meet Christ in the air. According to the Bible, this entire event will happen in a twinkling of an eye. The word, "Caught up Together," is where the idea of a rapture event comes from. The literal meaning to this phrase could be described as being suddenly caught up or snatched away with force from imminent danger. It would be an event similar to a child playing in the street literally being snatched away with force and rescued from being run over by a speeding vehicle. The Bible goes on to tell us when the righteous of God are caught up in the air to meet Him, from that moment on we will be with Him forever. Paul then instructs the brethren to comfort one another with these words. Notice what the Bible also states in 1 Corinthians concerning this same event.

> Now this I say, brethren, that flesh and
> blood cannot inherit the kingdom of God; nei-
> ther doth corruption inherit incorruption.
> Behold, I shew you a mystery; We shall not
> all sleep, but we shall all be changed,

> In the moment, in the twinkling of an eye, at the last trump: for the trumpet shall sound, and the dead shall be raised incorruptible, and we shall be changed.
>
> For this corruptible must put on incorruption, and this mortal must put on immortality (1 Corinthians 15:50–53).

This old tent or body we currently live in will one day put on immortality. Our bodies will one day no longer ache, be sick, be tired, and finally experience death. We will be like the angels in the sense we will be immortal, and our bodies will no longer be of flesh and blood. Here again, the Bible gives us the sequence of these events. In a moment in the twinkling of an eye, a shout will be given, a trumpet will sound, the dead will be raised, and we who are alive will be changed. Notice the Bible refers to this event as a, "Mystery." For some reason God has chosen to keep some of the details and times of this event a mystery. I believe there may be a two-fold purpose for the concealment of this event. A first possible reason would be to keep information from Satan and his spiritual hierarchy. I currently believe the catching away of the bride of Christ which includes the removal of the restrainer will be a key event throwing the world into chaos. This will allow a literal spiritual darkness to immediately envelope the world. Secondly, I believe the concealment of this event gives reason for the church saints to be daily living for Christ, and constantly looking for His appearing.

I believe this event is not referring to the event given in Revelation chapter 1 where all eyes will see Christ coming in the clouds, and all people on earth will mourn because of Him. I believe the event described by Paul taking place in the twinkling of an eye, is not referring to Revelation chapter 19 where Christ descends from heaven on a white horse. The event in Revelation 19 where the armies of Christ descend from heaven with Him, is for the purpose of rescuing Israel and judging those dwelling on the earth. The event where those people sleeping, "In Christ," and are alive, "In Christ," are caught up to meet Jesus in the air, is called a, "Mystery." Just like in the case of the bride in the Jewish wedding ceremony, the bride never knew the exact day or hour her groom would appear, so she needed to keep herself in a state of readiness.

I firmly believe this catching or snatching away of those, "In Christ," will bring the church age or age of grace to a close, and will start the prophetic countdown to the seven-year tribulation period. Although the entire seven years will be a time of trouble, Jesus referred to the last 3.5 years or forty-two months of this period as being a time of, "Great Tribulation." I believe the sudden disappearance of perhaps millions of people on the earth in the twinkling of an eye will bring chaos upon the earth. Again, I strongly believe the collective body of Christ on earth who are indwelled by the Holy Spirit is what the Bible refers to as the, "Restrainer." When salt and light is removed from the earth, the environment on this earth will immediately change for the worse. If you think the world is in bad shape now, you don't want to be dwelling on earth when the bride of Christ is caught away. No longer will the prayers and the presence of the bride indwelled by the Holy Spirit be holding back or restraining the spirit of antichrist from rising on the scene. This is exactly the message Paul is trying to warn the brethren in 2 Thessalonians.

> Remember ye not, that, when I was with you, I told you these things?
>
> And now ye know what withholdeth that he might be revealed in his time.
>
> For the mystery of iniquity doth already work: only he who now letteth will let, until he be taken out of the way.
>
> And then shall that Wicked be revealed, whom the Lord shall consume with the spirit of his mouth, and shall destroy with the brightness of his coming:
>
> Even him, whose coming is after the working of Satan with all power and signs and lying wonders. (2 Thessalonians 2:5–9)

According to the scriptures, the antichrist who comes with the power and authority of Satan will be revealed after the bride of Christ and the, "Restrainer," of evil is taken out of the way. Paul goes on to further identify this, "Wicked One," as the person Christ will consume and destroy with the brightness of His coming. As already stated, I believe the Bible makes it clear the, "Son of Perdition," arrives on the scene after the bride is snatched or taken out of the way. Quite honestly, I believe the next major prophetic event taking place is the removal of the Holy Spirit indwelling the bride of Christ from the earth. Once this event takes place, God will allow Satan for a short time to reign and rule the entire world. A person must also consider the physical effects immediately experienced on earth when millions of people will suddenly explode out of their graves. Didn't Einstein tell us for every action, there is an equal and opposite reaction?

For those of you who think this is impossible or ridiculous, I would say you haven't done your homework. There have been several people deeply involved in the occult and the New Age Movement publicly stating they have been instructed by, "Spirit Guides," to not be surprised if millions of people suddenly leave this earth. These, "Spirit Guides," who are literal demons, are instructing their followers Bible believing Christians are currently preventing the earth from entering into a new age of reality, so they must be removed from the earth. It's kind of sad Satan is preparing his believers for the sudden removal of the bride of Christ from the earth, but probably half of those attending church deny the words previously stated by Paul. Yes, those people who sleep, "In Christ," and are alive during this time will be caught up to meet the Lord in the air in a moment, in the twinkling of an eye.

One of the first books I purchased to study the New Age Movement was a book written by Constance Cumbey published in 1983. I would greatly recommend her book for Bible study and gaining valuable spiritual insight into the New Age movement. The title to the book is, "The Hidden Dangers of the Rainbow." A person will be shocked when they realize many of these New Age practices have been creeping into the church for the past thirty or more years. I have read several other books dealing with the New Age over the years. What was most shocking to me is a person will discover most doctrines of the New Age Movement align perfectly with the Bible relating to Satan's plan of global control through a one world government, one world economic system, and a one world religion. Some of the basic beliefs and goals of the New Age movement includes:

- Religious tolerance and moral diversity for all religions except for the teachings of the Bible, where Jesus Christ states He is the only way through which one can obtain salvation.
- Humans are considered divine and ultimately the hope of the world.
- The movement is composed mainly of Eastern influenced belief systems.
- The belief of Global unity.
- The evolving of man is pursued through such practices as astral projection, channeling spirits, and crystal usage.
- To create a world of pure relativism.

Jesus makes some very interesting comments in John chapter 16 concerning the Holy Spirit. Notice the spiritual insight Jesus gives us in these verses concerning the, "Comforter," or the, "Holy Spirit." For some reason unknown to us, Jesus seems to be referring He and the Holy Spirit cannot or will not be on earth during the same period of time. The Holy Spirit came to earth indwelling believers during Pentecost after Jesus finished His ministry here on earth. The Holy Spirit is identified as the, "Comforter," and the, "Seal," of our heavenly inheritance. Could it be the Holy Spirit is the restraining force keeping Satan at bay until He is removed from the earth? I believe so.

> Nevertheless I tell you the truth; It is expedient for you that I go away: for if I go not away, the Comforter will not come unto you; but if I depart, I will send him unto you.

And when he is come, he will reprove the world of sin, and of righteousness, and of judgment:

Of sin, because they believe not on me;

Of righteousness, because I go to my Father, and ye see me no more;

Of judgment, because the prince of this world is judged. (John 16:7–11)

For all those who are, "In Christ," there is amazing grace and amazing hope. This book has been an incredible journey for me, and it is my hope and my prayer this book has the answers for many of the questions about the Bible you may have struggled with. The Bible speaks a message of truth for all willing to listen. The Bible informs us of what has taken place in the past, and what will again take place in the future. There really is nothing new under the sun. Mankind has been dealing with the same issues over and over for thousands of years. When it's all said and done, we really don't learn much from the past. Man says I want to do it my way, and God tells us its already been paid for. All we have to do is put our faith and trust in Him. God gives us all of creation as a witness and a testimony to His majesty. God gives us the Holy Bible with all of its thousands of historical names, places, dates, and facts. God even gave us His Son. What more could He give. The choice is yours.

Accept Christ today while there still is an open door, and while there is still time. We are not promised tomorrow. Just like it was in the days of Noah, people have to make a choice of what they believe and whom they will serve. A day is coming in the future when the door of opportunity to obtain righteousness will again be shut. I would like to end this book with a few other verses having a tremendous impact on my life, now that I truly understand their meaning. Read these verses and learn to understand their meaning. Yes, all these things will surely come to pass. Are you ready? Do you have oil in your lamp, and are you looking for His appearing?

Watch ye therefore, and pray always, that ye may be accounted worthy to escape all these things that shall come to pass, and to stand before the Son of man. (Luke 21:36)

And behold, I come quickly; and my reward is with me, to give every man according as his work shall be.

I am the Alpha and Omega, the beginning and the end, the first and the last.

Blessed are they that do his commandments, that they may have the right to the tree of life, and may enter in through the gates of the city.

For without are dogs, and sorcerers, and whoremongers, and murderers, and idolaters, and whosoever loveth and maketh a lie.

I Jesus have sent mine angel to testify unto you these things in the churches. I am the root and the offspring of David, and the bright and morning star.

And the Spirit and the bride say, Come. And let him that heareth say, Come. And let him that is athirst come. And whosoever will, let him take the water of life freely. (Revelation 22:12–17)

References

The Kings James Bible: All scriptural references.

The Book of Enoch tr. by R. H. Charles 1917, www.sacredtexts.com

The Book of Jasher Published by J. H. Parry and Company 1887, www.sacredtexts.com

Hitchcock's Bible Names Dictionary

Wikipedia, The Free Encyclopedia, The Seven Churches of Asia, Description of Lamassu, Bible Names, Lists of Egyptian Deities, Ancient Egyptian Deities

Dr. Chuck Missler, YouTube, Genesis chapter 6, The Days of Noah

An Autobiography of Buffalo Bill (Colonel W. F. Cody) Public Domain Cosmopolitan Book Corporation Farrar & Rinehart Incorporated, On Murray Hill, New York Illustrated by N. C. Wyeth 1920

The Hidden Danger of the Rainbow, The New Age Movement and Our Coming Age of Barbarism by Constance Cumbey, Huntington House, Inc. P.O. Box 53788 Lafayette, LA 70505 Copyright Constance E. Cumbey 1983

Apollyon Rising 2012: The Lost Symbol Found and the Final Mystery of the Great Seal Revealed, November 24 2009 Paperback by Thomas Horn

The Nephilim The Great Pyramid and The Apocalypse by Patrick Heron, DVD

Shutterstock, Ancient Babylonia and Assyria Sculpture Painting From Mesopotamia, Andrea Izotti, Photo ID# 655775740

Shutterstock, Ancient Sumerian Stone Carving, Fedor Selivanov, Photo ID# 530678590

Shutterstock, Ancient Sumerian Stone Carving, Fedor Selivanov, Photo ID# 530678398

Book, Bringers of the Dawn by Barbara Marciniak, New Age Author and Channeler, Teachings from the Pleiadians, Bear and Co., 1992

About the Author

Russell Nickel is fifty-six years of age, and currently resides on a farm near the small town of Aline, Oklahoma. Mr. Nickel has been married to his wife Ginger for thirty-three years. They have two beautiful daughters, Rachael and Crystal, and two great sons-in-law, Josh and Grayson. He also has three grandchildren named Rylee, Brax, and Gatlin. Russell attended Tabor College in Hillsboro, Kansas, and Northwestern Oklahoma State University in Alva, Oklahoma where he received a bachelor of science degree. Russell was active in sports most of his younger years competing in four years of college baseball as a pitcher. Mr. Nickel is currently employed as a park manager at the Great Salt Plains State Park in Jet, Oklahoma. He states managing a park has been one of the most exciting and rewarding jobs of his life. Russell enjoys living the country life, spending time with family, hunting, fishing, and being outdoors enjoying nature. Mr. Nickel believes unlocking the mysteries of history, biblical prophecy, and discovering new truths in the Bible, is one of the most exciting, challenging, and rewarding subjects a person can study.

CPSIA information can be obtained
at www.ICGtesting.com
Printed in the USA
BVHW070410161221
624023BV00011B/1035